James Schouler

Historical briefs

James Schouler

Historical briefs

ISBN/EAN: 9783743349308

Manufactured in Europe, USA, Canada, Australia, Japa

Cover: Foto ©ninafisch / pixelio.de

Manufactured and distributed by brebook publishing software (www.brebook.com)

James Schouler

Historical briefs

James Schouler

HISTORICAL BRIEFS.

BY

JAMES SCHOULER.

𝔚𝔦𝔱𝔥 𝔞 𝔅𝔦𝔬𝔤𝔯𝔞𝔭𝔥𝔶.

NEW YORK:
DODD, MEAD AND COMPANY.
1896.

Copyright, 1896,
By Dodd, Mead and Company.

University Press:
John Wilson and Son, Cambridge, U.S.A.

TO THE

AMERICAN HISTORICAL ASSOCIATION,

AT WHOSE ANNUAL MEETINGS MANY OF THESE ESSAYS HAVE BEEN READ, AND FROM WHOSE MEMBERS, COLLECTIVELY AND AS INDIVIDUALS, I HAVE RECEIVED THE CHIEF LITERARY ENCOURAGEMENT OF MATURE LIFE,

This Volume

IS AFFECTIONATELY DEDICATED BY

THE AUTHOR.

PUBLISHERS' NOTE.

WITH the exception of two Review articles, which it was thought best to omit,[1] this volume contains all of Professor Schouler's Historical Miscellanies which have hitherto been read or printed by him; and in order to complete the range of discussion pursued by the general essays contained herein, he has added two — "Historical Monographs" and "Historical Style" — which are published in this book for the first time. Our author's lecture courses, and the many professional papers from his pen which have appeared in the legal periodicals, are of course omitted.

The Biography will be found a unique and important feature of the present volume, and the publishers trust it may prove interesting and helpful to the general reader. The narrative is prepared from fresh and original materials supplied by the author himself, and its truthfulness may be relied upon.

---

[1] "Our Diplomacy during the Rebellion," *North American Review*, April, 1866; "The Hawaiian Conquest," *The Forum*, February, 1894.

CONTENTS.

I. HISTORICAL BRIEFS: PAGE
    FRANCIS PARKMAN 1
    HISTORICAL GROUPING 16
    SPIRIT OF RESEARCH 22
    HISTORICAL INDUSTRIES 34
    HISTORICAL MONOGRAPHS 48
    HISTORICAL TESTIMONY 60
    HISTORICAL STYLE 71
    LAFAYETTE'S TOUR IN 1824 85
    MONROE AND THE RHEA LETTER 97
    PRESIDENT POLK'S DIARY 121
    PRESIDENT POLK'S ADMINISTRATION . . 139
    REFORM IN PRESIDENTIAL ELECTIONS . 160

II. BIOGRAPHY:
    I. 169
    II. 177
    III. (1839–1846) 188
    IV. (1847–1855) 206
    V. (1855–1859) 223
    VI. (1860–1866) 242
    VII. (1866–1872) 261
    VIII. (1873–1896) 281

HISTORICAL BRIEFS.

FRANCIS PARKMAN.

THE illustrious scholar and historian, whose death we have deplored so recently, found physical drawbacks to his work to hinder and discourage. But all the greater is his meed of success because he surmounted them. His life was, on the whole, a happy one, and rounded out in rare conformity to its appointed task; he passed the Psalmist's full limit of years, as few of our English-speaking historians have done; and, however slow or painful might have been his progress, he completed in his riper years the great enterprise which he had projected in early life. Like one of those fair roses which in hours of recreation he so fondly cultivated, his literary reputation has lingered in full blossom, dispersing its delicate fragrance and beauty among all beholders.

Circumscription in the activities of the present life, when once felt to be inevitable, will turn the studious mind to closer communion with the past; and a lasting solace, no less than a source of usefulness, may be found in identifying one's self with those earlier generations of mankind, among whom he moves superior, with his own little particle of Divine om-

Reprinted from "Harvard Graduates' Magazine," March, 1894.

niscience, cognizant of the consequences where they had groped blindly, and feeling for them accordingly a human sympathy somewhat allied to compassion. Two eminent historians at least [1] have Massachusetts and our own Harvard University sent forth to the world, especially consecrated thus to their vocation, — William Hickling Prescott and Francis Parkman; and it must surely prove strange if the individual career of the earlier of these studious invalids did not largely influence the later. Both came of native New England stock, in which culture and taste were hereditary; both were true-hearted gentlemen by temperament and training; both had strong social and family roots in proud, intellectual Boston, so that seclusion simply clarified their acquaintance. Each inherited a fortune sufficient to relieve him from pecuniary anxiety. The literary tasks of the two were closely related in subject and method of development; Mr. Prescott's theme comprising Spanish dominion in the New World, Mr. Parkman's the later dominion of France; and each directing his research to distant European documents, while out of pictorial incidents which involved the native races he constructed narratives which, grouped together, might vividly illustrate a broad historical period, without assuming the pronounced garb of consecutive history. Their struggles against partial blindness and disability from the outset were singularly alike, and to some extent their experience in the assistance of an amanuensis. Some new tale of patience and iron perseverance under literary obstacles may possibly await us from Mr. Parkman's surviving family. But long ago he must have been deeply impressed in his own

---

[1] Unless tradition errs, a third might fittingly be named, in Richard Hildreth.

person with the facts of Mr. Prescott's beautiful life, which, as written by the felicitous pen of George Ticknor, is certainly the most stimulating biography for studious aspirants that ever was written. Mr. Prescott's fame was at its meridian when Mr. Parkman's star first dawned, and his most popular work, "The Conquest of Mexico,"—a dramatic episode and a tragedy, as is also the "Conspiracy of Pontiac,"— came out while Boston's younger delineator was at college. Often, indeed, must this junior explorer of colonial history have felt in his own heart, whether prompted or unprompted, as he pursued his studious round, what Mr. Prescott has so fittingly recorded: "On the whole there is no happiness so great as that of a permanent and lively interest in some intellectual labor. No other enjoyment can compensate or approach to the steady satisfaction and constantly increasing interest of active literary labor, the subject of meditation when I am out of my study, of diligent and stimulating activity within; to say nothing of the comfortable consciousness of directing my powers in some channel worthy of them, and of contributing something to the stock of useful knowledge in the world."

Francis Parkman was born in Boston, September 16, 1823. He came of a line of honorable Massachusetts ancestors, among whom were college graduates and Congregational clergymen with literary acquirements. From his grandfather, a wealthy and prosperous Boston merchant, he seems to have inherited that decided taste for floriculture which became a marked accomplishment; fondness for books and study being, in a broader sense, a family trait. His father, whose Christian name he bore, had been a favorite pupil and admirer of Dr. Channing, whose liberal tenets he preached at the New North Church in Boston, of which he was pastor for many years. His uncle, George Parkman, was a physician. Both father and uncle gave freely from their ample means to Harvard University; the one to aid the Divinity and the other the Medical School; and the Parkman professorship of pulpit eloquence and pastoral care commemorated in our college catalogue the family surname years before a son's literary fame promised it an academic lustre far greater than beneficence alone could bestow.

An inbred taste for letters combined from early boyhood with a love of woodland adventure to direct the youth's destiny. Frail when a child, Francis was sent to the country home of a maternal relative, near the Middlesex Fells, where he remained for several years. That magnificent forest tract, still in its primitive wildness, gave him a first sympathetic acquaintance with out-of-doors life, which he never lost. Returning home, when turned of twelve, he pursued his classical studies at a private school in Boston, and entered Harvard College in 1840, just seventeen years of age. Here once more the fondness for forest life was manifested; he spent one college vacation in camping and canoeing on the Magalloway River, in northern Maine, to this day a favorite haunt of the sportsman; and in the course of another, he explored the calm waters of Lakes George and Champlain, a region redolent with traditions of the old French and Indian War. Sickness once more diverting him from his regular studies, he was sent on a voyage to Europe, from which he returned in season to graduate with his class in 1844. In the course of his foreign tour he visited Rome, and, lodging in a monastery of the Passionist Fathers, he learned something by observation, for the first time, of those missionary agencies which the Roman Catholic Church had employed in former centuries with so much effect for reclaiming the red tribes of our great interior wilderness.

By this time, and indeed as early as his sophomore year at college, and before passing out of his teens, young Parkman had formed the distinct design of writing a history of the French and Indian War; and what to others might have seemed the casual recreation of youth bore immediately, from his own serious point of view, upon a precocious purpose. Heeding the wishes of his elders, he gave some two years after graduation to the dry study of the law; but destiny proved paramount, and in the summer of 1846 he was seen starting for the far West, with a young kinsman and college-mate for a companion, ostensibly seeking personal adventure, but in reality resolved upon preparing himself by personal observation for the great literary task of life. A printed volume, which gathered in the course of three years a series of sketches he had meantime contributed to the "Knickerbocker Magazine," descriptive of these wild experiences, was his first exploit in authorship; and under the style of the "Oregon Trail," these sketches with their original title first modified, and then restored, made up a book still prominent in our literature. Here the narrator himself is traveller and pioneer, supplying materials of contemporaneous description for historians of a later day to draw upon. An acute comprehension of strange scenery and strange people remote from conventional society, faithfulness to facts, and the power of delineating with humor and picturesque effect whatever may be best worth describing, are evinced in this earliest effort; and the impressiveness of the volume is greatly enhanced by the preface which the author inserted in a later edition, recalling vividly from the retrospect of another quarter of a century the wild scenes and lonely cavalcade which were already of the remote past, never in that once remote and lonely Pike's Peak region to be beheld again. It was in 1846 that the Mexican War was declared, whose first announcement reached our young explorers while they were far out on the plains, though in season to give them that summer a sight of Doniphan's military expedition, as well as of those more peaceful emigrant bands whose winding way was toward Oregon, California, and the Salt Lake wilderness, ignorant of gold and bent only upon agriculture. Curious observers only of such momentous caravans, the two Boston youths indulged their bent by camping among the Sioux Indians, and living upon rough and precarious Indian fare, listening to Indian legends, studying Indian traits and customs, and hunting the buffalo with their roving companions. The young historian gained the information he sought; but he paid dearly for his rash opportunity, for he was confirmed in invalid habits for the rest of his life.

"The Oregon Trail" is autobiographical, and so too are occasional passages in the prefaces which Mr. Parkman has written for his later successful works, more strictly historical. Of the probable influence upon his labors of the renowned Prescott, his older fellow-sufferer and fellow-citizen, we have spoken. To Washington Irving's "Astoria," Mr. Parkman's "Oregon Trail" makes familiar reference; and very likely to recitals of Indian hardships borne by his New England ancestors were added, by the time he became a college student, the fascinating delight of Cooper's "Leather Stocking Tales," whose romance of the French and Indian period has not yet lost its attractive hold upon American youth. Fortified further by his own practical contact with primitive life, whose recital had marked his first launch in literature, he buckled down to the graver task of historian and portrayer of the past. But the star of strength and of the unconquerable will he had now full need to invoke. From the day he returned from the far West to the day of his death he was never again entirely well. Chief among the obstacles to retard his progress was the condition of his sight; and for about three years the light of day was insupportable, and every attempt to read or write completely debarred. Indeed, as Mr. Parkman has recorded, there were two periods preceding 1865, each lasting several years, during which such labors "would have been merely suicidal," and his health forbade reading or writing for much over five minutes at a time, and often forbade it altogether. Only by the most rigid perseverance and economy of strength could such disheartening obstacles be overcome. In sifting materials, and in composition, he had to rely largely, like Mr. Prescott, upon memory and the sense of hearing. His amanuensis would repeatedly read the papers aloud, copious notes and extracts being simultaneously made; but instead of composing in solitude and having recourse to the stylus and noctograph, he relied rather upon dictation to his secretary, who would write down the narrative as he pronounced it. "This process," he adds cheerfully of his own general plan, "though extremely slow and laborious, was not without its advantages, and I am well convinced that the authorities have been even more minutely examined, more scrupulously collected, and more thoroughly digested than they would have been under ordinary circumstances."

The habit of travelling, to visit described localities,

— favored as it is so greatly in later times by our improved facilities of travel, — is one for every narrator of events to turn to account; for not only may interesting traditions be gathered on the spot, but one procures details of local coloring which others could never catalogue for him, and gains besides the inspiration of great surroundings. To Mr. Parkman, with his delicate constitution, such journeys must have afforded a relaxing relief and diversion, besides the indulgence of a strong natural taste and disposition. Through wild regions of the North and West, by the camp-fire or in the canoe, he had already gained familiar acquaintance, and he still continued to visit and examine every spot, near or remote, where the important incidents which he described occurred. The extensive seat of the final French and Indian struggle, the whole region of Detroit, the St. Lawrence, and Plains of Abraham, as well as remote Florida, became thus familiar to him. "In short," as he wrote in 1884, reiterating what he had said in other volumes already, "the subject has been studied as much from life in the open air as at the library table."

But none the less was Mr. Parkman a steady worker in his library; and his search for original documents and among masses of rare material was incessant. Whatever might be the immediate subject, he gathered such valuable collections of papers, in any way accessible, as might aid his description. The truth of the past, and the whole truth, he diligently inquired into. He was not content with secondary authorities, but searched for primary ones in the most conscientious and thorough manner; and he founded each narrative as largely as possible upon original and contemporary materials, collating with the greatest care, and only accepting the statements of secondary writers when found to conform to those who lived in the times. In short, as he expressed himself, he was too fond of his theme to neglect any means within his reach of making his conception of it distinct and true. All this was necessitated to a considerable extent by the crude and promiscuous character of the publications offered in the present choice of subjects; for the history of the French colonization in America was as wild, when Mr. Parkman took it up for research, as that colonization itself. "The field of the history," as he forcibly observes, "was uncultured and unreclaimed, and the labor that awaited me was like that of the border settler, who, before he builds his rugged dwelling, must fell the forest trees, burn the undergrowth, clear the ground, and hew the fallen trunks in due proportion." Yet under the old French régime in Canada the pen was always busy, and among reports to be found in the French archives were voluminous records. To make his investigations closer he visited Europe in 1858, soon after the death of his wife, and prosecuted his researches among the public collections of France, Spain, and England. Other visits followed in 1868, 1872, 1880, and 1881, after the scope of his historical work had enlarged, chiefly at Paris. His preparations for composition were thus exhaustive, and he spared neither labor nor expense. Nor with all his preparation did he feel that his work could be satisfactory unless as a narrator he could enter fully into the atmosphere of the times he described. "Faithfulness to the truth of history," as he justly observed, "involves far more than a research, however patient and scrupulous, into special facts. Such facts may be detailed with the most minute exactness, and still the narrative, taken as a whole, may be unmeaning or untrue. The narrator must seek to imbue himself with the life and spirit of the time. He must study events in their bearings, near and remote; in the character, habits, and manners of those who took part in them. He must himself be, as it were, a sharer or spectator of the men he describes."

Two other observations from Mr. Parkman's pen are so apt and admirable that we cannot refrain from quoting them. One relates to historical citation, a matter in which critics are apt to be over-exacting, as though historians ought to load down pages with pedantic notes, the usual display of second-hand assistance, and not be trusted at all upon their responsible statements. Observing on his own behalf that his citations are much less than his material, most of the latter being of a collateral and illustrative nature, "such," he well adds, "is necessarily the case, where one adhering to facts tries to animate them with the life of the past." And, again, seeking to be fair and impartial in his estimates of men and measures, he challenged the descendants of those who thought him otherwise to test his proofs. "As extremists on each side," he wrote finally at the close of his labors, "have charged me with favoring the other, I hope I have not been unfair to either."

With views of his vocation so just and honorable, Mr. Parkman, slowly of necessity, but with firm tenaciousness, wrought out his literary plans. His first work, "The Conspiracy of Pontiac," in two volumes, was published in 1851: the subject being a dramatic one of war and of conquest, and chosen by himself most happily for the portrayal of forest life and the Indian character. It was not until January, 1865, that his next volume appeared, on "Pioneers of

France in the New World;" and meanwhile he had made an unsuccessful venture with a work of pure fiction. So long a gap in his historical labors he never left again; for by this time he had accepted sickness and physical trial as permanent incidents of his career, while his historical plan had widened into its fullest scope. At first intending to limit himself to the great closing struggle for supremacy between France and Great Britain, he had decided at length to cover the whole field of French colonization in America. Under such an arrangement, "Pontiac's Conspiracy" would take its place as a sequel to his works written later, while its own introductory sketch served as the base of more extended and consecutive narratives to follow. Other volumes were accordingly under way when "Pioneers of France" appeared; and in 1867 he published "Jesuits in North America," a thrilling record of missionary labors, which was followed in 1869 by "La Salle, and the Discovery of the Great West," a recital of explorations about the upper Mississippi. "The Old Régime in Canada" came out in 1874, treating of the transition period of 1653–1680; and to this succeeded, in 1877, "Count Frontenac, and New France under Louis XIV.," the story of the bravest warrior and viceroy France ever sent to this continent. These works, following the earliest, were in single volumes, each taking its independent place in a series of narratives entitled "France and England in the New World." By this time the patient scholar had reached the full prime of life, and time admonished him to economize his remaining strength to the utmost. He interrupted the course of description sufficiently to make sure of that romantic period, the British conquest of Canada, which had first captivated his youthful imagination. "Montcalm and Wolfe," a work of two volumes, was therefore his next undertaking; this he finished by 1884, soon after rounding his threescore years; and leaving the climax of battle upon the Plains of Abraham for a closing scene, he now turned back once more with his veteran pen to fill the intervening gap. In 1892 two more volumes, entitled "The Half-Century of Conflict," and embracing the period 1700-1748, preceded "Montcalm and Wolfe" in the completed series. Mr. Parkman's monumental work, in spite of intervening obstacles which prolonged its execution, was now finished, with the same conscientious, thorough, and painstaking devotion which had always characterized him, and he now took final leave of his labors. His calculation of allotted strength had not been wide of the mark, for the very next year after laying down the historical pen his earthly limit was reached. He died a gentle death on the 8th of November, 1893.

Mr. Parkman's peculiar merits as a historian we have already indicated, — thoroughness of preparation, a painstaking accuracy, justness in balancing authorities, scholarly tastes and comprehension. and the constant disposition to be truthful and impartial, to which were added skill and an artistic grace and dignity in composition. His style was crystal-clear and melodious as a mountain brook, which flows obedient to easy impulse, setting off the charms of natural scenery by its own exquisite naturalness. The aroma of the woods and of woodland life is in all his books, among which, perhaps, "The Conspiracy of Pontiac" will remain the favorite. Here and constantly in dealing with the Indian, with the primeval American landscape and its primeval inhabitants, his touch is masterly and unapproachable; and so, too, in describing the sympathetic contact of France with a race which British interference doomed to destruction. French explorers, French missionaries and warriors, stand out lifelike from these interesting narratives, since he wrote to interest and not merely to instruct. Generalization and the broader historical lessons are to be found rather in the pages of his preface, as Mr. Parkman wrote, than in the narratives themselves, most of his later subjects being, in fact, extended ones for the compass of the book; and with his wealth of materials he kept closely to the tale. But in these preliminary, or rather final, deductions may be found pregnant passages of force and eloquence.

A life so symmetrical in its literary scope and occupation, and so minutely adjusted to the drawbacks of ill-health, could hardly have projected far into the active concerns of his age. On a few occasions only Mr. Parkman was tempted to discuss problems of the day in the magazines, when the conservatism of his temperament became manifest. His clear preference was for literary topics and subjects cognate to his studies. He felt, however, and felt deeply, the tremendous tumult, culminating in bloody strife, which went on without his domestic cell, and the preface to his "Pioneers of France," a volume published just before that fratricidal conflict ended, and dedicated to young kinsmen "slain in battle," reads like a solemn requiem. Somewhat later, after victory for freedom and the Union developed evil tendencies, his mind once more compared the régime of earlier centuries, and noted those vices in which democracy and autocracy approach one another. A home atmosphere made his studious seclusion redolent of lifelong friendships and attachments. A widower for half his life, with two daughters who have married and survived him, his winters were usually passed in the heart of his native Boston, and his summers in a once picturesque suburb, long since comprised within the same civic confines. He dedicated his various volumes to kinsmen dear to him, to a choice friend or two who had lightened his studies by helpful sympathy, to his college class of 1844, and, finally, and for the last time, to Harvard College, the *alma mater* under whose influence, as he acknowledged, his life purpose had been conceived.

To the Massachusetts Historical Society, of which he was vice-president and a most honored member, Mr. Parkman gave from time to time his collections of manuscript material used in the preparation of his works, which formed, when completed, some seventy volumes, mostly in folio. Harvard honored him with its degree of LL.D., and he served upon its Board of Overseers, and more lately as one of the Corporation Fellows. But his immediate interests extended elsewhere as his fame increased. In recognition of his taste for gardening he was chosen president of the Massachusetts Horticultural Society, besides occupying for two years a chair in the Agricultural Department of his own University.

When in 1880 was formed in Boston the St. Botolph Club, whose especial aim was to bring together men of talent and eminence in art, literature, and the professions, wealth being regarded secondary, Mr. Parkman was its conspicuous choice for president, and for six years he filled that trust with marked zeal and fidelity; and after declining health compelled him to retire, he still stood upon its list as vice-president. Faithful in these earlier years to its interests, he was constantly to be seen at its Saturday evening gatherings, genial and approachable to all, and promoting its hospitalities by as cordial a solicitude as though he were host in his own private parlors. Many of other circles in life, who met him then and there for the first and only times, were surprised to find him in appearance, when approaching threescore, not an invalid bent with years and sufferings, delicate, with pallid face furrowed with wrinkles, but decidedly elastic in step, fresh and handsome in appearance, with an impressive aspect of well-preserved and even healthful maturity. His height could scarcely have been an inch under six feet; his whole frame was compacted and even sturdy-looking; his hair, though tinged with gray, was abundant, and his head and full neck were firmly set upon broad and capable shoulders. He showed a high forehead, a face closely shaven, which exposed strong and resolute features, a chin and mouth bespeaking firmness and persistency, at the same time that his beaming eyes, of a soft brown color, were full of kindly and even tender expression. In his whole demeanor he showed dignity and an innate gentility happily combined. A portrait of two thirds length, painted at this period and an excellent likeness, is among the ornaments of the club in its new house; and on the evening following Mr. Parkman's funeral, when the members gathered for a memorial meeting, and this oil painting in its appropriate frame, decked with crape and laurel, stood in the picture gallery with a full light thrown upon it, it truly seemed, while one after another in sombre shadow pronounced a tribute, that the gentle and graceful figure was about to glide forward from the canvas to give a parting hand-grasp in silent and sympathetic benediction.

HISTORICAL GROUPING.

NOT far from where I am now standing, a grateful city has erected a stately monument to its soldiers and sailors who died in the late Civil War. This monument was erected about fifteen years after the war was over. At the base from which rises its pure granite shaft, may be seen bas-reliefs in bronze, one for each side, which depict appropriate scenes, with portraits to recall the heroic men who bore part in them. One of these metallic studies idealizes the departure of a Massachusetts regiment, in 1861, for the seat of war. How often do I recall that scene, as I many times witnessed it in impressible youth! Most fitly, the artist's central figure is that of our immortal war governor, John A. Andrew. But among the images grouped about him, that of the man is absent who, next to the governor himself, bore the chief part in organizing and despatching our State troops, and whose face was scarcely less familiar to our Massachusetts soldiers, whether departing or returning. Others historically associated with such scenes are wanting; while among the embossed likenesses more or less appropriate, which are here preserved for posterity, one is that of a distinguished citizen who in 1861 was crying down war, and urging that Southern States be permitted to secede in

Read before the American Historical Association, at Boston, May 23, 1887.

peace; another likeness recalls a son honored here indeed, years later, but who through this whole period of fraternal strife resided in a far distant State and city. I do not bring up this circumstance for reproach, but because it fitly introduces and illustrates the point to which I wish briefly to direct your attention. My subject is Historical Grouping, or what, perhaps, I might better style Historical Background. Whatever memorable scenes of the past it may be the function of historian or historical painter to recall, he should delineate with scrupulous fidelity to truth the lesser as well as the greater surroundings; his canvas should group those together, and only those, who were actually related to the event and worked out in unison the great issue. Two chief considerations enforce this duty: (1) That in the mad zeal of our modern age for present and future, the past is easily overlaid and obliterated; (2) That while Fame takes decent care of her chief hero, of the actor most responsible, she easily neglects the subordinates, however indispensable their parts might have been. "Set me down as I am" is the common appeal of patriots of every rank to posterity and the impartial historian; and the true relation to the event which the scholar must consider is not that of one individual, but of many, in the nicely graded proportion of foreground and background.

The Chief Executive, the warlike commander, the great personification of his time, him we follow with the eye; we discuss and re-discuss his achievements; we analyze his traits, over and over, even until we obscure them by our own ingenuity; we study his individual growth from infancy up, anxious to discover in a single brain, if we may, the seed which must have germinated in other minds and dispersed results to germinate again and still more widely, before the perfect flower and perfect opportunity could possibly have bloomed. The great hero of the age is still, as ever, the man most responsible for what was successfully accomplished; yet what hero ever achieved a great success, except by happily combining the wisdom, skill, and valor of others whose ideas, whose lives were intertwined with his own, and by bringing this whole subordinate force to bear properly upon the occasion? Let us look more particularly to the manifold influences and counter influences which work out the great problems of an age and republican system like our own. The public movements of American society in the present century are not accomplished without the combined force of elements more or less hidden from the casual vision, which in a large degree are coequal. The scholar, the recluse philosopher, the poet, the orator, the editor, the teacher, the legislator, the statesman, gives each an impulse and direction to affairs far greater, in normal times, than the professional warrior. Nor is it the individual mind that sways American politics, but rather the majority or average mind, the mind that has been brought by toilsome precept and discipline to the point of earnest conviction. History has its leaders still; but the leader who unites the highest expression of thought and action rarely appears in the modern days; our foremost administrator is apt to be more vigorous than original, and in this country, at least, we look no longer for the autocrat, the warrior chief, who plans conquests and drains his people that he may march an army whithersoever he will. A further thought rises in this connection; namely, that the reputation once achieved has now no sure bulwark to protect it. The sacrificial days are over. The people observe no longer the calendar of their demi-gods. Ulysses cannot reckon upon offices of tenderness, when he is gone, from his blameless Telemachus. So great and so constant becomes the pressure and counter pressure of ideas in our modern life, that civilization seems to wear into the solid land itself, like some turbulent torrent, washing away at one bank and bringing down alluvium at another. The past, with its traditions and examples, is ignored; not that we mean to falsify, but that we are indifferent to it; novelties absorb the present attention; the son cavils at the faults and limitations of the father; and in the headlong and incessant push and jostle of men, parties, and ideas, it is not enough for fame that a man filled well the measure of his own age, if a new age requires new measures.

Such being our present situation, in place of the few ambitious great, we find the scope fast enlarging for the many men and their petty and manifold ambitions. And no easier or cheaper means of gratifying a petty ambition can be found than in clustering about the leaders who have gained recognition and come into fashion, buzzing at their ears, and borrowing somewhat of the lustre and prestige of good neighborhood. Of the deserving recipients of applause some die late, some early; all do not leave their papers sorted and ready for posterity to judge of their own admitted inspiration. Here, then, is the opportunity for the parasite, the flatterer, the eleventh-hour convert, indeed, for all survivors who can grasp the key of the situation for themselves and their friends, to work seasonably upon the platform and into the conspicuous background, when the artist appears: just as loiterers elsewhere insinuate themselves into a group when they see the camera mounted. The picture is taken and placed on exhibition for the admiration of posterity. Who are not friends, who are not enthusiasts, when the man, the cause, has triumphed? And as for the artist whose handicraft was thus employed, why should he be less susceptible to the kindness of benefactors than the great masters into whose immortal paintings of saints and martyrs, and of the Holy Family itself, were introduced the portraits of their own patron bishops and duchesses?

Against all this false grouping for historical effect, wherever it may be found, this sordid commingling of souls noble and ignoble, this separation of the acknowledged leader from associations which combined to produce his great action, and gave him strength, dignity, and sympathy at the momentous opportunity, I invoke the justice, the scholarship, and the incorruptible honor of the historian. Let him take his impartial stand among bygone men and events, and, so far as in him lies, reproduce the past as it was. Let him extricate reputations from the dust of oblivion and cunning entanglements, and award posthumous honors anew without fear or favor. Let him observe the laws of perspective, and bring foreground and background into their just and harmonious relation. Let him distinguish scrupulously between the recognition which follows success and that rarer sort which precedes it in the day of personal sacrifice. And in order to do all this, let him not trust too closely to epitaphs placed on tombstones of the dead by the immediate survivors, nor to effigies bronze or brazen; for much depends upon the bias and worldly hopes of the men who set them in position. To rescue history from the age most dangerous because most likely to pervert its truth, and yet at the same time the age most plausible in its expression — that age, I mean, which next succeeds the event — should command one's diligent effort. For every epoch is best read and explained by its own light, by its own contemporaneous record; and every other record ought to be held but secondary and subservient in comparison by the student who searches for the real truth of events. This last observation may be thought a trite one; but I am well convinced that it is at the very foundation of historical study and criticism, such as a society like ours ought to practise and inculcate.

SPIRIT OF RESEARCH.

WHAT, let us ask, is history? And by what image may we present to the mind of the student a proper conception of that department of study? Emerson, our American Plato, pictures as a vast sea the universal mind to which all other minds have access. "Of the works of this mind," he adds, "history is the record." That idea is a leading one of this philosopher. Man he considers the encyclopædia, the epitome of facts; the thought, he observes, is always prior to the fact, and is wrought out in human action.

Such a conception may suit the philosophic mind; it may commend itself to men of thought, as contrasted with men of action. But it seems to me too vast if not too vague a definition for an appropriate basis to historical investigation. No one can project history upon such a plan, except man's Maker, the Universal Mind itself. Thought itself may precede the fact, but the two do not coincide nor form a perfect sequence. The empire of thought differs greatly from that of personal action; we each live but one life, while we may propose a hundred. The works of the mind involve all knowledge, all reasoning, all experience. Nor can we with accuracy picture the human mind as a tranquil sea tossing only in its own

Read before the American Historical Association, at Washington, December 31, 1889.

agitations, but rather as an onward force working through strong physical barriers. History, in truth, is the record of human thought in active motion, of thought which is wrought out into action, of events in their real and recorded sequence. The individual acts upon his external surroundings; those surroundings react upon him and upon his fellows. Men, tribes, nations, thus acting, mould one another's career and are moulded in return. History leaves the whole boundless empire of unfettered mental philosophy, of fiction, of imagination. It deals with facts; it notes and narrates what has actually transpired and by whose agency; and it draws where it may the moral. History, in short, is the record of consecutive events, — of consecutive public events.

This broad truth should be kept in view, that the human mind (under which term we comprise volition, and not the intellectual process alone), that the individual character acts upon the circumstances surrounding it, upon external nature, upon external fellow-beings. These persons and things external not only modify and influence one's attempted action, but modify his thought and feeling; they react upon him, form and influence his character, his destiny. This makes human history, and it makes the forecast of that history forever uncertain.

The picture, then, that we should prefer to present to the imagination is not of one vast universal mind, calmly germinating, fermenting, conceiving; not of one mind at equilibrium, having various inlets — but of a torrent in motion. They did wisely and naturally who mapped out for us a stream of history flowing onward, and widening and branching in its flow. Downward and onward, this impetuous torrent of human life obeys its own law of gravitation. It advances like a river, with its feeders or its deltas; or like the march of an immense army, now re-enforced, now dividing into columns, now reuniting, — but going forever on and never backward. Let us reject, therefore, the idea of an *à priori* history and whatever conception conjures up a human mind planning history in advance and then executing it. Buckle was oppressed to death by the burden of such an idea as that of reducing the whole history of this world's civilization to a law of natural selection. There is no rigid scientific development to the human race. The particle of divine essence which is in man formulates, creates, compels to its will, changes because of its desire for change; though, after all, it bends to the laws of natural necessity. The man of genius may invent; he may construct a wonderful motive-engine which propels by steam or electricity; yet he may be battered to pieces by this same machine, if ignorant or careless of some latent physical cause. We speak, too, of prophecy; but prophecy is vague. "Westward," says Bishop Berkeley, "the course of empire takes its way;" and he looked through the vista of a century. But who, of all our statesmen and philanthropists who flourished forty years ago, — and wise and great, indeed, were many of them, — foretold with accuracy how and through what agencies the problem of American slavery, which they so earnestly discussed, would reach its historical solution?

To take, then, our simile of the onward torrent from distant sources, or the army advancing from afar: observe how absorbed was ancient history with the larger streams fed by hidden fountains; how its narrative was confined to the great leaders of thousands and tens of thousands. But in modern history each individual has his relative place; and looking as through a microscope we see an intricate network of rills from which the full stream is supplied. In this consists the difference between ancient and modern life, ancient and modern history. Simplicity is the characteristic of the primitive age; complexity is that of our present civilized and widely multiplied society. The ancient force was the force of the pre-eminent leader, — of the king, the warrior chief; but the modern force is that rather of combined mankind, — of the majority. Individuals were formerly absorbed under the domination of a single controlling will, but now they are blended or subdued by the co-operation of wills, among which the greatest or the pre-eminent is hard to discover. The course of history all the while is consecutive, knowing no cessation. There is a present, a past, and a future; but the present soon becomes the past, the future takes its turn as the present. And, after all, the only clear law of history is that of motion incessantly onward.

As students of history, we seek next a subject and a point of view. Look, then, upon this vast chart of the world's progress. Retrace its course, if you will, and choose where you shall explore. Do not choose at random, but with this great universal record to guide you as a chart; as a chart capable, indeed, of correction, but in the main correct enough to serve the navigator. Having thus chosen, circumscribe your work: confine your exploration to a particular country, to a particular period, say of twenty, thirty, or a hundred years; let your scrutiny be close, and discover what you may to render the great chart fuller and more accurate than hitherto. If universal history be your subject, you will not go far beyond tracing the bold headlands, while on the other hand, with a small compass of work, you may contribute much information of genuine value to your age. Explore from some starting-point; you can descend upon it like a hawk. You may require some time to study its vicinity, to look back and consider what brought the stream to this point. But your main investigation will be not by exploring to a source, but by following the stream in its onward and downward current. In the present age one must be ignorant of much if he would be proficient in something.

Our chart of history opens like an atlas; it presents page after page of equal size, but with a lessening area for the sake of an increasing scale. One page exhibits a hemisphere, another a continent, another a nation; others, in turn, the state, the county, the municipal unit. From a world we may thus reduce the focus, until we have mapped within the same spaces a town or city, or even a single house; from a population of millions we may come down to a tribe, a family, or even (as in a biography) to a single individual, and we retrace the human course accordingly. Or we may trace backwards, as the genealogist does, in an order reverse to biography or general history. As we have projected, so we work, we investigate. In such an atlas as I am describing, how different appear both civil and physical configurations at different epochs. Compare, for instance, a map of the United States of our latest date with earlier ones in succession from 1787. Not only in national names and boundaries do they differ, not only in the obscure or erroneous delineation of lakes and rivers in unexplored regions, but in that dotting of towns and cities, that marking of county divisions, which positively indicates the advance of a settled population and settled State governments. Maps of different epochs like these, where they exist, are part of a permanent historical record.

Involved in the study of any civilization is the study of its religion, of its literature, of its political and military movements, of the appliances of science, of the changes and development of trade, commerce, and industries. Each of these influences may be traced apart, or their combined influence may be shown upon the course of some great people. In this present enlightened age, nations intersect one another more and more in their interests, and you may feel the pulse of the whole civilized world through the daily press. How different the task of preparing such a history as the nineteenth century requires, from that of ancient Athens, of China, of mediæval Britain, of early America. But in all tasks unity and selection should be the aim, and above all circumscription. One must measure out his work with exactness, make careful estimates, and work the huge materials into place, besides using his pencil with the dignity and grace of an artist. In a word, he should be an architect. It is because of this union of the ideal and practical that Michael Angelo deserves the first place among men distinguished in the fine arts. And for this reason, too, we may well rank Gibbon as the foremost among historians; as greater, indeed, than Thucydides, Sallust, or any other of those classical writers who have so long been held up for modern reverence. And this is because, with skill equally or nearly as great as theirs, he conceived and wrought out a task far more difficult. In historical narrative the greatest triumph consists in tracing out and delineating with color and accuracy a variety of intricate influences which contribute to the main result. And who has done this so well as the author of the "Decline and Fall of the Roman Empire," that greatest of all historical themes, that most impressive and momentous of all human events? See the hand of the master unfolding the long train of emperors and potentates; painting the revolt and irruption of distant nations, of remote tribes; gathering upon his canvas the Greeks, the Scythians, the Arabs, Mohammed and his followers, the fathers of the Christian Church, the Goths and northern barbarians, who were destined to shape the civilization of modern Europe; leading his readers with stately tread through the whole grand pathway down which the highest type of a pagan civilization sank slowly into the shades and dissolution of the dark ages. I will not deny that Gibbon had faults as a historian; that his stately pomp might become wearisome, that he partook somewhat of the French sensuousness and scepticism which surrounded him as he labored. But of his profound scholarship and artistic skill there can be no question. Contrast with a task like his the simple narrative of some brief strife under a few heroes or a single one, — like the history of the Peloponnesian or Jugurthine war, or like that of the Cortes invasion of Mexico which our own Prescott has so admirably described, — and see how immense is the difference. Yet I would not be understood to disparage these other writers with simpler subjects. They have instructed and interested posterity and their own times; their fame is deservedly lasting; there is room in historical literature for them and for all. And our Anglo-Saxon appears to be, of all historical explorers, the best adapted to portray the manners and events of foreign nations and distant times. Thucydides and Xenophon wrote each of his own country alone; and so did Sallust, Livy, Tacitus.

But Gibbon perfected himself in a foreign literature and tongue so as to write of other lands; and so, too, did our Prescott and Motley.

Here let us observe how much easier it is to be graphic, to interest and attract the reader, when one's story has simple unity and relates to personal exploit. Biography, or the study of individual leaders, is at the foundation of the narratives which are most widely read and most popular; in the Bible, for instance, in Homer, in the wars of Alexander, Cæsar, or Napoleon. Biography excites interest because it develops, as in the reader's own experience, the growth of a certain individual life to which all other lives bear but an incidental relation; and for this reason, too, biography is partial. The modern temperament, however, leads us to investigate, besides, the growth of the people who were ruled, the development of their laws, manners, customs, and institutions. In either case the interest that moves the reader is human. That military and political course of a community with which history is chiefly engrossed moves far differently, to be sure, under an absolute monarch than in a democracy; in the former case foibles and caprice are those of a person, in the latter they are those of a whole people. Yet we observe in all but the ruder ages of mankind the refining influence upon rulers which is exerted by philosophy, by religion, literature, and the arts. Note this, for example, under the reign of Solomon, of Pericles, of Alexander, of Constantine; and yet it is a lasting regret to posterity that out of epochs like theirs so little is left on record concerning the daily lives and habits of the people they governed. That must be a rigid tyranny, indeed, whose government has not recognized to some extent the strong though insensible force of popular customs. Custom constantly crystallizes into laws, which the legislature, the court, or the monarch stamps with authority; and thus are local institutions pruned and trained like the grape-vine on a trellis. We find in the most primitive society wills and the transmission of property recognized; buying and selling; trade and commerce (whence come revenue and personal prosperity); marriage and the seclusion, greater or less, of the family circle. How seldom has the reader associated all these with the wealth of Solomon and the Queen of Sheba, with the vicissitudes of Crœsus, the voluptuous pleasures of Xerxes, Cleopatra, or the later Cæsars; and yet it is certain that unless the subjects of monarchs like these had pursued their private business successfully, amassed fortunes of their own, brought up families and increased in numbers, the monarch could not have been arrayed with such luxury; for royal revenues come from taxation, and the richest kings and nobles take but a percentage from the general wealth. The customs of one nation are borrowed by others; Moses, Lycurgus, Solon, among the great lawgivers, framed codes each for his own people after observing the institutions of other and older countries, and considering how best to adapt them. Government has rightly been likened to a coat which is cut differently to fit each figure, each nation; and, more than this, the garb itself may differ in pattern, since the object is to clothe different communities appropriately to the tastes and habits of each. We shall continue to regret, then, that the ancient writers have left us so little real illustration concerning the habits of these earlier peoples, — how they worked and sported, and what was their intercourse and mode of life. Research in archæology may yet supply such information in a measure; and of the institutions, the embodied customs, we have, fortunately, some important remains. No contribution survives, more valuable to this end, than the books of Roman jurisprudence which were compiled under Justinian. Though one of the lesser rulers of that once illustrious empire, he has left a fame for modern times more conspicuous than that of Julius or Augustus Cæsar; and this is because he brought into permanent and enduring form for the guidance and instruction of all succeeding ages the wisest laws, the best epitome of human experience, the broadest embodiment of customs, which ever regulated ancient society in the mutual dealings of man and man.

As for the progress of our modern society which emerges from the mediæval age succeeding the Roman collapse, its advance in knowledge and the arts, in the successive changes of manners and pursuits, there is much yet to be gathered and exposed to view for illustration; though with respect to England we owe much to Macaulay for setting an example of investigation upon that broader line which Niebuhr and others of his school had initiated for Roman history. And Macaulay achieved the additional triumph of making such investigation attractive. Statutes and judicial reports (to quote Daniel Webster) are overflowing fountains of knowledge respecting the progress of Anglo-Saxon society, from feudalism down to the full splendor of the commercial age. And from the modern invention of printing, let us add, and particularly since the growth and development of the modern press, we find (with all the faults of fecundity and fallibility which are peculiar to journalism) a picture of the world's daily life set forth which far surpasses in its vivid and continuous detail any collection of ancient records. Our modern newspaper may pander for the sake of gain; it may avow no higher aim in affairs than to please a paying constituency; and yet, for better or worse, it wields and will continue to wield an immense power. The reporter may be brazen-faced, inclined to scandalous gossip and ribaldry; the news may be spread forth disjointed, founded on false rumor, requiring correction; editorial comments may be wilfully partisan, or thundered from the Olympus height of a safe circulation; but, even at its worst, so long as it is duly curbed by the laws of libel so essential for the citizens' protection, what with advertisements, business news, the discussion of current topics, the description of passing events and the transient impression made by them, our newspaper holds the mirror up to modern society; while at its best, journalism sits in her chariot, pencil in hand, like that marble muse herself in our national capitol, over the timepiece of the age. The newspaper's truest revelation is that unconscious one of the passions and prejudice of the times, and of that cast of popular thought under which events were born; it preserves imperishable the fashion prevailing, for posterity to look upon with reverence or a smile. But in the present age the journalist should beware how he presents his columns to bear the double weight of universal advertiser and universal purveyor of knowledge, lest he make a chaos of the whole. As in the former centuries records were scanty, so in the century to come they will be found superabundant, unless fire or deluge diminish them. Pregnant facts, such as in the past we search for in vain, lie buried, under prevalent methods, in bushel-heaps of worthless assertion. To know the old era, you must search with a lantern; to know the new era, you must winnow.

Research is a fitting word to apply in historical studies; for by this word we import that one is not content to skim the surface of past events, but prefers to probe, to investigate, to turn the soil for himself. It is original exploration which makes such studies attractive and stimulating. We walk the streets of buried cities and roam through the deserted houses, once instinct with life, piercing the lava crust of careless centuries; we place our hearts and minds, richer by accumulated experience, close to the passions and intellects of an earlier age; and we listen to the heart-beat of a race of mankind who reached forward, as our own race is reaching and as all races reach in turn, to catch the omens of a far off destiny. The grand results and the grand lessons of human life are ours in the retrospect, and in the retrospect alone. And while retracing thus the footprints of the past, we shall do well if we deduce the right moral; if we judge of human actions dispassionately and as befits scholars of riper times and a broader revelation; if we keep under due constraint that laudable but dangerous passion for new discovery, so as neither to revive buried calumnies nor to weigh evidence with a perverted bias to novelty. Let our judgment give full force to the presumption that the long-settled opinion is the true one, and let our spirit of research be imbued at all times with the fearless purpose to know and to promulgate the truth.

HISTORICAL INDUSTRIES.

Historians are sometimes said to be a long-lived race. To historical students, at all events, this is a comfortable theory. Recent examples of a productive old age, such as Ranke so long supplied, and our own illustrious George Bancroft, may have lent strong force to the supposition. History herself, no doubt, is a long-winded muse, and demands of each votary the power of continuance. But I doubt whether statistics would bear out strongly this theory of a long-lived race. Among modern historians, well-known, who have died a natural death, neither Niebuhr, Gibbon, Macaulay, nor Hildreth reached his sixtieth year; both Prescott and Motley died at about sixty-three.[1] On the other hand, to take poets alone whom many of us may have seen in the flesh, both Longfellow and Lowell passed, well preserved, the bounds of threescore years and ten; while Bryant, Whittier, and Holmes, the last of whom still vigorously survives, enjoyed life much beyond fourscore; and of English composers the most famous, both Tennyson and Browning mellowed long before they dropped.

Undoubtedly, however, steady and systematic brain-work without brain worry, conduces to health and

Read before the American Historical Association, at Chicago, July 11, 1893.

[1] Francis Parkman has recently died at the age of seventy, longer spared for his work than any of those above mentioned.

long life, whatever be the special occupation; and who may better claim that precious condition of mind than the average historian? For of all literary pursuits none on the whole appears so naturally allied to competent means and good family. Public office and influence — the making of history — have belonged in most epochs before our own to the aristocracy, superior station being usually linked in the world's experience to wealth; and it is the scions and kindred of those who have been actors and associates in events, if not the actors and associates themselves, whose pens describe past exploits most readily. These have gained the readiest access for their studies to the public archives, — ransacking, moreover, that private correspondence of illustrious leaders defunct, which family pride guards so jealously; and with mingled urbanity and scholarship they maintain the polish of easy intercourse in the courtly circles of their own times. One ought to be a man of letters and liberal training for such a life, a close student, and yet, in some sense, a person of affairs. It costs long leisure, and money too, to collect materials properly, while the actual composition proceeds in comparison but slowly. Nor are the royalties from historical writings, however successful and popular, likely to remunerate one greatly, considering his aggregate outlay; but rather than in any enhanced pecuniary ease, his reward must be looked for in the distinguished comradeship of the dead and of the living — in the satisfaction that he has performed exalted labors faithfully for the good of his fellow-men, and found them in his own day fairly appreciated. Happy the historian, withal, whom fame or early promise has helped into some collateral and congenial employment of indirect advantage to his task.

Calmness and constancy of purpose carry us on steadily in work of this character, with powers of mind that strengthen by habitual exercise. It is not brilliancy of assault, it is not the pompous announcement of a narrative purpose, that determines the historian; but rather silent concentration and perseverance. The story one begins will never be thoroughly finished while the world stands; and on the one hand is the temptation of preparing with too much elaboration or fastidiousness to narrate rapidly enough, and on the other of trying to tell more than the circumscribed limits of preparation and of personal capacity will permit. Men who are free from financial anxieties will be tempted aside from the incessant laborious work by the seductions of pleasure. Thus Prescott, the blind historian, with excuses much stronger than Milton ever had for social ease and inaction, found himself compelled to overcome his temptations to sloth by placing himself habitually under penal bonds to his secretary to prepare so many pages by a given time.

More, however, than the gift of time and income the world will scarcely look for in a literary man. It is the publisher, rather, who projects encyclopedias and huge reservoirs of useful information, and who embarks large money capital in the enterprise. A few celebrated authors, to be sure, have figured, some in a dormant sense, as publishers of their own works; like Richardson, the English novelist, for instance, the Chambers brothers, and, most disastrously for himself, Sir Walter Scott. Many literary men of means own their plates, while putting firms forward to print and publish for them notwithstanding.

But it is reserved, I believe, to America, and to the present age, to furnish to the world the first unique example of bookseller, book collector, historian, and publisher, all combined in one, whose fortune is devoted to the fulfilment of a colossal pioneer research. We must count, I apprehend, the living historian of "The Pacific States" among the wealthy benefactors of our higher learning; for that prolific brood of brown volumes such as no other historian from Herodotus down ever fathered for his own, can hardly have repaid their immense cost and labor of preparation, even with the ultimate sale added of the famous library whose precious contents gave them substance.

Mr. Bancroft's "Literary Industries," a stimulating and well-written book, recounts fully the methods he employed, with a corps of literary writers under his personal direction, in ransacking the contents of that huge library, since offered for sale, to furnish forth his own compendious treatises upon the archæology, history, and ethnology of our Pacific Coast, hitherto but little illustrated by its latest race of conquerors. And he felicitates himself that an enterprise, otherwise beyond any one man's power of execution, was brought by his own organized efforts within the compass of some thirty years.

I will not undertake any direct criticism of such comprehensive methods as his, nor seek to disparage labors so generously and withal so successfully rounded out to a close. But this present age runs very strongly, as it seems to me, — and perhaps too strongly, — to vast executive projects in every department of human activity. We are apt, in consequence, to sacrifice high individual thought and mental creativeness to feats of technique and organized mastery; while our trusts, our syndicates, and combiners of capital seek so constantly to monopolize profits, both moral and material, for themselves, by welding and concentrating the lesser resources of individuals, that single endeavor faints in the unequal rivalry. Such a development artfully conducts the human race back, sooner or later, to a species of slavery; it hands over the many to the patronage of the powerful few; and, unless checked, it must prove eventually fatal to the spirit of manly emulation. Just as the surf of property accumulation breaks fitly at each owner's death upon the broad bulwark of equal distribution among kindred, so would it be wise, I think, could public policy contrive by some indirection to limit in effect the achievements of a lifetime in every direction to what fairly and naturally belongs to the scope of that single life in competition with others; and at the same time that it lets the greatest prizes go to the fittest, could it but encourage each member of society to achieve still his best.

At all events, if you will, let huge engineering, let the products of organized exploit, go to increase the material comfort of the race; but for art, for scholarship, for literature and religion, for whatever appeals most to imagination and the moral life, I would keep the freest play possible to the individual and to individual effort. One forcible preacher reaches more hearts than the composite of a hundred preachers. And, furthermore, in gathering historical facts, we should remember that what may be convenient for simple reference is not equally so for consecutive reading. There is a natural progression, coincident with the stream of time, in all history, all biography, all fiction; and to attempt to read backward, or on parallel lines, or by other arbitrary arrangement, produces nausea, drowsiness, and confusion of ideas. In Washington Irving's grotesque dream in the British Museum, the bookmakers at their toilsome tasks about him seemed suddenly transformed into masqueraders decking themselves out fantastically from the literary clothes-presses of the past about them.

Co-operative history, or the alliance of various writers in one description of past events, is a favorite device of publishers in our late day, for producing volumes which may give each talented contributor as little personal exertion as possible. Of such enterprises, that which assigns to each author his own limited period or range of events, is the best, because the most natural, and here it is only needful that each should confine his labor to his own portion, avoiding the dangers of comparison. Less satisfactory, because far more liable to contradiction and confusion, is that co-operative history which distributes topics such as the progress of science, education, religion, or politics, for a general and detached review, and, instead of any proper narrative at all, supplies a mass of heterogeneous essays. The latest plan of the kind which publishers have brought to my notice, is history upon an alphabetical arrangement, resembling a Gazetteer, — which proposes, of course, the use of scissors more than pen or brain. Mr. Hubert Bancroft's plan is, finally, that of a literary bureau, with salaried workers more or less trained, over whom presides the one nominal historian.

In this nineteenth century you may thus see historical chasms bridged, and jungles, once impenetrable, laid open to the sunlight. But where can one safely define here the limits of original authorship? At what point does the elucidation of facts rise above the dignity of manual labor? And how far, in fine, may you trust the chief executive of such an enterprise for his responsible scholarship; rather than merely as the editor of a vast compilation, or as one who rubs into shape, and gives a literary gloss to materials of doubtful authenticity?

Let me address myself, then, rather to the encouragement of that great majority of historical students and writers whose purpose is to accomplish, and to accomplish conscientiously, results which may fairly be comprehended within the space of a single and unaided human life. Even they who plead most forcibly for co-operative investigation in history distinctly recognize the advantage of unity in research and expression, and they concede that, where one may master his own subject seasonably enough, the single skilled workman is preferable to the many. For my own part, not meaning to boast, but to encourage others, I may say, that legal and historical works — the one kind by way of relief to the other — have fairly occupied me for twenty-five years, with considerable ground covered in their publication. Another worker may produce better solid books than I have done, but he will hardly be moved to produce a greater number within the same space of time, or to pre-empt a wider range of research. Whether it be from an innate distrust of hired sub-workers, or for economy's sake, or from the pride of responsible authorship, or because of habits which I early formed in life of concentrating and warming into interest wherever I personally investigated, — or whether, indeed, from all these considerations combined, — I never employed literary assistance of any sort, except for sharing in the drudgery of index-making, for copying out my rough drafts in a neat hand for my own revision, and for transcribing passages from other books which I had first selected. And once only, when engaging my amanuensis (a very intelligent man), where historical controversy had arisen upon a minor point, to examine and collate the accounts of various old newspapers, I found, upon reviewing his work, that he had overlooked a single circumstance among these numerous descriptions, which was almost decisive of the issue. In fine, every real research, where I have published, and every page of composition, has been my own; and having regularly contracted with my publishers to create a book, instead of hawking about its manuscript when completed, and having always been permitted when ready to hand my copy to the printers, without submitting it to any mortal's inspection, — I have pursued my own bent, in shaping out the task as I had projected it. I have shown my manuscript to no one at all for criticism or approval; nor have I received suggestions, in any volume, even as to literary style and expression, except upon printed sheets from the casual proof-reader, as the book went finally through the press.

The counsel of genuine and disinterested literary friends, if you are fortunate enough to have them, is doubtless sweet and stimulating; and for the want of it a book will often suffer in matters of expression, as well as of fact. But the recompense, on the other side, comes after a time, in one's own confirmed skill, self-confidence, individuality, and the power to despatch; and often as I have reproached myself for little slips of language (revising and even altering my plates, upon opportunity), I have seldom seen reason to change the record or coloring of historical events, and never an important deduction.

Instead, then, of employing other persons, trained or untrained, to elaborate or help me out with the responsible task of authorship, I have sought, as the most trustworthy of expert assistance, where such aids were needful, the labors of accomplished scholars who had gone through the ordeal of authorship before me. Books and authors, in fact, I have employed for special investigators, and an amanuensis for amanuensis work alone. Original records and information are preferable to all others; but secondary sources of knowledge I have largely accepted as a labor-saving means, where I could bring my own accumulated knowledge and habits of verification to bear upon them, so as to judge fairly of their comparative worth. I have not disembowelled nor re-distributed their contents; but I have learned to dip into them for the quintessence of information they could best impart. To all authors, to all earlier investigators, I have applied diligently whatever materials of consequence were inaccessible to them, or derived from my own later and more advantageous study.

Special assistance, I admit, may be very valuable, when of an expert character. Eminent historians who have University pupils, eminent barristers as the patrons of the shy and briefless, — often employ junior minds, well-trained young men of poverty and ambition, upon the drudgery of their own more affluent investigation. In law-suits the judge will often put out the analysis of complicated facts at issue to some member of the bar, to investigate as auditor and make a report which shall stand as *primâ facie* evidence of the truth. Much the same confidence may you repose in the published monograph of some reputable historical scholar, if you desire economy of labor. Such assistance is trained already for your purpose, and one obvious advantage of employing it is, that you may cite the author and throw the responsibility of your assertion upon his shoulders. Yet, after all, one should be prepared to do most of his own drudgery; for nine-tenths of all the successful achievements in life, as it has been well observed, consist in drudgery. Whatever subordinate or expert assistance, then, may be called in by the responsible historian, let him always reserve the main investigation to himself. In no other way can he rightfully blazon his name upon the title-page of his book, or approach the true ideals of excellence and thoroughness. The trained assistance one employs with only a mercenary interest in the study accomplishes but little, after all, as compared with the one mind inspired for its task, which concentrates the best of its God-given powers upon precisely what it seeks, and gains in skill, quickness, and accuracy by constant exercise. Judgment and intuition may thus move rapidly forward and seize upon results. The student absorbed in his subject brings to bear at every step of preliminary study his own discrimination, analysis, and comparison, qualities which he can never safely delegate; even in crude facts he is saved the alternative of accepting promiscuous heaps from journeymen at second-hand, or of verifying personally their labor, which is the worst toilsomeness of all. And it is by thus throwing himself into the very time of which he treats and becoming enveloped in its atmosphere, that the narrator may hope to kindle his own imagination and grow deeply sympathetic with his subject. Fiery phrases, pictorial hints, startling details, suggestions of effect, meet here and there his quick, artistic eye, which a subordinate would never have discovered among the dull rubbish of surrounding circumstances. Pen and memory learn to aid one another in the exploration; one needs to abstract nothing from the books which serve him as a basis, nothing indeed, anywhere, but what may best aid his immediate purpose; the drift of long correspondence, speeches and documents of merely subsidiary value, he gathers at a glance, and a few trenchant passages will serve for his quotation. What self-directing scholar has not felt his pulse quicken and his heart beat high when in such close communion with the great actors and thinkers of the past, or as he reads contemporary reports of the event, and lives transactions over again amid their original surroundings? And, if in such personal exploits among the buried cities, new pregnant facts, new points of view are revealed corrective of prevailing misconceptions; if some sudden insight into motives, public or personal, lights up his lonely induction, — how does the soul dilate with that greatest of all the triumphs of research, — the triumph of discovery.

Nor let it be said, as an objection to such expenditure of time, that an economizing historian ought to reserve his best strength for the loftier task of arrangement and final composition. Let us not turn literary skill to meretricious uses; let us beware how we steer blindly among conflicting statements, or accept for facts what only our paid pupils have collected. Due preparation is no less essential to the historian than the art of telling his story; for he has never of right the free range of his imagination. There should be a time to study, and a time to compose; the one task should aid and alternate with the other. Nothing, I am sure, so relieves a laborious literary life as to diversify its pursuits, — to change the subject or the mode of occupation. And in historical literature, if we would save ourselves the excessive strain which soon exhausts, let us turn the pen which has been vigorously employed for a sufficient time upon the narrative to prosaic annotation and abstracts. Let us leave the recital of results for one chapter or volume, to gather material and study for the next. We need not fear to roam the broad fields of investigation over, if we hold fixedly to our purpose. The bee culls sweetness from the flower cups, before treading out the honey. And the indolence which every investigator should chiefly guard against is that of subsiding into the intellectual pleasure of filling and refilling his mental pouch for his own delectation, while never setting himself to manufacture that others may derive a profit.

As a most important means of economizing time and personal labor, we should fix clearly in advance the general scope and direction we mean to pursue, and then adhere to it, limiting the range of investigation accordingly. Authorship in history requires resolution, and an intelligent purpose besides in the development of the original plan throughout its entire length and breadth. For as the area of mental research is of itself boundless, the individual should fence off for himself only a certain portion. Chance and opportunity may unquestionably lead us on from one task of exploration to another. We may, like Gibbon, carry our work purposely to a given point, and then leave a still further advance to depend upon health and favoring circumstances. Or, as Prescott, Motley, and Parkman have done, we may let one dramatic episode, when fairly compassed and set forth, conduct to another and kindred one, so as eventually to group out the life's occupation, whether longer or shorter, into one symmetrical whole. But to attack mountains of huge material blindly, without a just estimate of life and physical capabilities, can bring only despair and premature exhaustion.

It is not strange at all, if, after announcing and planning a work of so many pages or volumes, you find the burden of materials increasing on your hands; but you are a novice in book architecture, if, nevertheless, you cannot build according to the plan; and you are certainly the worst of blunderers, if you throw the superabundant materials blindly into form, as they come, and still strive to erect by contract, as a cottage, what should have been only undertaken for a castle. In all literary workmanship, or at least in historical, there should be specifications, and the specifications should correspond with the plan; the rule and compasses should be applied so as to give due proportion to every part of the work. In the lesser details one must be prepared to compress, to sacrifice, to omit. and no reader will miss what is judiciously left out as does the author himself.

By thus keeping within one's intended space, as carefully mapped out in advance, — and I would advise every projector of a book to get practical suggestions from his publisher, and then clearly settle as to size and subject before he tackles to the task, — by thus doing we circumscribe at once the field of investigation; and by apprehending well that in which we mean to be impressive or original, by conceiving fitly our main purpose in authorship, we are prepared to apply ourselves to the real service of our age. Some writers set their minds to work upon manuals, upon the abridgment of what they find at hand for a certain period and country, some upon amplifying; but no one should undertake to narrate history with the same fulness as one who has told the tale before, unless he is confident that he can truthfully put the facts in a new light, or add something really valuable which has not been already set forth elsewhere.

Let it be admitted, in fine, in all historical writing, that much patient and minute study must be bestowed for one's own personal gratification alone; that one may spread the result before his readers, but not the processes. Whatever the historian may print and publish for the edification of the public, let him endeavor to make the result apparent for which he prospected; let him tell the tale, unfold the particulars, and inculcate the lesson with the pertinence and force which best befit the character of his undertaking; and let him show his essential excellence precisely where the public has the most right to expect and desire it.

HISTORICAL MONOGRAPHS.

Some of my friends think that I do scant justice to co-operative methods of historical work. Perhaps they have misapprehended my meaning. The main object of my former essay [1] was to oppose to all boasted advantages of new and monopolizing plans of literary labor — of capitalized scholarship, if I may be allowed such expression — the immense synthetic power of which the single trained and healthy scholar is capable who pursues his own consistent course of literary production with diligence and constancy. To a generation intent upon vast undertakings, and in all departments of industry setting so much store by organized co-operation and so little by individual achievement, I have dared to plead something for the individual. The illustrations of what an average life, rightly and systematically conducted, may accomplish with the pen, are, indeed, easily multiplied. Inventive writers stand necessarily apart; and where invention and learning happily combine, the accumulated written expression of a single human brain may prove prodigious. Bring together, if you will, the manuscripts of some illustrious preacher, journalist, public officer, or business director, accumulated in chronological mass at his decease, and the prolific results are amazing.

[1] See preceding paper.

In the realm of intellectual thought and study, what achievement worthy of a lifetime should be thought impossible, if we regard fairly, as individuals, our average limitation; if we curb the desire of selfish aggrandizement, content to begin where others have left off, and to end where others still may follow? As for the individual task well in hand, one accomplishment leads to another, and the lesser development opens to view the greater. Habit and experience smooth out the earlier difficulties, and by a little arithmetic despondency may be corrected. For that which looms up so formidable prospectively to the imagination is readily built when you figure out that just so much labor and so much progress from day to day for a given number of years will bring you to the finish.

But I am far from meaning to disparage those wider possibilities of literary usefulness which the employment of co-operative or subordinate labor may afford. Especially valuable must be such labor in the collection and classified array of solid facts. The more concrete and simple those facts and the clearer the general scope of the unified undertaking the better can the task be apportioned. For some comprehensive dictionary, cyclopædia, or catalogue, for instance, combined labor is essential; nor is a newspaper or magazine otherwise made readable, where the popular taste demands selection and variety. A labor-saving contrivance is needed in the one instance; in the other a feast for various appetites. But for history or biography, and where facts themselves are found complex and scientific deduction inappropriate, — and where, too, characterization, consistent summary, and social application must find a place, — the reader's continuous interest can only be engaged by the closest unity of design. And so, too, should it be said, wherever any one tells a story. Co-ordinate work finds here a closer environment, and if not laid off by eras or spaces of narration can scarcely be laid off well at all. In poetry and fiction you are content with the product of one creator; one vivid mind illuminates and instructs. Midway, it seems to me, between the collector of facts and the imaginative writer stands the historian; like the prophet in the valley of dry bones who gathers the fragments of dead men together and makes them live again. His mental equipment is not complete if he is a collector alone, nor if he is a narrator alone. The molten mass should flow from his own heated crucible into the moulds he makes for it.

To waive for a moment the question of co-ordinate aid, a capable historian may and ought to know how to use much subordinate assistance to advantage. There is the drudgery of the amanuensis, of the secretary, of our modern type-writer, of copying out compositions for the press, and of revising proofs. Passages which the responsible author has marked in other books may be thus drawn off; parallel statements collated, citations written out. So, too, under one's judicious supervision, reference lists or an index may be compiled, statistics tabulated, and explorations made into newspapers and bulky public documents for special statements, facts simple in themselves or readily verified, which laborious search can alone reveal. After considerable experience one may train this clerical subordinate into an intelligent hunter for special material, or teach him to make good briefs and abstracts, and in various ways save wearisome details to his employer. But the scenting of the game is one thing and bringing down and bagging it is quite another. All such secondary assistance — for I speak not yet of scholars and experts competent to co-operate — must be of moderate scope, and a proper training takes time. The mind that can appropriate and apply such labors must have wrought out its own broad experience, and carried constantly its consecutive plans. Like senior counsel in a case, like the Attorney-General with a "devil," or the judge whose logical processes are aided by the precedents which some secretary has arranged for his inspection, our present investigator, knowing better than to estimate the weight of authorities by the weight of books, applies his own sense and discrimination to all testimony thus brought before him, making sure that it has been sought in the right quarters and rightly gathered. His own mind has been trained to conduct dry investigation and connect results by quicker divination than any subordinate can apply for him.

But now to speak of historical monographs, — a species of publication to which I have repeatedly alluded, and never without respect and commendation. Here we have treatises to consult which have been thought worth printing, and for whose accuracy in each instance some trained scholar vouches over his personal signature. Such studies deserve more credence than the gathered pile of some unknown clerk whose chief aim in life may have been to earn his daily pittance. For the monograph, be it brief or extended, purports to supply the results of an expert investigation into some recondite topic; and its credibility acquires weight from the circumstance that the person who prepared it was one of our own craft, of liberal attainments, who worked presumably under the strongest inducement to be accurate. He seeks scholarly reputation; and the higher his reputation already, the more confidence, if he be unbiassed, do we incline to give him. Special investigations of this kind, for which there is always an ample field in the study of social institutions, I have elsewhere likened to that of an auditor or master of chancery, in legal practice, whom a court will appoint for its own convenience, to take testimony on complicated details of fact and submit his report. This auditor or master is no common citizen, drafted into the service casually as men are drawn for a jury, but an honored member of the bar worthy in that particular case to have sat upon the bench or served as counsel. Nor, with even such high assurance of his capacity and fidelity, is his report (which is a sort of monograph) taken for more than it is worth. It is *primâ facie* evidence of conclusions on a particular branch of the case and no more. The tribunal has still to survey the ampler field of controversy, and finally to adjudicate upon the general merits of the whole cause where this investigation may have disposed of a particular.

I hail the auspicious efforts of those higher University instructors who are busily training young men of the present generation to become experts and co-laborers in the grand universal study of the past; who organize and send forth new exploring expeditions to those hidden sources of human history where rich treasures of fact have long lain buried. And as a marked triumph of such new instruction the decision of our Federal Supreme Court, last year, in the income tax case, serves for illustration, where, by the virtual admission of its grave majority, a reversal of past precedents was due, most of all to an exhaustive historical presentation, for the first time, of those essential conditions under which the State resources of taxation, at first exclusive, were bestowed in 1787-89 upon the new and more perfect Union.[1]

Why American scholarship has done little in its earlier growth, for such leading investigations, is obvious. Americans, until thirty years ago, had but little leisure or money to waste upon books and pursuits unremunerative in cash. A liberal college education went almost exclusively to the mental equipment of young men for one of the three grand professions or for mercantile pursuits. General graduate studies were not encouraged in this country to any great extent. Hence history was taught at our higher institutions, not to train men to habits of individual research, but rather so as to memorize past events and hang great examples round the chambers of the mind on the pegs of chronology. As for historical productions, moreover, whatever literary market might exist was confined to the narratives of heroic prowess or text-book abridgments for the common schools. Monographs, in such an age, if prepared at all, were but the chance diversion of men otherwise actively employed, or the orator's staple for an occasional address. Patriotism or family pride might be stirred on some choice anniversary, but the college educator gave no great impulse to solid study in the historical direction nor to a combination of critical results. We had two or three grand historians, but they were stranded men of ample fortune. Even learned societies found not readily their mission in those days. How often, still, does that brief epitome of ephemeral facts, prepared like a school-boy's composition, serve as the prelude to some general chat or a more solid hot supper! In the

[1] Pollock v. Farmers' Loan & Trust Co., 158 U. S. 601 (May, 1895); Chief Justice Fuller's opinion.

publication of monographs, or better still, in a systematic effort to collect and print rare letters and manuscripts, a growing field has been found for associations which bring congenial men together in State or local organization, whose hobby otherwise is genealogical lore, or the biography of deceased members. And more useful still for future promise, is that systematic training of critical investigators which our highest Universities are of late developing. It was the Johns Hopkins University, scarce twenty years old, which first adapted the Heidelberg historical methods to American use under its munificent endowment; and now, with splendid equipments of their own, Harvard, Yale, Columbia, and other leading institutions of the land extend like facilities for post-graduate instruction.

Under such admirable education a race of native investigators, I trust, is growing up, whose enthusiasm, if not rewarded as it deserves, with the highest trusts of political office, will yet impress upon our local communities convincingly how public affairs ought to be administered. They will strengthen the cause of good government on the people's side and rule at the polls by disseminating correct ideas and information. Their combined research will be directed to comparative facts which illustrate domestic, business, and social manners and customs, legal and political institutions. For the Freeman apothegm[1] — though perhaps embodying the truth without the whole truth — opens regular search in the right direction.

As a further result of this new systematic training, we may look for a better classification, a more thorough gathering of archives and private papers which

---

[1] "History is past politics; politics is present history."

evidence great events. The indexing of documents in our American State Department is a step taken in the right direction; and worthy of all commendation is the fresh editorial work which has lately begun upon the hoarded correspondence of our earliest Presidents. To turn on the fullest light becomes the prevalent historic disposition and the true one, avoiding, nevertheless, as we ought, the scandalous invasion of private life and of matters unessential to public and popular development. Our American Congress has made its own noble benefaction to history by throwing open for universal inspection the whole record of our late Civil War, Union and Confederate, in the nation's possession, — a monument in multiplied print, unparalleled probably in the world's experience, to the modern power of public opinion. Scholars have in this voluminous testimony the right materials upon which to base a military narrative of events while yet the public judgment is impressible; and the danger once imminent that the battles and leaders of the Civil War would be recreated from the false, contradictory, and slipshod statements of casual survivors has been averted as it ought to be. For — let alone the differing bias of the concurrent and the retrospect, the personal disposition to shift and justify where circumstances have changed and one's cause was lost, the boastful swell that the swaggerer takes on when rivals and cross-examiners are dead — a sufficient warning against implicit reliance on such testimony may be found in the honest lapses of memory alone. On this point let me mention my own experience. My part in the Civil War was humble enough, but my disposition to recite what I had seen as honest as any man's. Details of the picture which youthful memory engraved gradually on my mind were materially changed, when a diary which I had carried on my person through a whole campaign disappeared from among my papers and turned up again for inspection some twenty years later. For no testimony so surely and so often confounds the subsequent tale of the same witness as his contemporaneous.

A needful stimulus has been given to the production of monographs by the increased means of placing them generously before the public. Formerly a rich man only, or a few interested subscribers, would bear the cost of printing; for publishers saw no profit in such essays, and see none still, while the periodicals admitted them but rarely. But latterly our learned societies have furnished printed collections of their own, and still more recently our foremost Universities. The American Historical Association and the American Historical Review are among the latest hopeful agencies in this useful direction, and with especial reference to national exploration. Two things seem highly desirable for the widest usefulness of such critical and co-operative labors: one, that the collection of our monographs be intelligently directed to the most obvious wants of the age; another, that a reference index, well classified and arranged, and kept up to date, shall direct the consulting scholar for any topic or period to such monograph literature as may assist his search for information.

Yet, after all, however valuable the writing of monographs may become, however essential to the elucidation of historical truth in the by-places, we should not overestimate its practical importance, nor, as it seems to me, expect such essays to supplant that more comprehensive survey and description of the past which historians have hitherto considered their natural task. For the writer of a historical monograph is the historian in his workshop, or, if we prefer, the historian's own skilled assistant, whose product must enter into the tissues of his own task like all other nutritious substances. Often is the conductor of a comprehensive narrative led into these recondite channels or feeders which he pursues at leisure and describes in monographs of his own. I still recall the analogy of that complicated suit in chancery which one directing tribunal expects to work to final results notwithstanding the incidental issues of fact which may have been put out for a finding. There is no royal road to capacious learning, still less to capacious wisdom. Monographs serve the special effort, just like a magazine article. The writer of a monograph may elaborate farther. Many monographs may make a narrative of events; but not unless they are consecutive, in just accordance with a master-plan, and with the thread held fast by a master. The more persistent and systematic our exploit into realities, the broader becomes the range of our knowledge and experience, and the better is one qualified to write of human life, past or present, in its amplest relation. Specialized investigation, taken by itself, is like boring for a well, and the deeper we dig the closer we find our environment; we may reach a new water-spring far below, but the starry sky above us is but a small disk in sight, while the topography of the earth's vast surface about our entrance-place has vanished. Some ampler surveyor, some intelligence more comprehensive, must direct these literary divers, or at least apply what they have dipped out in discreet combination. The hidden treasures brought thus to light must be coined into money and made to circulate. Culture finds little to attract, little artistic delight, in a bare wilderness perforated with the pickaxe. Who is this director of research, this medium for moral lessons, this guide of posterity, but the true historian, whose own wide range of philosophy and study entitles him to the confidence of the public? From the literary standpoint alone we find that the books describing human life and invention which influence us the most, which are the most readable, are, on the whole, of individual fruition and not co-operative; for though each vivacious intellect that finds admirers will find censors as well, the public seeks still, as it has always sought, its prime inspiration from single minds of a superior cast capable of much continuity and impressive presentation. This you cannot look for in works where different writers, differently brought up, and with a different growth of ideas, strive to give you their composite thought. A dictionary or gazetteer for ready reference may be thus constructed, but not a narrative. Different eras for treatment may of course be apportioned among different narrators; for this is merely to subdivide, and the story or history remains what it always was, an unfinished tale. Concrete facts, in a word, bottom facts, are not enough to make books readable; there must be a dignified marshalling of matter, pictorial grouping, effective massing, vivid characterization and description, a sound political and social philosophy.

In preparing materials for any extensive exposition of history one should first draw up carefully a rough sketch of the main epochs or topics to be embraced. It is well, I think, to keep some handy blank-book for such a sketch; and in preparing the classified plan to mark each running chapter or subdivision which one proposes to occupy by some arbitrary sign, such as a letter of the alphabet. This same blank-book may also contain a list of the authorities which the writer has examined or means to examine under each topic. Slips, note-sheets, and large paper, distinguished each in an upper corner by the arbitrary sign of its topic, such as I have suggested, can then be used, as convenience may serve, for the notes, citations or abstracts, adduced in the course of one's preparatory study; and by large envelopes for the slips, rubber bands or pins to connect the sheets, and packages or portfolios to keep these alphabetical topics apart, an author's amplest materials become easily arranged for special review and comparison when active composition begins. As for secondary narratives fit for basing one's own story upon, a rapid worker may, by keeping several such books open before him at parallel pages, compose as he writes, and so economize his time and labor. Where your materials first collected have since been condensed and digested, and one draft of composition follows another, writing paper of different color or quality may serve to distinguish the revised from the unrevised portion. At all events, one should before composing make careful plans for his book and fix upon a rough outline, however much he may change the plan in details as his book progresses; for brain-work systematically applied is indispensable to all long-sustained productive effort.

HISTORICAL TESTIMONY.

Our common law, which is not given to flattery, pays a delicate compliment to writers of history, in permitting their works to be cited in court with something of the authenticity of official documents. This privilege, which books of art and science have not yet attained, and books of speculation never can, should confirm us in the conviction that the truth of history is above everything else what historians should strive after; that the accurate and diligent presentation of past events, of past public facts, of past manners and customs, must constitute after all the basis of their permanent renown and usefulness. Opinions change from age to age; but facts well interpreted once are interpreted forever. Hence the deductions, the moral lessons of history, one should hold subordinate to a candid, conscientious, and courageous exploration for the truth and the whole truth; all hypotheses should be kept under curb: the writer's imagination ought to be like that of a painter whose model is kept before his eyes. We should not seek unduly to stir the passions of our readers, nor to color artfully for effect; it is enough if we can interest and gain their sympathy. Fancy, theorizing, false ideals, and false inferences have no place in such sober efforts; conjecture should not supplement study, nor

Read before the American Historical Association, at Washington, December 27, 1895.

ought the fagots of study to be piled as fuel for that *ignis fatuus*, the philosophy of history. For the realm of the historian is the actual, and his art should be to reproduce life's panorama.

Not only, then, does every historical writer who goes into print owe it to the public to be as accurate as possible from the commencement, but errors or omissions of fact and misleading deductions which he afterwards discovers should be promptly and heroically corrected. He cannot afford to set up for a guide, and remain to the end a false one. That which he has once published ought to be published under his tacit pledge to make afterwards all needful correction; and he may fairly ask to be judged by his work only as he finally leaves it. There should be vision and revision. Not a single monograph which clears up minor particulars, where he had not personally searched, should be wasted upon his notice; not a criticism by one competent to correct, however harshly and unfeelingly expressed. It is better, of course, to be wholly right at first; but that is not easy. Knowledge which in a measure we must all of us gain at second-hand cannot be infallible; and the best we may promise is, to purpose right and maintain that purpose. So positive is it, as Cicero has eloquently stated the maxim, that each historian should dare to say whatever is true and fear to record a falsehood.

Nor can we, I think, pay the common law a better compliment in return for its flattering confidence, than to adapt to our own use for investigation some of its familiar rules and methods for the right eliciting of truth from testimony. Historical scholars are investigators; and they should be trained to investigate, — to weigh and measure together the authorities, and not merely to collate and cite them. We relax, of course, as we must, that rigid distrust which the old common law showed in excluding from the witness-stand all interested parties. We adopt that better rule of modern tribunals which hears all testimony founded upon direct knowledge of the matter at issue, applying a strict scrutiny, however, and a searching cross-examination to each individual witness. We ask his means of knowledge, his character for truth and veracity, the bias or prejudice under which he testifies. We reconcile contradictions, balance probabilities, consider presumptions and the burden of proof, compare and adjudicate. What is deliberately written down we prefer for exactness to the oral; primary authorities to secondary; what one admits against himself to what it suits him to declare; testimony solemnly given under oath, or upon the death-bed, to the careless and casual utterances of every-day life; that which is corroborated to that which is unsupported or denied; the probable to the improbable. Whatever one says when the event is recent, we trust sooner than that which he says far subsequent, in reliance upon a too treacherous memory; and for ourselves we choose, wherever we may apply it, the observation of our own immediate senses to that hearsay, upon which, in spite of himself, each investigator of the past, each historian or chronicler, must so greatly rest.

The scholarship, then, and the reputed honesty of every writer whose works we are to study, become of prime consequence in judging of his credibility; and so, too, though perhaps in a less degree, the conscious or unconscious bias under which he wrote. Patriotism itself gives to each loyal citizen a bias or prejudicial direction; and this is sure to affect historical narrative, since one does not easily separate his task from the lesson he has in view. This bias becomes very strong where one's country or State was a belligerent, or his immediate fellow-citizens engaged in civil war. The prepossessions of religion and politics have also an immense influence. You do not expect a Macaulay to do entire justice to Tories, nor an Alison to Frenchmen, nor a Lingard to Protestants and the English Reformation, nor a Gibbon to the Christian religion. Our American school histories glorify without stint the heroes of 1776 and the American Revolution; over the causes and course of our latest civil strife they become politic enough. What American youth, however, is trained to apologize for the King and Parliament that strove patriotically to maintain the integrity of British dominion, or to do honor to our colonial loyalists who remained loyal? One of the most valuable contributions to American history, of recent years, embraces a narrative of the Mexican War as the Mexicans wrote it. Will the time ever come, in the advance of race education, when the negro or the red man may compose a history of this continent and its civilization from the standpoint of his own race experience?

Impartial treatment, and the effort to deal fairly by all races and all nations and all men, are qualities praiseworthy in any writer; yet we must confess that a cold and colorless narration fails of effect, and that each one of us dearly desires the applause of his own countrymen and constituency. There are special risks to be run, therefore, when writing of times and contentions which have not yet cooled down and solidified, so to speak; and here is it that they have the advantage as narrators, who, like the British Gibbon and Arnold, and perhaps our own Prescott and Motley, devote their literary skill and scholarship to describing some period of the distant past, and to countries and civilizations only remotely connected with their own. Or if, like Freeman of the one country and Parkman of the other, or like Guizot of France and the great investigators of modern Germany, they search into the institutions of their own native land, they stake out some period for their toil far enough back to admit of a passionless perspective. And yet, after all, the vivid portrayers of their own times and countries have hitherto enjoyed the surest posthumous confidence, especially when, like Herodotus, Thucydides, Xenophon, or Cæsar, the writer describes scenes and events of which he has personally partaken.

In biography, again, where history is seen teaching by example, we find an obvious bias of the writer to ascribe all the influence possible to the hero of his tale, — to make him, if he can, the radiator of events, the centre and sun of the system, round which all other luminaries of his age revolved. The official biographer, more especially, to whom family papers are confided, is apt to be one of the family seeking to keep up the ancestral renown, or some family friend trusted for the pious duty; and hence the laudatory strain, the panegyric, the effort to revivify the dead man's friends and to slay his slain, that we not unfrequently witness in such narratives, with amiable emotion, but withal a little sceptical. More candor, certainly, we look for in a family biography than in an epitaph or a funeral oration; but we should be disappointed enough not to find from such a biographer the strongest defence of his hero, as to all controverted points of his career where public opinion had been in suspense or misinformed; and we should expect, moreover, a fair peep into the private portfolio for family letters and confidences, which history would feel free to appropriate in its own way as its own authentic material, regardless of the family injunction. All filial prepossessions, all that personal partiality which close intimacy exacts as its tribute, let us treat with reverence, provided we are left to estimate for ourselves and to supply the corrective that justice to others may demand. For my part, I do not envy the man who is too callous to become intimate at all; who can explore a kindred human heart as though he held a surgical instrument in his hand; who can enter the recesses of a noble soul, whatever its human shortcomings, without one throb of emotion. Love, compassion, need not, of course, be that emotion in every instance; there is the earnestness of sympathy in one biographer, and the earnestness of antipathy in another. Let us, however, have earnestness; for the writer, historian, or biographer to be most distrusted, is he, in my opinion, who gains no earnestness at all from his subject, but remains wholly neutral, negative, and external, — critical, quizzical, or cynical, as the mood may move him, — or extending the arm of judicial patronage, like some self-chosen Rhadamanthus who practises before the looking-glass.

There is still another bias to which all literary authorship is peculiarly liable, now that our great purchasing public supplants the influential patron to whom a book was formerly dedicated. I mean that of pampering, for the sake of immediate circulation and profit, instead of writing out what one thinks at heart, and supplying to those who seek knowledge the strong meat of correct information. So immense has become the power of fiction in the community of late, that facts themselves are too readily accepted with a fictitious embellishment; and readers, even of the more solid books, will, many of them, ask chiefly to be amused or excited, and not to have their own complacency disturbed. Publishers often seek what is popular, what will sell readiest and coin money; and their mercenary estimates may distort the views of an author, so as to hinder him from remaining constant to his best ideals. God forbid that an author should not make himself interesting if he can, or write books that are salable; but the higher grade of scholarship will refuse to suppress or misrepresent for the sake of popularity, or to make the unripe fruits of study look tempting by applying the high polish of a brilliant style. He will not degenerate from historian into a gossip, nor like a gossip shift his views of men and measures to suit his trivialities.

Here let us distinguish, as the law of evidence bids us, between the two great classes of authorities offered in testimony,—the primary and the secondary. No one should investigate into historical facts, without this fundamental distinction well borne in mind. Under primary authorities we comprehend, of course, all public records and documents, official reports, every original source of information; and we may fairly refer to the same head for ourselves the private and contemporaneous statements and correspondence of those who were actors or eye-witnesses in the events or experiences which they describe; and, furthermore, though with cautious reserve, reports of the contemporary press, from contemporary observation. Secondary as to classification, and quite subordinate and subsidiary to all this, let us reckon newspaper comment and generalization, and the literary remnants, materials, and memoranda of those who simply relate what others have told them. All such materials are but secondary; and so, necessarily, are those other narratives, however trustworthy, which we are compelled to consult, more or less, under any circumstances, because primary evidence is not accessible, or our own power and opportunity for research are limited.

Works of travel afford much coloring matter for history; but only so far as the traveller tells what he saw with his own eyes. The very book we toil upon with pains and put forth, whatever our own primary sources of information, becomes but secondary proof to our readers, so far as we have not stated facts as eye-witnesses. Hence, in historical studies, you may separate quotations from the context for trustworthy matter, or accord to the same writer more credence in one connection than in another. Quotations may be verified; and with the help of citations we may go over the whole original ground for ourselves, though we are not likely to do so. Writers themselves like to be trusted; they cannot turn the processes of their own investigation inside out, nor display to the reader all the testimony which the *res gestæ* afforded them. Time enters into the essence of all human labor; and one would hardly be a laborer himself if he did not hope to save labor to others.

Primary evidence, then, under some such classification as I have endeavored to indicate, should in all cases be preferred by the investigator to secondary, wherever available; for in spite of what literary indolence may claim to the contrary, you gain thus not only greater moral satisfaction, but often an economy of time besides. You are saved a comparison of collateral statements with the added danger of restating errors. Fill your pitcher at the fountain-head and you need not scoop and scrape further down among a hundred rills. Seek original records, original reports, original letters, original documents, or the authentic publication of them, — not content with mere extracts or abstracts which others have made, — and you will be often surprised to find how some suggestive phrase or turn of expression, which did not attract the writer who read the whole instrument before you, — since his standpoint was a different one, — will flash out from the dull verbiage with a new and forcible application. For the standpoint of the present does not coincide with that of former times, nor does the array of facts that immediately interests, or the desired application of past experience to present action, cease to vary with varying eras. How different must be the method of historical research among primary documents which illustrate our present annals from those of earlier centuries! Far behind us lie the chronicles, the musty archives, the rare manuscripts of those feudal governments which flourished when printing was unknown and literary appliances were rude. We live in the parting radiance of a great century of popular development, looking towards the horizon of a new, and, as we hope, a greater one. Government, once conducted in secret councils, now pursues its routine out-of-doors, observed of all men, until the official evidence of the times becomes an overwhelming mass. Public documents are printed, multiplied, scattered broadcast from the press, so that you may burn or make pulp of the share which falls to your own use, and yet leave copies behind in superabundance for the information of posterity. Current literature, current journalism, current reading matter, good and bad, swell the stores elsewhere accumulating for that ideal personage, the future historian; besides those official publications, State and national, executive, legislative, and judicial, which overflow the huge public basins built to hold them. On yonder hill[1] legislation, one department of government alone, has stretched far its marble wings northward and southward, and at length added great catacombs down deep underneath the foundation walls of its temple, to hold the buried treasures of Congressional committee-rooms. There rest in a common tomb the corpses of bills safely delivered and of bills still-born, shrouded petitions, and the reports upon petitions; this immense mass displaying for posterity's information the whole embryo process of legislation, — all the minutiæ, in short, that political science might ever wish hereafter to exhume, except, indeed, the mysterious lobbying and log-rolling that may have so often influenced their delicate creation. To historically reconstruct the earlier centuries, it might be enough to compare the meagre secondary authorities extant, or through official favor gain access to lean archives mysteriously locked; but to reconstruct this nineteenth century you must thrash out the golden grains from storehouses already crammed with chaff, whose doors stand open.

Besides that keenly discriminating scent for the useful among old rubbish, our future historian will need, like us earlier brethren of the craft, habits of careful comparison as to whatever materials, whatever evidence, he admits into his case, — not mingling primary and secondary proof indiscriminately, as though of equal value; not taking any witness upon his *ipse dixit*, apart from his means of knowledge, his probable bias, and his general worthiness of credence; not deciding issues by numerical count of the authorities, like that old Dutch judge who summed up in

[1] Capitol Hill, Washington, D. C., where this paper was read.

favor of the litigant producing the greater number of persons on the stand; not interpreting a great constitutional document, as some would interpret Shakespeare, so as to make it the text of their own fanciful inspiration; but reading all authors, all testimony, in the light of the age in which they existed, and illuminating the whole pathway of past events with the fullest lustre of surrounding circumstances.

Furthermore, on weighing and determining where witnesses contradict, as they often must, and the truth of events is not clear, our scholar will consider the presumptions proper in each case; he will not reject that which has passed into established belief, for the sake of novel and ingenious estimates, without putting the burden of proof where it belongs, and taking the new proof for simply what it is worth. Nor will he disdain that popular verdict, always deliberately and upon good evidence rendered, and always presumptively correct, though liable of course to final reversal, which is known as the judgment of history. Some important element in the formation of a country's earlier civilization, or some individual influence, may have been overlooked or too lightly regarded, in posterity's estimate; happy, then, is the historical scholar who can produce new testimony, and set opinion right; but he asks more than the law of presumptive evidence will grant him, when he undertakes, on the strength of that testimony aided only by conjecture, to set the past judgment of history wholly aside, and reconstruct past civilization upon his new theory, as though the burden of proof did not rest still upon his own shoulders.

HISTORICAL STYLE.

I DOUBT whether I ought to discourse at all upon this particular topic. There are various critics for whose literary opinions I cherish high respect, who have not scrupled to berate me as one of bad taste in historical expression. Even when they have come to acknowledge that there is some force in the new materials brought to light in my five volumes, and that my work has after all some merit in point of scholarship, they still maintain their disapprobation of its rough, harsh, and "swashbuckling" style. "I cannot get over your facts," writes very frankly one New England professor, whose critical acumen is reputed so great that I am almost tempted to believe him; "but I must still say that I think your style very inelegant."

And yet there are other critics, equally competent, who have gone out of their way to commend this same historical composition as warm, vivid in its coloring, lucid, epigrammatic, and "intensely interesting;" which is praise enough for any man. And years ago the present author was pronounced in a leading law periodical "the best law-writer of our day in point of style." All these are the unsought comments of personal strangers to myself, and not my own. I conclude, therefore, that men of good critical acquirements differ among themselves in their estimates of what should constitute a meritorious style. This, I imagine, is partly due to the fact that some whose ordained function it is to criticise and not perform, set up an ideal of all-round perfection that neither they themselves could have attained nor any other man who ever lived; but more still I ascribe it to that difference in prepossessions and affinity with which they encounter the particular book and its subject-matter, and hence to a differing capacity for sympathy with the writer. If what an author has written reaches his reader's heart, moves him to better thought and action, and makes the responsive chord of patriotism beat quickly, all close analysis of style merges in the immediate effect produced. Some critics have warm feelings, others are cold, negative, unresponsive, even where their opinions are much alike; some flatter the well-assured only, others wish to extend a helping hand to new-comers. "Live and let live" is a good reply for all literary writers to make to their critics. The patient fruit of twenty years' thought and study, as the sage Montesquieu reminds us, is not to be estimated lightly nor dismissed with a cursory glance. Let us recall modestly the instance of Macaulay, who, after his splendid success and popularity, looked over the volumes he had written, and, owning their deficiencies in many respects, took final courage in the thought that he might after all have written much worse, and at all events had done something with his pen for the advancement of learning.

In recalling a former apology for my literary shortcomings,[1] I am pleased to find that Gibbon, the writer of history whom I most admire, made his extensive work his own original product, sending his own written copy to the press, as his memoirs inform us,

[1] See paper on "Literary Industries."

without external aid or suggestion. Yet external aid may improve particular expressions; Jefferson's draft of the Declaration of Independence is in point, which critical debate in Congress modified into a model document fit for immortality. High-sounding phrases, such as a fervid mind works out in its lonely chamber when excited with its subject, need often to be pruned. But for all this the best of revisers in the long run is the writer himself; and to write history well requires, as Jefferson himself has observed so fitly, "a whole life of observation, of inquiry, of labor and correction."

A few observations on this same subject of historical style I would ask leave to offer as the result of my own matured reflection. First of all, an author's style should be the image of himself, and if it exposes him instead as the copyist of other minds, it must fail of impressiveness. A literary writer need not be a genius, but he should be genuine; he should be sincere and true to his preconceived purpose; he should put forward his stock of erudition and influence, as one who thinks for himself, judges for himself, seeks the truth, and writes accordingly. Carlyle was not perhaps a historian in his breadth of judgment, but he wrote on historical subjects with pictorial skill; and though rough and impetuous in style, exaggerated and at times almost hysterical, he delivered his message as one who felt the Deity within, and after his own characteristic method was profoundly effective. He wrote in rugged earnest, and the world believed him honest. Emerson, on the other hand, a contemporary and friend, who harmonized with Carlyle in many ways, was in concrete expression the antipodes. The calm mood of the Greek philosopher suited his own more tranquil contact with life; he equally was in earnest and true to himself; but his method was to string pearls of thought together in apothegms. Was this smooth composition in a literary style? Yet many writers may well have envied Emerson's literary influence. Among American statesmen famed for their mastery of expression, the clear and peremptory diction of Hamilton in his correspondence stands in marked contrast with Jefferson's graceful and philanthropic flow; Calhoun and Webster could no more have exchanged in debate their respective methods of oratory than their political views or their strikingly different physical frames. Yet each and all of these men, and many more who might readily be mentioned for illustration, found scope for a wide popular impression because the style of each was appropriate to the individual and characterized him; not one of them was weak enough to model himself after a contemporary.

Next, to borrow the advice of our admirable Prescott, whose literary taste was exquisite, one should chiefly "be engrossed with the thought and not with the fashion of expressing it." For the chief thing after all in effective writing is to put clearly the idea intended. Private and familiar letters often exceed in interest the formal ones more sedulously composed, because there is more of a person's plain self in them, and moreover a pith and directness that shows the writer to be intent upon imparting what he has to say. And the same holds true of familiar conversation with those you know intimately enough to speak as the heart prompts you. Contrast, for instance, as printed in the same volumes, the confidential family letters of our second President with his ceremonious official responses which exchanged lofty platitudes; and yet John Adams was a forcible writer. We might compare many a scholar's chance notes jotted down, while he was warmly pursuing his facts, with the stately composition he afterwards elaborated for the printer, and we should see that the preparatory work, however hasty, was often in point of readableness superior because he was not engrossed with the expression. "Tacitus," once remarked Dr. Johnson, "seems rather to have made notes for an historical work than to have written a history;" but for all that, among the world's historians Tacitus ranks with the greatest; and deservedly so, assuming that his notes were accurate.

It has been said of some great English statesman whose style was pellucid and forcible — I think it was Cobden — that he would formulate carefully the substance of what he had to express and then express it in the first words that occurred to him. Many a bright man tells well the tale of his own personal adventure, since he has only to renew his sensations and describe them with effect, whereas to throw one's self into another's sensations and reproduce them well requires a certain sympathetic creativeness. In either case one should be intent upon the symptoms and due sequence and keep to his narrative. Clear thinking and clear expression go naturally together.

But all this we may fairly qualify by observing further that expression, to be adequate, requires much training, like skill in any physical pursuit. For the choice and command of language, as Gibbon well tells us, is the fruit of exercise. There is no perfection in nature without skill. In art, not chance, lies true ease in writing, as the poet says; by which I understand is meant that art which has attained to something of the perfection of a second nature. The musician, the dancer, the gymnast, the actor, the consummate orator, moves us deeply because he strains after nothing, but in his higher plane seems perfectly natural; his grace, his strength, his power to interpret and apply, is but the superior endowment which incessant training has made supreme. The man who guides you among the high mountain summits has lived and lingered among them most of his life. Compare Shakespeare's earlier and later plays and you will see how the imagination, at first so labored in its expression, embodied its rich ideas in his prime as freely as the pen could move. Daniel Webster's compacted power of statement, simple as it seems, was the result of long effort and experience; and with all Clay's impassioned imagery which appealed so strongly to the heart, we cannot doubt that, spontaneous as he appeared, he was a most carefully trained orator. Public speaking and the writing of public history are closely allied; and if in either pursuit the utterance finds real dignity, it is invariably because study and sustained effort have lifted one to a higher plane of intellectual life, so that in his greatest mood grandeur of expression comes from grandeur of feeling.

Elegant extracts, quotations kept in a castor to be peppered over one's composition so as to give an affected spice of learning and loftiness, I hold in little estimation. But to feel the stir in your soul of the noble passages remembered which others have written is quite another matter. It is the memory of such passages, of bosom-lines, of past fables or fancies, which well up in the thoughts while one is writing, and whose verification may be left for another time, that may well mingle with his own composition. Burke for a prose writer, Milton for a poet, have formulated grand and inspiring ideas and images that may well lie slumbering in your recollection until the glow of solitary writing calls them from the inner chamber of the brain. What critic but a stupid one would take Webster to task for having paraphrased "Paradise Lost" in so many of his most eloquent passages, instead of reciting by lengthy verse? That great master of speech knew that eloquence lay in impetuous imagery and not in the display of pedantry; hence when he quoted at all it was rather by pregnant phrase or allusion than by rote. We writers, knowing wherein our literary work shall consist, may gain skill likewise by the study and absorption of master composers, master passages, which stir us to our best. And in perfecting our own individual style of literary composition let us not only observe the idioms, the construction of sentences, the general arrangement, in compositions which other authors have made effective and which affect ourselves, but enrich our own vocabulary besides by figurative and appropriate words and epithets, such as we find in our casual meditation or whenever we are reading.

There is somewhat of a changing fashion in literary style just as there is in dress and architecture. A century ago or more men seeking intellectual culture were so enamoured of the "Spectator" that they would transcribe its essays again and again to acquire that elegant grace of good breeding and classical persiflage which gave the Addisonian school such renown. Dr. Johnson set the fashion of pompous and well-balanced sentences, which, though of somewhat ornate and imposing construction, gave doubtless a dignity to high discourse in prose. For a choice English style, appropriate to orations and history, I doubt whether anything will ever prove so truly classical and rich as that nearer the simplicity of the Elizabethan age, with which Webster, Irving, and Prescott supplied our literature half a century ago; though the prevalent and latest fashion tends rather to pith and a familiar directness of expression, with less wealth of reading and imagery thrown in, and more of the French repartee and sententiousness. Macaulay introduced into historical writing an English style peculiarly his own which many have admired, — that of the modern reviewer, brilliant, dogmatic, ephemeral in its application, with a vast outpouring of contemporary detail over the main narrative, and a glittering array of statistics in the background. He has bred many imitators; as, for instance, in that emphatic "I purpose" of the first paragraph in the introductory chapter which unfolds the historian's plan to the reader, — a plan, by the way, which he did not live to fully execute. This is a Homeric introduction; and Thucydides (in the third person, however) begins after much the same strain. Such an opening smacks of egotism, as some would say; but perhaps it marks rather an effort to dispense with the usual "preface" which other solid writers employ more familiarly for a like purpose.

Imitation is always a sign of dependence or immaturity; but some writers are so imbued with its spirit that they transport their shrine from one object of worship to another; and authors who have formed a good style of their own have been known to spoil it by coming under the captivation of some new master. We should do well to get rid of such subservience and stand on our own pedestal. But when one is about to engage in some great literary task of invention, it may strongly stimulate him to explore the production of some master mind and study its grasp of similar work. Prescott prepared himself for his famous "Conquest of Mexico" by reading other narratives of individual enterprise, — Voltaire's "Charles XII." and Livy's "Hannibal." Dignified reading stirs the blood for dignified composition; and yet to write well the first chapter of a dignified narrative costs many a futile effort before the will gains dominance. Any book meant to be popular needs most of all to be lively and entertaining; but for all that it need not fail of lofty expression when developing the serious drama of governmental life. One should make good use of the concrete; and there is much choice for good taste to exercise among historical material. Look for facts of kindling suggestion, and for such as illustrate most clearly and give at once most vividly a deep insight into the age. It is well for the narrator to strike into some new path; to shape an easy transition from one scene or topic to another, so as not to fatigue the reader by keeping his gaze too constantly in one direction.

As to one's final composition for the press, Prescott's idea is the correct one: that the only rule is to write with freedom and nature, even with occasional homeliness of expression, and with such variety in alternating long and short sentences (and paragraphs too, we might add) as may be essential to harmonious effect. With "Ferdinand and Isabella," his first work, this conscientious self-critic was not well satisfied, for he felt that he had elaborated it too carefully. Indeed, as his biography shows us, he wrote and worked over those two maiden volumes for ten years, and even then felt almost afraid to print until his father told him it would be rank cowardice not to do so. "After all," as the scholarly Prescott well concludes, "it is not the construction of the sentence, but the tone of the coloring, which produces the effect. If the sentiment is warm, lively, forcible, the reader will be carried along without much heed to the arrangement of periods, which differs exceedingly in different standard writers. Put life into the narrative if you would have it take. Elaborate and artificial fastidiousness in the form of expression is highly detrimental to this. A book may be made up of perfect sentences and yet the general impression be very imperfect."

As an author's habits and experience in composition may be of use to others, let me follow so laudable an example and state my own. We shall admit that a creative and highly imaginative writer, and a poet most of all, must wait for his inspired moments and forge his best work in the heat of some glowing occasion. But they whose intellectual occupation requires a study and prolific product should habituate themselves to continuous and systematic labor of the pen and make inspiration their handmaid; and among such steady producers we may reckon the preacher, the journalist, and the regular historian. Concentration of the faculties, where imagination must be brought into play, with the application of realities, and a full style is of consequence as well as a flowing one, is gained with difficulty, to be sure; but habit triumphs in securing it. In my law treatises, which, inclusive of changes in the various editions, cover some six thousand ample pages of text and notes, and in whose treatment clearness in the development of principles was of the chief consequence, I have, with rare exceptions in certain paragraphs, sent regularly my first and only draft to the printer as written out with the running pen, keeping the general plan and proportion of each volume well in view, and feeling my own way from one legal doctrine to another, so as to impart knowledge by induction as my own mind comprehended it. The summary of law or general conclusion on any topic followed thus the exposition; and as for the introductory chapter to each volume, so-called, which took a general survey of the field, I usually wrote it last, gathering pertinent suggestions as the main investigation proceeded. The professional mind intent upon illustrating and tracing out rules and their subtle limitations, as applied by our courts, compares and comments upon the mass of cases, and may leave warmth of coloring to take care of itself, so long as he applies a logical analysis and sound sense and is himself interested.

In historical composition, on the other hand, one feels the greater sublimity and scope of the task, in a literary aspect, and having rules less ready at hand to rest upon and the *ipse dixit* of others, trusts less to his first simple expression. Political maxims, metaphors, images, comparisons, troop forth from the mind into the pen, and obstruct the limpid course of his narrative. The first expression needs condensing in such a case even after it is clear. Macaulay himself is recorded as having reduced a day's stretch of writing to a third of its original bulk; and most historical manuscript, I apprehend, will bear a careful revision and compression. I formed early a plan for such historical composition which I recommend to others. After working out the daily task I would hand the manuscript with its rough alterations to my amanuensis, to be neatly copied on good paper and spread out on wide lines ready for my final revision. This copy was laid aside, and after some convenient interval of weeks or months, I would turn from rough composition and devote a good space of time, when full of the particular chapter and in a glow with the subject, to revising a batch of this convenient copy with a free and rapid pen. Manuscript in this final shape was sent to be printed. To print and read proofs of the earlier pages while you are still composing the later ones keeps you fully absorbed and abreast of your main subject, and urges the mind on to harmonious completion. One is pleased to find that so much that looked bad in the manuscript beams out neat, concise, and attractive from the printed page. I at least have found this a great encouragement; and yet I admit it is not safe to begin the press-work of a volume while you are composing it, unless your good health and spirits, and leisure too, may be reckoned upon.

The hardest thing of all in such responsible composition is to pitch to the right key at the start and sound the dominant chord. Even Gibbon, who is said to have acquired such final ease of expression that he would send his first rough and unaided copy to press, relates that he experimented long before he could hit the middle tone between a dull chronicle and rhetorical declamation. His first chapter, he tells us, was composed three times and his second twice, — an experience, I dare say, which many later writers of a similar pursuit have repeated. Another habit which he formed, and which I think worthy of all emulation, was that of arranging well in his mind the facts and form of expression before he sat down to the desk. It surely saves much manual labor to think before you take up the pen. At the close of each day's task, and while the mind is still excited, you are likely to discern a clew to the next day's commencement, or some better expression of what you have just written; and in either case you might jot down a memorandum. Rumination on a quiet afternoon's walk will aid you to memorize materials and give them some sort of shape for the next day's pages; and after a peaceful night's rest such details as you may have scanned or thought over group themselves so fairly that you enter your morning study sufficiently advanced in thought to begin the new day's work intelligently and in a becoming frame of mind. It is better to guide your thoughts thus gently into the right channel than to attempt to force them at command in your study-chair, with pen in hand and eyes rolling idly to seek that spontaneous inspiration which does not descend.

There is one thing, however, which it seems to me that every author should observe who hopes to build with success the lofty prose. He must aid the triumph of continuity of thought by keeping continuity itself down to a reasonable span. Whether by pure recreation or by changing the mental movements, he should give his brain all the relaxation it regularly needs. Some great historians have risen with the sun and lighted their winter fire while their household slept; and at all events the morning hours which end with noon seem to me decidedly the best for smooth writing, because the mind comes fresh and recuperated to its toil. But whatever hours or time of the day one may prefer, he should fix his routine and hold fast to it. Nor should he under any circumstances give more than three or four consecutive hours of each day to real intellectual composition. For the rest of one's daily course of work, be it longer or shorter, let him examine proof-sheets, attend to his business affairs, study materials or collect and arrange them, and keep up his correspondence. For those of us mature mortals not of iron constitution, a full third of every day belongs to out-of-door exercise, light reading, and social intercourse, and another third to sleep. The mind that moves steadily on, oppressed by no spasms of exertion and no worry, accomplishes far more in the end than that which races recklessly on unchecked and then succumbs to over-effort. And even for our intellectual hours it is well, as my personal experience convinces me, to turn from one mental employment to another; to vary composition with study and note-taking; and to compose, if one may learn to do so, in different places of abode and among different local surroundings, as where one changes from his winter to his summer home, from the roar and rush of city life to the birds and the green pines. The brightest intellect fades and flickers out where the will has abused it; just as the diamond itself, which is after all but a crystallization, dissolves, when we are foolish enough to apply the blow-pipe, into the same dross as common charcoal.

LAFAYETTE'S TOUR IN 1824.

Lafayette's final visit to the United States, in 1824-25, was in two aspects most remarkable. A venerated hero returned after an absence of full forty years, to see our prosperous nation enjoying in peace the independence in whose cause, when first he stood on this soil, his sword was drawn. And this hero was himself a foreign nobleman; one who in youth had so generously given of his treasures and his blood to the American people as to seem an American by adoption; and who yet became afterward identified, in the prime of manhood, with the cause of liberty in his own native land, as the conspicuous, perhaps the only, revolutionary leader of France of those times whose record left nothing to blush for. A guest like this no nation was ever likely to entertain a second time. The splendor of Lafayette's later reputation in the old hemisphere heightened his earlier renown in the new. His whole life had been consecrated to the cause of liberty and human rights. Republicanism itself was ennobled when one so illustrious could be claimed as friend and father.

No wonder, then, that on Lafayette's return to the United States, after so long an absence, the heart of this whole people was poured out in salutation. To use Clay's felicitous expression, it seemed a realization of that vain wish that the patriot-father might

Reprinted from 10 Magazine of American History, 243 (1883).

revisit his country after death, and contemplate the intermediate changes which time had wrought. But that figure of speech was inadequate; for the man who now revisited America, and stood in the midst of posterity, was not like the risen dead, but rather as some long-absent champion, who, leaving America free, had gone out to liberate new worlds. There had been no grave, no oblivion, to close over the patriot in this instance, but the bond of sympathy which united this people and their benefactor had remained constantly unbroken. Seas had divided, but absence made hearts fonder.

The season of his arrival was most propitious for thus pledging anew this most precious of international friendships. Our second war with Great Britain had in its happy termination secured a permanent confidence at home and abroad in American institutions, and divorced the United States forever from Europe. Under the long and eminently prudent administration of Monroe, now drawing to its peaceful close, our people enjoyed a constantly growing prosperity. What they remembered of dangers past, served most of all to endear the recollections of the great founders of this republic, their sufferings and sacrifices. The memories of '76 were peculiarly tender; battle monuments had been planned and liberal provision made for aged survivors of the revolutionary struggle. Children refused to nourish the old party feuds of their parents; we had ceased to be partisans of England or France; in politics we were all Americans and republicans. Those leading spirits of the late momentous half-century of war, hatred and bloodshed, were disappearing. George III. and Bonaparte had recently died, within a few months of one another. The few survivors of

American independence who lingered on the scene inspired reverence, but they had ceased to participate actively in affairs. Monroe was of necessity the last President of the United States identified with the revolutionary epoch. And Lafayette himself, once the young companion of Washington, had now become the sole surviving general officer of Washington's immortal army.

In honoring Lafayette thus publicly our government appears to have irritated, willingly enough, though not purposely, the Bourbon family, who once more (for a brief spell as events proved) occupied the throne of France. Congress at the same session, in fact, which opened with that celebrated Presidential message announcing what has since been styled the "Monroe Doctrine," passed its resolution of February 4, 1824, complimentary to Lafayette, which, in view of his intended visit, authorized a national ship to bring him over. Our new minister to France, James Brown, bore to Lafayette almost simultaneously an autograph letter from the President which made a like offer, and assured the marquis of the sincere attachment of the whole American nation and their ardent desire to see him once more in the United States. Monroe's timely protest against any further extension of Europe's political systems to the American continent, had meantime, in connection with England's disfavor, operated to check the scheme which France and the "Holy Alliance" meditated, at the fall of Cadiz, for subjugating the Spanish-American republics and restoring the rule of royalty. Loyal to the principles he had always maintained, Lafayette had of late incurred the resentment of Louis XVIII. by speeches opposing the government policy in the French chamber of deputies. A corrupt ministry now succeeded in removing him from the national representation, and Lafayette was left free to accept his invitation to America. While offering no constraint upon his movements, either in departing or returning, the French government, nevertheless, by means of its police and gendarmes, checked the public expressions of love and gratitude which Lafayette's fellow-countrymen would eagerly have rendered.

Lafayette's star had risen and sunk repeatedly with the vicissitudes of France, and the time now approached when, the Bourbons finally dethroned, this veteran soldier of freedom would once more be worthily trusted by his countrymen. But in the mean time, and while in temporary disgrace, the opportunity was offered for visiting the United States, and accordingly Lafayette came.

I shall not attempt to set forth the narrative of Lafayette's memorable tour. The main incidents of the journey are well preserved in the published journal of Levasseur, Lafayette's private secretary, and in American newspapers of the day, particularly "Niles's Register." Quincy, in his "Figures of the Past," well describes Lafayette's visits to Boston. The hero traversed every State and every section of this Union, and wherever he went he was welcomed with love and respect. His health and his spirits improved almost constantly, and but one accident, and that hardly a serious one as to personal consequences, — the sinking of a steamboat on the Ohio, — interrupted the progress of the nation's guest.

What I wish in this paper is to state some historical facts connected with Lafayette's tour, which are not generally known, and which I have gathered from some unpublished correspondence, chiefly among the Monroe and Gouverneur manuscripts.

The general impression has been that Lafayette's visit to the United States was mutually intended for his pleasure and the public gratification, and for no more. This view, however, is not strictly correct. True, there was no special political significance attached to the tour, though this idea some Frenchmen entertained at the time, imagining that some plan of conquest was on foot in which he was to bear a part. True, too, that Lafayette's long-cherished wish to revisit the scenes of his youthful exploits had of late been constantly reciprocated by the American press and his private American correspondents. But in the present instance our administration was tacitly pledged to bestow upon the last of the illustrious revolutionary leaders some tangible proof of the public gratitude, such as, it was well understood, he had good reason to demand. Lafayette was far from affluent at this time, and the loss of royal favor involved a private sacrifice to one of his rank. He, a stranger to these colonies, and owing us nothing, had in our hour of peril voluntarily expended from his own means, sacrificed his ease, shed his blood, and risked his life in our service. As a revolutionary officer, he was entitled to public lands, and having, in fact, received a specific grant from Congress at the annexation of Louisiana, the location made by his agent in that territory near New Orleans proved to be in conflict with some earlier grants. Respecting that claim, Lafayette appears to have been in correspondence with Edward Livingston, who had recently been elected to Congress from Louisiana, and understood the embarrassments which had arisen. Hence President Monroe, and men prominent in influence with his administration, becoming acquainted with Lafayette's pecuniary affairs, encouraged him in his half-formed purpose of coming to this country, at the same time treating the claimant with the utmost tact.

The greatest delicacy was shown in all the arrangements prepared for Lafayette. And thus was it that, returning to America in the modest expectation of, perhaps, honorable attentions, he found at once, on his first landing in New York, a whole community's gratitude to be his welcome. Where, indeed, could one better be than in the bosom of a family like this? So astonished was he, so overcome, to find a great demonstration made for him where he had expected to land quietly and engage private lodgings, that his eyes flowed with tears, and, violently pressing both hands to his heart, he exclaimed, "It will burst!" But the same public demonstrations which greeted Lafayette on his arrival at New York were exhibited wherever else he went.

In the course of some fourteen months he traversed the whole country, visiting every State in the Union and all the leading cities, and received everywhere the same sincere token of reverence and affection, though the characteristic expression might differ. The nation's guest was felt to be the people's friend. With chief magistrates, national, State, and civic, to perform the honors on their own behalf, the great body of American citizens themselves constituted his host. They took Lafayette into their own keeping, carried him from place to place, and feasted and applauded him as long as he would remain. The wish, expressed on many a public occasion and cheered, was that he would become at length an American citizen, and end his days here. When at last he re-embarked for France, the round of hospitalities had been by no means exhausted, and many invitations were of necessity declined.

The tacit pledge of Congress, that the honor paid Lafayette should not be an empty one, was not forgotten. By an act approved on the 28th of December, 1824, the sum of $200,000 was voted him, together with a township of land, to be located on any of the unappropriated public domain, in consideration of his services and sacrifices in the war of the Revolution. This munificent grant readily passed both houses by a vote unanimous. A joint committee waited upon him with a copy of the act, asking him in behalf of Congress to permit this partial discharge of the national obligation. Taken by surprise as he was by this munificent donation, Lafayette could but accept it under the circumstances. Not only did the voice of the nation sustain Congress in its generous action, but several of the States, Virginia, New York, and Maryland, for instance, would have added their own largess, had not Lafayette himself repressed their generosity.

If Lafayette's appearance somewhat surprised, he did not long disappoint, the spectator. He presented a fine, portly figure, nearly six feet high; his weight of years was lightly worn, and his only apparent infirmity was a slight lameness, resulting from his old wound at Brandywine. That lithe, graceful youth, with elastic step and joyous face, whose bronze image is passed by New Yorkers of the present day in Union Square, had, indeed, vanished; yet Lafayette's appearance astonished by its vigorous contrast with those bent and gray-haired veterans who saluted him as their compatriot. This was partly the effect of French art, though more was owing to Lafayette's French vivacity and perennial good-nature. Looking closely upon his face, one saw traces of his sufferings; and Quincy tells us that the brown wig which set low on his forehead, concealing some of his wrinkles, did yeoman's service to one who rode so constantly in an open carriage, bowing with uncovered head. The old Indian chief, Red Jacket, who had been with Lafayette in 1784, frankly expressed his amazement that time should have left the general so fresh a countenance and so hairy a scalp.

We must remember, too, that Lafayette's American renown came to him remarkably early in life. He was scarcely twenty years of age when he bore to Washington a major-general's commission, which Congress had conferred upon a titled foreigner only as a mark of honorary distinction, but which soon became the credentials of his active service.

What, one may inquire, were the strongest impressions produced upon Lafayette himself by this American visit, so impressive to his American hosts? Of these, some indications are to be found in Lafayette's correspondence with American friends after his return home, as also in memorials of the tour which others have preserved. Lafayette himself appears never to have summed up the results of his experience here, nor could he have been expected to do so. That he was both delighted and surprised with the constant enthusiasm of his reception cannot be doubted. These honors from the land of his early exploits were substantial honors too. For himself, personally, it was a memorable episode in an eventful life; a relief from oppressive cares; a vacation tour during which old age revelled among the scenes and recollections of a well-spent youth, and where he could forget the vexations and responsibilities of official station. Here he was truly a benefactor; a successful philanthropist; a father visiting a distant son well established in his own home.

Lafayette was at heart a consistent republican, and a man of liberal principles, sympathizing fully with our political institutions. The nature of our government he had long intelligently comprehended. But as a Frenchman, and with reference to preserving firmly the essential liberties of his own countrymen, he believed that a constitutional monarchy was the form of government best adapted to the existing wants of France. Of the sincerity of that belief, already demonstrated on one signal occasion, he was to give a last proof soon after his return. Hence American institutions afforded Lafayette, at this time, no occasion for minute study; for the bent of his mind was practical, and for his generation, at least, France had done with broad experiments of self-government. Holding these views, Lafayette carried nevertheless a heart whose generous emotions had not been stifled by the hard vicissitudes of experience, and though himself of aristocratic rank, he felt a personal interest in mankind as brothers. The example of the American republic seemed precious in his estimation beyond any immediate reckoning. "Perpetual union among the United States," was his toast on one occasion: "it has saved us in our times of danger; it will save the world."

Gratitude to America for its own gratitude was doubtless the feeling predominant on this tour. Next, the rapid development of the American nation, under its constitutional government, doubtless impressed him: the immense extension of our territorial area since the revolutionary war; the threefold increase of population; the rapid development of the West; the original number of the States nearly doubled. Here, too, he saw that every one had his pursuit in life, so that many who accosted him seemed to wonder how a French nobleman supported himself. More than once he observed chief rulers and high dignitaries travelling without peculiar distinction; a high cabinet officer, who had served in European courts besides, preparing his bed upon the saloon floor of a crowded steamboat; the governor of a State pulling in a skiff to help unload a sunken vessel; statesmen often seeming to receive social honors as secondary to some private citizens. The only time during his tour that Lafayette's carriage was stopped for a toll was once when he rode with the President of the United States. But the universal respect for law and order moved him to admiration. It seemed as if the largest crowds that gathered to honor his approach had resolved not to disgrace American institutions in the eyes of their fraternal guest. Lafayette's entrance into Philadelphia caused not the slightest disturbance of the peace, though its population of 120,000 souls was augmented by 40,000 strangers, who came to participate in the rejoicings. Multitudes huzzaed that day in the streets as the procession passed, and multitudes at night walked the streets for miles to witness the illuminations; and yet there was found no need of increasing the police, nor, as the mayor announced, was a single complaint reported the next morning.

As a Frenchman and a guest, however, Lafayette was less likely to draw such political comparisons than to comment upon what our general humanity inculcates. Two suggestions which he made in a fatherly way from this latter standpoint deserve our chief remembrance. They related to prison reform and negro emancipation, and were addressed frankly to those immediately responsible for existing systems and capable of changing them.

Visiting Philadelphia, where he was shown a new and commodious prison nearly finished, on the plan of solitary confinement, — a mode of punishment which Pennsylvania had within twenty years adopted in its fullest extent, — Lafayette, recalling his personal experience, observed that solitary confinement was a punishment which might lead to madness, and by no means, in his own case at least, had caused a reformation of opinions.

So, too, did the sincerity of Lafayette's convictions on the subject of human slavery force him to commend its abolition whenever a word of judicious counsel might aid the cause. The rapid development of New York, where traces of the former existence of this institution were now fast disappearing, he placed in sad contrast with the condition of other Atlantic States to the southward where the evil still remained. His heart was pained by the exhibitions of human bondage which he witnessed at the South just after his Northern tour. And as he found opportunity, while in Virginia, he discussed the delicate problem, and especially when visiting the ex-Presidents Jefferson and Madison, never failing on his part to defend the right which all men, without exception, have to liberty. Most Virginians with whom Lafayette thus conversed treated his suggestions with entire courtesy; they frankly condemned the principle of slavery, and though citing strong objections to a general and immediate emancipation, appeared ready to rid themselves of the curse, could only some feasible method be shown.

For that ancient State of proud revolutionary traditions and illustrious leaders, Lafayette undoubtedly felt a peculiar tenderness, with perhaps a pang of disappointment at its present condition. There reposed the ashes of his paternal friend and exemplar, the first in war and peace. Jefferson, too, who died soon after his visit to Monticello, was a beloved compatriot. The later survivors of the famous Virginian trio, Madison and Monroe, were, and continued after his return to France, Lafayette's cherished correspondents. Hearing in later years that Monroe had been struggling with poverty, after retiring from public station, Lafayette generously offered his purse; but Monroe, with a delicate sense of honor, refused to be thus relieved.

There is an autograph letter among the Monroe papers probably never published, which the writer has been permitted to read, written from Paris in 1829, in that neat, angular, half-feminine hand, so characteristic of Frenchmen, — one of the last ever penned by Lafayette to his Virginia friends. This letter was written in view of the approaching Virginia convention of that year, and was addressed to ex-President Monroe himself, who presided at that convention. It contains Lafayette's final appeal for bringing Virginia into the sisterhood of free States. "Oh, how proud and elated I would feel," he writes, "if something could be contrived in your convention whereby Virginia, who was the first to petition against the slave trade and afterwards to forbid it, and who has published the first declaration of rights, would take an exalted situation among the promoters of measures tending first to ameliorate, then gradually to abolish, the slave mode of labor." Happily might the Old Dominion preserve that letter in a golden frame had she followed voluntarily his disinterested advice.

MONROE AND THE RHEA LETTER.

The Seminole War of 1817-18 was hardly worthy of its imposing title, so far as concerned the belligerent parties themselves and their encounters; but in respect of the political controversies, domestic and international, which General Jackson's conduct of that war provoked, it assumes in our history a memorable importance. Roving Indians from East Florida, a province which Spain at that time held by a feeble and loosening grasp, approached Fort Scott on the Georgia frontier, surprised a boat-load of United States troops with their wives and children, who were ascending the Appalachicola River, and cruelly butchered the whole party. The administration at Washington, on receiving the startling news, ordered General Jackson to the front. The hero of New Orleans displayed his customary energy and promptness. Having raised an additional force of volunteers, he marched rapidly from Nashville to the southern frontiers, and drove the bloodthirsty Seminoles into Florida. Pursued to St. Mark's after a slight encounter, the enemy escaped southward into their inaccessible swamps, and in less than six months from the date of the massacre this Indian war was over.

But Jackson was not content that hostilities should end thus easily. Two British subjects had come into his hands, Arbuthnot and Ambrister, and these, having been tried by drum-head court-martial on the charge of giving aid and comfort to the enemy, he caused to be summarily executed, — the one hanged and the other shot. Next, turning aside from the homeward march, he captured Pensacola, as he had already captured St. Mark's against the protest of the Spanish commander, and hoisted the stars and stripes in place of the Spanish colors; here once more alleging that the king's officers thus displaced had instigated the Seminoles to make war over the American borders. The British people were greatly incensed at what they called the murder of two fellow-countrymen; and as Castlereagh told Minister Rush there would have been a war over this "if the ministry had but held up a finger;" but the British ministry, having at this time the strongest motives for maintaining cordial relations with the United States, waived apologies. As for Spain, King Ferdinand betrayed an impotent rage; but President Monroe promptly disavowed General Jackson's acts and restored the Spanish posts, at the same time sustaining in the main our general's charges of Spanish complicity; in which posture of affairs the leading European powers refused to espouse Spain's quarrel, and the king after much hesitation signed a treaty which finally ceded the Floridas to the United States for $5,000,000 upon stated considerations. This cession, negotiations for which had been pending some fifteen years, was not in the end procured without a skilful management of these Seminole difficulties, and to the happy result Jackson's rude exposure of the imbecility of Spanish domination doubtless contributed.

Not less memorable is the Seminole War for the

influence which it came to exert upon the internal politics of our country. Jackson's summary seizure of the Spanish posts was a popular act, and such he had meant it to be. Our people, and those especially of the Western States, had long borne with impatience the delays of a fruitless diplomacy, confident all the while that in order to obtain a full settlement of spoliation claims, old and new, and gain title to a territory once paid for, as to West Florida at least, when Louisiana was purchased, nothing could be easier than to march a resolute body of troops into Florida, dislodge the Spanish garrisons, and take possession in the name of the United States. This Jackson did on his own responsibility; and already the most conspicuous man of the age among our military generals, he leaped at once into prominence as a candidate for the next presidency. All presidential candidates in that day belonged, so to speak, to one party; and civilians like Crawford and Clay, who themselves were ambitious rivals and competitors for the succession, committed the fatal error of setting on foot a Congressional investigation; hoping thereby, as Jackson's friends have claimed, to procure a public censure and crush this new popular favorite. But the President himself stood firmly by the general at this crisis, as also did Adams and Calhoun of the cabinet, and the result of the investigation was the utter discomfiture of those who started it, Jackson becoming a stronger and more formidable candidate than ever. From Jackson's gratitude the Secretary of War presently reaped a tangible reward in his own successful advancement to the vice-presidency; but in the moment of his highest elation, and while he reached out his hand for the chief magistracy, Calhoun received a fatal stab in the back. Crawford, his quondam associate and bitter enemy, betrayed to the old general the Cabinet secrets of 1818, showing that Calhoun had declared, when the seizure of Pensacola was announced, that Jackson ought to be court-martialled. Being asked to explain, Calhoun sought to excuse himself. All the papers and traditions of the Seminole War were ransacked for his justification; but the angry President remained implacable, and under the deadening weight of Jackson's displeasure Calhoun with his national aspirations sank as in a quicksand. No longer influential with the mass of national voters, he devoted his commanding talents thenceforth to the philosophy of nullification, to State rights, and Southern secession. In fine, the Seminole War and its controversies bore, indirectly, no slight influence in producing the tremendous civil conflict of 1861.

In recalling the story of the Seminole War, I came upon a letter of General Jackson's, written January 6, 1818, which played a very singular part in the discussions which that war elicited. I print it in the foot-notes, as it appears in Parton's "Life of Jackson," with the essential passage denoted by italics.[1] That

---

[1] This letter reads as follows. See 2 Parton's Life of Jackson, 433:

General Jackson to President Monroe.

NASHVILLE, 6th January, 1818.

SIR: A few days since I received a letter from the Secretary of War, of the 17th ult., with inclosures. Your order of the 19th ult. through him to Brevet Major General Gaines to enter the territory of Spain, and chastise the ruthless savages who have been depredating on the property and lives of our citizens, will meet not only the approbation of your country, but the approbation of Heaven. Will you, however, permit me to suggest the catastrophe that might arise by General Gaines' compliance with the last clause of your order? Suppose the case that the Indians are beaten: they take refuge either in Pensacola or St. Augustine, which open their gates to them; to profit

passage may be considered as the text of the present article, my object being to lay before the public, and I may confidently say for the first time, a full and true narrative as to what for convenience I shall style "Jackson's January letter." Parton, in his "Life of Andrew Jackson," follows Benton; and Benton, in preparing his "Thirty Years' View," was misled — honestly, no doubt — by a lengthy document on the subject of the Seminole War which he found among Andrew Jackson's posthumous papers, but whose publication Jackson himself never positively

by his victory, General Gaines pursues the fugitives, and has to halt before the garrison until he can communicate with his government. In the meantime the militia grow restless, and he is left to defend himself by the regulars. The enemy, with the aid of their Spanish friends and Woodbine's British partisans, or, if you please, with Aury's force, attacks him. What may not be the result? Defeat and massacre. Permit me to remark that the arms of the United States must be carried to any point within the limits of East Florida, where an enemy is permitted and protected, or disgrace attends.

The executive government have ordered, and, as I conceive, very properly, Amelia Island to be taken possession of. This order ought to be carried into execution at all hazards, and simultaneously the whole of East Florida seized, and held as an indemnity for the outrages of Spain upon the property of our citizens. This done, it puts all opposition down, secures our citizens a complete indemnity, and saves us from a war with Great Britain, or some of the continental powers combined with Spain. This can be done without implicating the government. *Let it be signified to me through any channel (say Mr. J. Rhea), that the possession of the Floridas would be desirable to the United States, and in sixty days it will be accomplished.*

The order being given for the possession of Amelia Island, it ought to be executed, or our enemies, internal and external, will use it to the disadvantage of the government. If our troops enter the territory of Spain in pursuit of our Indian enemy, all opposition that they meet with must be put down, or we will be involved in danger and disgrace.

I have the honor, &c.,

ANDREW JACKSON.

HON. JAMES MONROE,
    President United States.

sanctioned. Parton, if not Benton himself, has been puzzled by the mysteries involved in that January letter. Those mysteries, however, are solved in part by the later published volumes of that most valuable historical work, John Quincy Adams's "Diary," though no one, I believe, has called attention to the point; and they are essentially cleared by the testimony of the Monroe manuscripts now in possession of the government, and of the Gouverneur papers which are still held in Washington by the last of Monroe's lineal descendants. I believe I violate no confidence in using the substance of their contents for the purpose of this narrative, in connection with the publications I have referred to, well knowing that the American people value truth and justice in history, and that they would not willingly suffer false imputations to tarnish the fame of an honored President, who has reposed more than fifty years in the grave.

Jackson's January letter, it is perceived, indicates on the general's part a personal wish to carry the war into Spain precisely as he afterwards did. Heedless, perhaps, of the duplicity, of the lawlessness to which such a course must have committed the responsible Executive of the United States, Jackson urged Monroe to drop only a sly hint, and in sixty days the Floridas would be ours. The secret channel indicated was through John Rhea, better known to statesmen of the day as "Johnny Rhea,"—a member of Congress for many years from Tennessee, a native of Ireland, a man never of much reputation, who is remembered in history only as one of Jackson's constant parasites. It is well known that this January letter was written from Nashville before Jackson had received the marching orders which were already on their way to him from Washington, and in ignorance of their contents. Those orders directed him to proceed to the scene of war and take command, observing the restrictions already imposed on his predecessor, General Gaines, — restrictions of whose import Jackson's own letter shows that he was already apprised. In other words, Jackson might cross the Florida line, provided the hostile Indians could be reached and punished in no other way; but on no account was he to molest or threaten a Spanish post; and should the enemy find refuge within a Spanish fortress, he was to relinquish the pursuit and take no further steps without receiving new and explicit orders from the war department.[1]

Jackson was resolute, headstrong, self-reliant, disinclined to obey orders from any one, strongly persistent in his own views, and by no means considerate toward those he fought or argued against. Monroe, on the other hand, was at this epoch, as all accounts agree, patient, tolerant, slow in reaching conclusions, but magnanimous and considerate, — an Executive who both sought counsel and encouraged the confidence of his counsellors; a chief magistrate who took just and comprehensive views of public policy, who was sensitive that all his official acts should be rightly performed, and as a man the soul of generous honor. What impression would such a private letter from a commanding general have been likely to produce upon the mind of such a President, under circumstances like these? Much the same, we may imagine, as McClellan's famous letter on the slavery question, written while engaged in his Peninsular campaign, produced upon President Lincoln's mind. The general had meantime received his military orders and

[1] See 2 Parton's Jackson, 433.

was bound to pursue them; consequently, personal advice on delicate questions of a political character, whose tendency was to compromise the Chief Executive, would be weighed but not discussed by the latter at such a juncture. In truth, free advice from Jackson was nothing new to Monroe; he had been receiving it ever since his election to the presidency; and, appreciating Jackson's friendship as well as the originality and force of all he might say, he had constantly encouraged him to speak his mind freely, but at the same time pursued the tenor of his administration after his own deliberate convictions.

In point of fact, however, Monroe never read nor reflected upon Jackson's January letter at all until after Pensacola had fallen. This will conclusively appear in the course of the present narrative.

For historical facts one should trust most of all to contemporary testimony. Later narratives, solely derived from personal recollection, are not to be depended upon; for not only do events fade from the memory after a long lapse of years, but they are grouped differently as viewed in the prospect or the retrospect; important links may in time have disappeared, while the bias of the narrator must be to make the sequence of anticipation coincide with that of actual results, — a state of things which rarely occurs in real life. Let any one who doubts this tell from memory the story of his own personal experiences, dating ten or fifteen years back, describing the time, the persons, the surroundings, and the impressions he received, and then compare this story with the details recorded by him in some letter or note-book when all was fresh in the mind. Nothing, then, which admits us to the inner secrets of the Monroe administration upon the Seminole question can be so trustworthy as the correspondence in 1818 of the parties concerned and John Quincy Adams's scrupulous Diary.

As Adams himself, Monroe's Secretary of State, while thoroughly conscientious, was a keen and unsparing critic of his political associates and chieftain, in what he thus jotted down, and at the present juncture the only one of them all who showed a disposition to sustain Jackson's conduct to the utmost, we may trust his recorded impressions as not too indulgent toward the administration. His minutes of the Seminole discussions show clearly enough that the capture of Pensacola was an entire surprise to the Cabinet, Calhoun included, and to the President, who had summoned them for counsel. The question for consultation here was not (as Jackson, long years after, chose to believe) whether to punish the general commanding for disobedience, but whether to approve or disapprove of his proceedings. Not only did Monroe state the capture as a breach of orders, but the news of Pensacola's surrender came at the very moment when, under the favor of the French minister at Washington, negotiations with Spain for the purchase of Florida had been taken up anew, with fresh hopes of success. Despatches relating to the execution of Arbuthnot and Ambrister had miscarried, and hence the full scope of Jackson's conduct did not yet appear; but, as to the Spanish posts, all the Cabinet finally concurred in the conclusion that their capture must be disavowed as having been made without authority. The President generously admitted that there might be justification for taking Pensacola under some circumstances, but that Jackson had not made out his case.

Adams gives further incidental proof of the President's good faith. He says that, while candid and good-humored as to all that he, the Secretary of State, had suggested in Jackson's favor, Monroe was firm on the main conclusion. And once more, in November, 1818, Adams records in his Diary that when revising the draft of the official despatch, in which, as it is well known, the Secretary of State made, for European impression as against Spain, a most brilliant and successful defence of the administration policy, Monroe altered the document, saying: "You have gone too far in justifying Jackson's acts in Florida." "I am decidedly of opinion," was his recorded substance of the President's comment, "that these proceedings have been attended with good results and are in the main justifiable; but that certainly they were not contemplated in any of the instructions issued to Jackson. I think the public will not entirely justify the general; and the true course for ourselves is to shield and support him as much as possible, but not commit the administration on points where the public will be against us." Adams, who felt the force of the criticism, observes in his Diary that this view of the case is wise, just, and generous.[1]

Monroe's whole course toward Jackson, indeed, corresponded with this same wise and generous view of his public duty. Had he made Jackson's rule of conduct his own in this instance, there might have been war with the allied powers of Europe, and, what was worse, American diplomacy must have been stigmatized as perfidious. But, making all allowance for Jackson's idiosyncrasies, Monroe candidly acknowledged the positive service Jackson rendered, as events turned out; and positive proofs of a con-

[1] See 4 John Quincy Adams's Diary (1818).

tinued confidence were given soon after, as when, for instance, he commissioned Jackson to receive the cession of the Floridas from the Spanish authorities after the treaty with Spain had been ratified.

In his message, on the reassembling of Congress, Monroe states the official facts clearly, but considerately.[1] Monroe's most confidential correspondence of this date with his own friends is consistent with the same theory. To Madison (whom he constantly consulted on all the great points of his administration), he wrote, February 7, 1819, while the Seminole debates were progressing in the House, that everything not already communicated to him was before the country; and, reciting the policy pursued on the receipt of Jackson's Pensacola despatches, and the justice done to Spain by restoring the posts, he proceeds to blame the Spanish authorities themselves for conniving at or permitting the Seminole hostilities, and to defend himself in not punishing Jackson " for his mistake."[2] Monroe wrote, March 17, 1819, to Minister Rush in a similar strain after the Florida treaty had been concluded at Washington.[3]

But how was the delicate affair managed with

---

[1] In this message the President observes that only by returning these posts were amicable relations preserved with Spain, *and that for changing those relations Congress and not the Executive has the power.* — Annual Message, November 17, 1818.

[2] Madison's Writings (1819); Monroe MSS.

[3] "The right to make war," says Monroe, "was not only not assumed by the Executive, but explicitly disclaimed. The General transcended his orders, but that was no breach of the Constitution; he chastised all those as well in secret as open hostility to the United States. But as soon as the orders of the Government reached him and those under him, a prompt obedience followed." And Monroe further observes (once more defending himself for not censuring Jackson), that had he censured our commander and exculpated the Spanish authorities in Florida, the cession just made would not have been procured. — Monroe MSS.

Jackson himself, so as to soothe an insubordinate commander while reversing his acts? Most skilfully, as the correspondence to be found in Parton's Life will show, and with an obvious endeavor on Monroe's part to assure the general of his personal sympathy and at the same time point out his breach of official orders. This correspondence, which was carried on after Jackson's return from Florida to Nashville, and extended from July to December, 1818, shows that Jackson merely claimed to construe his orders differently from the War Department, arguing that they gave him a broad discretion. And Parton, who relies upon the hypothesis (whose origin will be noticed at length hereafter) that Monroe had actually sent Jackson some secret sanction through Rhea, in response to Jackson's January letter, confesses his own surprise that these epistles should have contained no allusion to that subject.[1] There is, however, not only an allusion here, but a full explanation as to the receipt of the January letter, which Parton has either overlooked or intentionally perverts: namely, in the last of the series, Monroe's response of December 21, 1818, to Jackson's of November. Monroe says at the close of that response: "On one circumstance it seems proper that I should now give you an explanation. Your letter of January 6 was received when I was seriously indisposed. Observing that it was from you, I handed it to Mr. Calhoun to read, after reading one or two lines only myself. The order to you to take command in that quarter had before then been issued. He remarked, after perusing the letter, that it was a confidential one, relating to Florida, which I must answer. I asked him if he had forwarded to you the orders of General Gaines on that subject.

[1] Parton's Life of Jackson, 518–528.

He replied that he had. Your letter to me, with many others from friends, was put aside in consequence of my indisposition and the great pressure on me at the time, and never recurred to until after my return from Loudoun, on receipt of yours by Mr. Hambly, and then on the suggestion of Mr. Calhoun." [1]

Here, then, is a complete explanation on Monroe's part, contemporaneous with the events, as to the effect of Jackson's January letter, and, so far as history is aware, it satisfied Jackson, for he made no rejoinder nor ceased to cultivate Monroe's friendship. But why did Monroe volunteer this explanation, considering that Jackson's letter of November, to which it responded, made no direct allusion to the subject? Possibly there was the barest hint in that direction in the November letter, though Parton himself fails to discover it. A chance passage in John Quincy Adams's Diary will, I think, if taken in connection with Crawford's later assertions, supply the reason. "At the President's [notes Adams, of date December 17, 1818] I met Secretary Crawford, who was reading to him a violent attack upon himself in a letter from Nashville, published in the 'Aurora' of the day before yesterday." [2] Crawford, recalling the

---

[1] For this letter of December 21, 1818, in full, and those preceding, see Monroe MSS.; also "Correspondence relating to the Seminole War," prepared by Calhoun, and printed at Washington in 1831, where the date is incorrectly given as "1830," instead of "1818,"— an obvious misprint, as the context alone might show. This letter is strangely garbled and misplaced in Parton's Life of Jackson, Vol. II., pp. 434, 527.

"Loudoun" refers to Monroe's Virginia home, and, as John Quincy Adams afterward pointed out, it was Hambly who brought the Pensacola despatches upon which the Cabinet consultations were held, so that the allusion of the text is to Hambly's arrival in July, 1818.

[2] John Quincy Adams's Diary.

same circumstances to Monroe's mind, in 1830, states that they both agreed in this interview that the essay had been written either under Jackson's direction or by some one who had access to Jackson's confidential papers.[1] And to that conclusion the candid reader will arrive if he examines, as this writer has done, the files of the "Aurora" for December 15, 1818, and reads that Nashville letter. In the course of it, the unknown writer, "B. B.," observes that the government knew the general's views upon the capture of the Spanish forts before he marched his army into Florida; and if this be so, he adds, why, if those did not meet their own views, were not specific orders to the contrary given him?[2] This anonymous inquiry in the public prints touched Monroe; and hence, as we infer, his explanation to Jackson, made but a few days later, and the only one ever given, which the long record of Monroe's administration discloses.

Years rolled on, and the Seminole controversy slumbered. Monroe's long administration closed with applause. Among the numerous candidates in 1824 for the succession no choice was made by the electors, and the duty of a selection having devolved upon the House of Representatives, John Quincy Adams became the next President. But so formidable a coalition was presently made of Jackson's supporters that they soon gained the full control of Congress, blocked all administration measures, and prepared the way for an easy victory in 1828. In these political arrangements, Calhoun, already Vice-President, shifted his forces to Jackson, whose friends in turn

---

[1] Crawford's lapse of memory is to be noted; he called it "an essay in a Nashville paper."

[2] "Aurora" (Philadelphia), December 15, 1818. Observe that this epistle argues that to the January letter of Jackson no reply was ever given.

agreed to support him for re-election on the Democratic ticket. In this state of affairs an old feud between Calhoun and Crawford broke out afresh in 1827; the friends of the latter now seeking to embroil their adversary with Jackson by charging him with duplicity in the old Seminole business. Appeal was made to ex-President Monroe for the facts; and among other issues of veracity raised between Calhoun and Crawford was that concerning the reception and use made of Jackson's January letter. Monroe transmitted his private correspondence for Calhoun to use strictly in his own justification; and at the same time perceiving, as he thought, a growing disposition on the part of Jackson's friends to pervert facts and rob the Virginia statesmen of merited honors for their own hero's glory, he recalled, with no little feeling, the generous interest he had always shown in Jackson's welfare. As for Jackson's January letter, Monroe here reiterated the explanation of 1818. "I solemnly declare," he writes Calhoun, "that I never read that letter until after the affair was concluded; nor did I ever think of it until you recalled it to my recollection by an intimation of its contents and a suggestion that it had also been read by Crawford, who had mentioned it to some person who might be disposed to turn it to some account."[1]

A further statement in this same confidential letter becomes of startling importance. "I asked Mr. Rhea in a conversation," proceeds Monroe, "whether he had ever intimated to General Jackson his opinion that the administration had no objection to his making an attack on Pensacola, and he declared that he never had. I did not know, if the general had

[1] Monroe MSS., January 28, 1827.

written him to the same effect as he had to me, as I had not read my letter, but that he might have led me innocently into a conversation in which, wishing to obtain Florida, I might have expressed a sentiment from which he might have drawn that inference. But he assured me that no such conversation ever passed between us. I did not apprise him of the letter which I had received from the general on the subject, being able to ascertain my object without doing so."[1]

Efforts were made, during the bitter campaign of 1828, to draw Monroe from his retirement; but he maintained in honor the strictest neutrality as between the candidates just as he had done in 1824. He rejected overtures from Adams's supporters to place him on their ticket as Vice-President; and both he and Madison refused to serve when selected to head the Virginia list of presidential electors on that ticket.

It is known that Monroe, like Jefferson, while above suspicion in all public pecuniary transactions, retired from the presidential office, weighed down with private debts, and that his last declining years were harassed with the humiliating struggles of pride and poverty. A claim pending before Congress after his retirement promised him, or rather his creditors, a partial relief; and meanwhile President Adams, with a tender consideration for his late chief, appointed Monroe's son-in-law, Samuel L. Gouverneur, postmaster of New York City, — a vacancy having occurred in the office by death, — in the expectation that some advantage would accrue from the office to Monroe personally. This, however, was not until the presidential contest of 1828 was settled, and that adversely, of course, to Adams himself. After Jackson came into the White House there was a vigorous proscrip-

[1] Monroe MSS. January 28, 1827.

tion among the officeholders; and Monroe saw with sorrow that the proscription extended to men long attached to himself in friendship and confidence. Jackson gave no direct proof that he had construed Monroe's neutrality to his prejudice; yet symptoms of this appeared. Early in 1831 the breach between Crawford and Calhoun became open; the latter, still Vice-President, had been expelled from the confidence of the administration, and the issues of the Seminole War burned fiercely in the public prints. Both Crawford and Calhoun turned once more to Monroe and to their Cabinet associates under his presidency for testimony to corroborate their respective statements.

With regard to Jackson's January letter a curious issue had now arisen. Crawford charged Calhoun with suppressing knowledge of its contents. Calhoun claimed in return that Crawford had purloined that letter from the War Department. Crawford insisted that the letter had been read in the Cabinet consultations of 1818 upon the fall of Pensacola; Calhoun, that it never was before the Cabinet at all. On this latter point Calhoun was doubtless right; for Monroe, Wirt, and Adams all sustained him, the last-named having his own Diary to refresh his recollections; and, indeed, the January letter now produced was to Wirt and Adams a new revelation. But Crawford, like Calhoun, appears to be fairly absolved from the imputation of falsehood in this matter, for Monroe was of the belief that both Calhoun and Crawford had been shown the letter; and Adams, comparing the several statements of this date with Monroe's explanation of December, 1818, suggested, fairly enough, that while the January letter was certainly not before the Cabinet at all when the Seminole questions were discussed, it might have been produced about that time, while only Crawford and Calhoun were with the President.[1]

By April, 1831, a partial allowance of Monroe's claim had been voted by Congress. The venerable ex-President was fast failing in health and spirits. His wife, whom he dearly loved, had recently died, also one of his two sons-in-law. He was troubled with a constant cough from which he could procure no relief. The solitude of his farm was insupportable, nor might he call the ancestral acres his own. He announced to Madison the intention of taking his widowed daughter with him to New York, there to remain for the present with the family of his other child, Mrs. Gouverneur. "My situation," he wrote in a letter of farewell to his life-long friend, "prescribes my course, and I deeply regret that there is no prospect I will ever see you again." It was not long after this departure that ex-President Adams, while passing through New York, found his illustrious predecessor confined to his sick chamber, extremely feeble and emaciated, and so exhausted by the exertion of speaking that Adams dared not protract the call, though he felt it to be a final one.[2]

While Monroe was thus suffering, a strange letter arrived at the house of his son-in-law, now installed as the ex-President's confidential secretary and the chosen custodian of his papers. Even to this day, that letter, deliberately composed and appearing to have been carefully copied out, bristles with hate and defiance, every line resembling a row of rattlesnakes. It is written and signed by John Rhea. It asks Monroe whether he received a confidential letter

---

[1] Monroe MSS.; John Quincy Adams's Diary, 1818, 1831.
[2] John Quincy Adams's Diary, April 27, 1831; Monroe MSS.

from Andrew Jackson, dated January 6, 1818. After identifying that letter it thus continues: "I had many confidential conversations with you respecting General Jackson at that period. You communicated to me that confidential letter, or its substance, approved the opinion of Jackson therein expressed, and did authorize me to write to him. I did accordingly write to him. He says he received my letter on his way to Fort Scott, and acted accordingly. After that war a question was raised in your Cabinet as to General Jackson's authority, and that question was got over. I know that General Jackson was in Washington in January, 1819, and my confidential letter was probably in his possession. You requested me to request General Jackson to burn that letter, in consequence of which I asked General Jackson, and he promised to do so. He has since informed me that April 12, 1819, he did burn it." Rhea closed with the request for a reply.

This letter, containing statements so utterly at variance with all that had ever been said or written hitherto upon the Seminole War, was opened by Gouverneur. Monroe had for weeks been confined to his bed, and those attending him had found it absolutely necessary to keep his mind free from all excitement or anxiety. In his astonishment and perplexity, the son-in-law consulted Wirt, the trusted legal adviser of former administrations. Wirt, agreeing with him that Rhea's story was not only utterly false, but invented for some hidden political purpose, urged that Monroe's solemn statement be procured. Gouverneur followed this advice; and accordingly on the 19th of June, 1831, the ex-President made his deposition in presence of witnesses, signing his familiar name firmly and legibly at the close. As to this Rhea letter shown him for the first time, and of which he never before had an intimation, Monroe declares on oath: (1) That it is utterly unfounded and untrue that he ever authorized John Rhea to write any letter authorizing Andrew Jackson to deviate from or disobey the orders sent him through the War Department; (2) That it is utterly untrue that he ever desired John Rhea to request Andrew Jackson to destroy any letter written by him to General Jackson.

This document is still extant, and I have read it with no little emotion. It is probably the last of State papers, if I may use that expression, which Monroe ever subscribed; and what must have passed through his mind, as to the vanity of fame and friendship, while his pen glided over the paper, the reader may imagine. On the ensuing 4th of July Monroe was dead; and with his death the Seminole controversy suddenly subsided. Whether the affair was dropped because this triangular quarrel between Jackson, Calhoun, and Crawford had ended in a permanent rupture of relations, or because the public would hear no more of it, or possibly because the administration and President Jackson personally had learned from some source that there was a statement made *in extremis* which might be forthcoming, history does not record. But it may now be positively affirmed that Monroe's most intimate friends were informed confidentially of this deposition, and that one of them at least — John Quincy Adams — has left on record an opinion as to the Rhea letter expressed in language sufficiently clear and vehement.[1]

---

[1] See John Quincy Adams's Diary, August 30, 1831. "There is a depth of depravity in this transaction," observes Adams, "at which the heart sickens." See further comments, etc.

No exigency ever arose for the production of Monroe's deposition while either Rhea or Gouverneur lived. Jackson, triumphant over all political foes, furnished no material for reviving the dispute. But, long after Jackson's death, Benton found among some chests containing Jackson's private papers, which were then and are still in the custody of the Blair family at Washington, a lengthy document which purported to contain an exposition of Jackson's conduct in the Seminole War from Jackson's own standpoint. This document, prepared evidently for publication in the heat of the Calhoun controversy in 1831, had for some reason been suppressed, or at least withheld from the public. Being then engaged in preparing his "Thirty Years' View," which was published about 1854, Benton made free use of it. As a chronicler he set the narrative forth at much length; and as a long-devoted partisan of General Jackson, and one moreover having slight personal knowledge of the whole affair, he accepted its allegations with no real effort to discriminate. But the careful critic must perceive that the document is not greatly to be trusted. The writing, as Benton observes, is that of some clerk, in a fair, round hand, with slight interlineations by the general, and the expression is sometimes in the third person and sometimes in the first. Plainly enough, the story is long and loosely put together, with hasty transitions from narrative to argument, with *ad captandum* thrusts, with assertions equally positive whether facts are alleged as of Jackson's personal knowledge or upon mere hearsay; its main purpose is to put Calhoun in the wrong and convict him of duplicity, and its whole strain is passionate and bitter. Though bearing Jackson's signature at the end, it is not sworn to; page after page might have been interpolated by a scribe; and finally there is no proof that Jackson himself ever finally accepted it as fit for publication, but rather the reverse.[1]

In this document appears a statement as to the Jackson January letter which singularly fits into Rhea's mysterious epistle of 1831. It alleges that while Jackson and Rhea were in Washington, during the winter of 1819 (or at the time of the Seminole debates), Rhea called on Jackson, as he said at the request of Monroe, and begged him on his return home to burn the letter authorizing the capture of the Spanish posts which Rhea had written Jackson in 1818. Jackson, it adds, gave Rhea the promise thus solicited; and accordingly, after his return to Nashville, he burnt Rhea's letter, and on his letter-book, opposite the copy of his January letter to Monroe, made this entry: "Mr. Rhea's letter in answer is burnt this 12th April, 1819."[2]

---

[1] See Benton's Thirty Years' View, Vol. I., p. 168 *et seq.*

[2] 1 Benton's Thirty Years' View, 168 *et seq.* This is the statement borrowed by Parton, to which allusion has already been made in this article, *supra*, p. 101. If it were needful, much might be said to discredit such a story. From the Jackson statement one gathers the impression that Rhea's letter, being already in Nashville, was burnt by Jackson at the first opportunity. But Rhea's letter to Monroe in 1831 supposes rather that Jackson had the letter with him while in Washington, which is the more consistent. The general had come all the way from Nashville to Washington, in order to produce his papers and justify himself before a Congressional committee; and is it to be supposed that a letter so material to his defence, if it existed at all, and he had relied upon it, would have been left behind? And if he had that letter with him, why, in utter disregard of the reasons which the Benton document puts forward so sedulously, should Jackson have so long deferred destroying it, when it was so easy to relieve Rhea of embarrassment by returning the letter or burning it before his eyes on the spot? Again, it is certain that Jackson saw the President and Secretary of War frequently, while on this visit to Washington, and that he was on the most cordial terms with both of them.

Monroe's own connection with Jackson's January letter has now, I think, been amply explained. And as for that Rhea letter, which, it is claimed, Andrew Jackson burnt at Rhea's request, only one of two theories appears tenable: (1) That Rhea imposed upon Jackson in the Florida business a pretended authority which the President never gave him, — a situation which might well explain his anxiety in 1819 that his letter to Jackson should be destroyed; (2) That the whole story was fabricated, in or about 1831, by Rhea and others in Jackson's confidence, for some political purpose, in connection with the Calhoun disclosures, which they did not see fit to press. The latter hypothesis, I regret, for Jackson's sake, to say, appears altogether the more probable; and that hypothesis Wirt and John Quincy Adams accepted, — men most competent to judge, and not more disposed to favor Calhoun than Jackson.

One word as to the private papers of Jackson to which I have alluded. Since the recent death of Hon. Montgomery Blair, these papers have been held by his executors, who intimate an intention to arrange them for publication. Congress, on the other hand, at the instance of Jackson's surviving relatives, is considering the propriety of purchasing them. In the interest of our national history, I trust that the question of title to these important documents will soon be settled, so that they may be opened to the

---

Why, then, should one of the general's astuteness have acted thus upon Rhea's oral request, unsupported by proof that the request came from the President, and without a suspicion of Rhea's motives in making it? And, once more, as Parton himself has suggested, is it not singular that, while we are told that Rhea's letter to Jackson was burnt, neither Rhea nor Jackson has pretended to state what was its substance, what the dates of Rhea's interview with Monroe, what the terms of the supposed authority, or any other details?

inspection of historical scholars and investigators, if not to the general public. I shall be glad to learn whether the Jackson papers throw any light upon the purposes which this falsehood about Rhea's backstairs mission — for falsehood it certainly was — was meant to subserve.

PRESIDENT POLK'S DIARY.

In the Lenox Library of New York City may be seen the literary relics of the late George Bancroft, which that institution purchased in 1893 from the executors of his estate, after Congress had delayed action upon their offer of the whole undivided collection to the United States government at an appraised value of $75,000, under a provision of the historian's will. The price paid privately was nearly ten thousand dollars more than that asked from the public; the entire collection numbering, in books, pamphlets, and manuscripts, about twenty thousand volumes.

Among the richest treasures of this collection, as well as its latest important accession during Mr. Bancroft's life, should be reckoned the private papers and correspondence of President James K. Polk; or rather, we should say, type-written copies of the original manuscripts, which were prepared under the venerable author's immediate supervision, and bound up, after careful verification, in handsome volumes of half-turkey morocco with gilt-letter titles. Mr. Bancroft, as the last survivor of a Cabinet and an administration whose policy was in many respects profound and far-reaching, suddenly conceived, at the age of eighty-six, the purpose of making an authentic and complete narrative of that political

Reprinted from Atlantic Monthly, August, 1895.

term; and accordingly, after writing to Nashville in April, 1887, he visited Mr. Polk's widow, and obtained full permission to take to his own home the mass of papers which had remained undisturbed as the ex-President left them at his death, nearly forty years earlier, and to make such use of them as he might deem fit. The scholar pursued his task with ardor, so far as to prepare and arrange the desired materials, a labor most congenial and easy to one of his long experience; he felt the first glow of this new literary undertaking, which was sure to bring hidden testimony to light. But his remarkable intellect and trained habits of industry were not equal, at so late an age, to the creative task of composition; his health declined, and on the 17th of January, 1891, he died. This final service of our historical sage in the interest of American past politics was a distinct and valuable one, but it was that of compiler, rather than of historian. He has, however, left on record the impressions made on his own mind by the perusal of the manuscript. "Polk's character shines out in these papers," he writes, "just exactly as the man was, — prudent, far-sighted, bold, exceeding any Democrat of his day in his undeviatingly correct exposition of Democratic principles."

Unquestionably, the chief historical value of the Polk collection consists in the twenty-four volumes of Mr. Polk's Diary, kept during nearly the whole term of his presidency; each volume averaging about a hundred type-written pages in the large octavo which Mr. Bancroft used. It must be a surprise to most of our fellow-countrymen to learn that another President besides John Quincy Adams kept an extensive journal while in office; and especially that an Executive so absorbed in difficult details as Mr. Polk should have found time to record his impressions from day to day at such great length, and with so obvious a determination to be exact and comprehensive. Such an enterprise steadily pursued, and with no full opportunity to change or suppress what at the time was written, reveals not only facts essential to a correct understanding of public actions, but, more unconsciously, the mental cast and political bias of the writer. Like his more erudite predecessor, Polk cherished — and probably with greater zeal — the purpose of vindicating some day his secret political motives and his public relations with other men; but his premature death, very soon after his four years' term had expired, left the Diary unrevised as its own expositor, an inner fountain of information unadorned. No two Presidents could have been more at the antipodes than were Polk and John Quincy Adams in political affiliations and designs. Yet each, after his peculiar fashion, was honest, inflexible in purpose, and pursuant of the country's good; and both have revealed views singularly alike — the one as a scholar, the other as a sage and sensible observer — of the selfish, ignoble, and antagonistic influences which surge about the citadel of national patronage, and beset each supreme occupant of the White House.

President Polk has stated the circumstances under which he commenced his Diary. On the 26th of August, 1845, he held with his Secretary of State, James Buchanan, an important conversation over the Oregon troubles, which he reduced at once to writing; and after reflecting upon this narrative in his own solitude, he determined to open a diary at once and continue the plan. Next day he procured a blank book, with this purpose in view, and began his entries regularly, concluding to make them longer or shorter as convenience and the events worth recording might determine. The conversation of August 26, however, he did not again transcribe, but left the written sheets separate, beginning his book on the 27th. The journal thus commenced he continued from day to day for the remainder of his remarkable term, which lasted from March 4, 1845, to March 4, 1849. Leaving office, feeble and in failing health, on the latter date, he died in the middle of the following June.

Whatever may be thought of Mr. Polk's official course in despoiling Mexico for the aggrandizement of his own country, one cannot read this Diary carefully without an increased respect for his simple and sturdy traits of character, his inflexible honesty in financial concerns, and the pertinacious zeal and strong sagacity which characterized his whole presidential career. Making all due allowance for any personal selfishness which might color his narrative, we now perceive clearly that he was the framer of that public policy which he carried into so successful execution, and that instead of being led (as many might have imagined) by the more famous statesmen of his administration and party who surrounded him, he in reality led and shaped his own executive course; disclosing in advance to his familiar Cabinet such part as he thought best to make known, while concealing the rest. Both Bancroft and Buchanan, of his official advisers, have left on record, since his death, incidental tributes to his greatness as an administrator and unifier of executive action; both admitting in effect his superior force of will and comprehension of the best practical methods for attaining his far-reaching ends. On the other hand, while the Diary shows that Mr. Polk held the one

Secretary in high esteem, it is plain that he appreciated the many weaknesses of the other, with whom he had frequent differences of opinion, which in these secret pages elicit his own sharp comment. In fact, the Secretary of State, whom he repeatedly overruled, felt, for the first sixteen months, at least, of this executive term, so much dissatisfied with various features of Polk's policy, and in particular, like others of Pennsylvania, so discontented with the famous low tariff measure which Polk was bent upon carrying, that in the summer of 1846 he arranged definitely to retire from the Cabinet, to accept a Middle State vacancy on the supreme bench, which the President promised him; though with an overruling discretion deferring the appointment until the new tariff act was out of jeopardy at the Capitol, when Buchanan himself at last concluded to remain where he was. Buchanan's presidential aspirations, notwithstanding a condition exacted by the President from all who entered the administration, that they should cease to aspire so long as they sat at his council board, annoyed him much as time went on. "He is selfish," says the Diary in March, 1848, "and controlled so much by wishes for his own advancement that I cannot trust his advice on a public question; yet it is hazardous to dismiss, and I have borne with him." And on another occasion Polk records, after repeatedly finding his Secretary timid, over-anxious, and disposed too much to forestall overtures from others which the administration knew were due and were sure to come, "Mr. Buchanan is an able man, but is in small matters without judgment, and sometimes acts like an old maid."

All hasty diarists are likely to repeat themselves; and no idea does Mr. Polk's Diary repeat so frequently as that of disgust with the constant pressure for office which our chief magistrate encounters. It is the same phase of human nature which John Quincy Adams beheld with a like antipathy, though with a more dogged determination not to yield to such importunity. President Polk delineates his tormentors in the shape of callers at the White House as they may still be seen: some to seek office, others to beg money, and others still to pay, or profess to pay, their respects. "A year gone," records the Diary, March 4, 1846, "and the pressure for office has not abated. Will this pressure never cease? I most sincerely wish that I had no offices to bestow. If I had not, it would add much to the happiness and comfort of my position. As it is, I have no office to bestow without turning out better men than a large majority of those who seek their places." Again in September is his loathing expressed at this "constant stream of persons seeking office and begging money." "Almost the whole of my embarrassment in administering the government," he writes in May, 1847, "grows out of the public patronage which it is my duty to dispense." But the pressure of these "loafers for office" lasted his whole term; even "females" (as he expresses himself) seeking personal interviews and pleading "for their worthless relatives." During the summer of 1848, at a time when there were no existing offices to bestow, the President was besieged by applicants, simply because Congress was going to pass a bill for creating a board of commissioners upon Mexican claims, which might or might not meet the executive approval; and so greatly were the places sought in advance of their creation that one woman pleaded for her husband as a commissioner, shedding tears freely, and distressing the President with a story of their poverty and great need of an office; while another person — a man with whom Mr. Polk had once served in Congress — occupied more than an hour in soliciting a place upon the board, "if the bill should pass." "I had," adds the diarist, "no idea of appointing him, and yet I could not avoid hearing him without rudeness." Even after the presidential election of 1848, in which Polk's own party candidate was defeated by the Whigs, the pressure upon this Democratic President continued strong, under the apparent conviction that the incoming Executive, General Taylor, was not likely to make many removals. "The herd of office-seekers," observes Mr. Polk at this late stage, "are the most unprincipled persons in the country. As a mass they are governed by no principle." And professing to be Democrats under him, he expected them to go *vice versâ* under his Whig successor, whom many of them had helped elect. "The patronage," he finally adds, shortly before leaving office, "will, from the day any President enters upon his duties, weaken his administration."

Judge Mason, of the Cabinet, told the President in April, 1848, of one office-seeker whose papers were filed at his department without specifying any particular office. The Secretary asked him what office he wanted. "I am a good hand at making treaties," he replied, "and as some are to be made soon, I should like to serve as a minister abroad."

The constant interference of members of Congress in these matters of patronage was another source of annoyance upon which Mr. Polk made frequent comment. "Members of Congress," he writes, "attach great importance to petty offices, and assume their right to make the appointments in their own States, thereby joining issue with heads of the departments in such matters." He was much annoyed when a prominent member of the House, who had already declined the mission to Russia, pursued him for an appointment to the court of France, not only in writing, but in person at the White House, and face to face, most persistently; and when, after much urging, the President yielded to his wishes, and the Senate rejected the appointment, this person grew angry because Polk promptly sent in another name, and he soon drifted into a semi-hostile position towards the administration. Two other members of the House, at the time the Mexican war was declared, desired appointments as military paymasters, under a new bill which they had done much to frame and push through Congress; but appointments trenching so closely upon the prohibition of the Constitution the President refused to make. Again and again did legislators at the Capitol oppose the executive wishes, or treat the highest incumbent with personal incivility over some quarrel of patronage. "Patronage is injurious to a President," was Polk's decided opinion, as he secretly expressed himself; and this partly because legislators did not stand by the consequences of their own recommendations. "Members of Congress," writes the President, December 16, 1846, "and others high in society make representations for friends on which I cannot rely, and lead me constantly into error. When I act upon the information which they give me, and make a mistake, they leave me to bear the responsibility, and never have the manliness to assume it for themselves." And yet few American executives had seen greater experience than Polk in congressional life, or proved more capable, while at the other end of the avenue, of managing our national legislature so as to achieve their most cherished plans.

John Quincy Adams, while detesting Polk's political principles and his narrow conceptions of party infallibility, does justice to his unquestionable capacity for toilsome work and indefatigable industry. The same habits which made this son of Tennessee so conspicuous in despatching legislative business while chairman of the Ways and Means committee or Speaker of the House insured his successful career as President. Failing though he was in health during these four consummate years, he did not hesitate to put his shoulder to the wheel whenever the work of the departments got into deep mire. This was partly because he distrusted others, and felt constantly disposed to keep all executive details, foreign or domestic, great or small, under his personal control. With the unexpected burdens thrown upon his administration by the Mexican war, he soon found his Secretary of the Treasury quite overworked, and in danger of death; and the President, sending him away for recuperation, took an active hand in the financial guidance of the government, at the same time aiding his Secretary of War, who also was taken sick. General Scott he disliked greatly, as the ranking military officer, and found his presence at Washington so embarrassing that he resolved to send him off; and he strongly suspected that the detailed chiefs of the quartermaster and commissary divisions were hostile to his Mexican policy. Some of these subordinates (so he writes) "appear to be indifferent to our contest, and merely go through their ordinary routine." On general principle, too, he felt disposed to check such lesser chiefs. "Bureau officers," he writes in November, 1848, "whose duty it is to prepare estimates, are always in favor of large appropriations. They are not responsible to the public, but to the Executive, and must be watched and controlled in these respects." After the adjournment of the long session of Congress, in August of the same year, Polk, who had not been three miles away from the White House (as he relates) for more than thirteen months, took a brief vacation trip for his health to the mineral springs of Pennsylvania, and was back again in ten days; attending to his duties at the capital in the hottest summer weather, receiving important secret despatches from abroad, and in fact conducting the government for a whole month without the aid of his Cabinet, who were mostly away. "So familiar am I," he records at this time, "with all the principles and details of the administration that I have no difficulty in doing so;" and he declared that he found himself better acquainted with the work than his subordinates themselves. But he confessed to himself, while thus engaged, that he found the presidency no bed of roses. "No President," he writes at the close of this year, "who performs his duty faithfully and conscientiously can have any leisure. If he intrusts the details and smaller matters to subordinates, constant errors will occur. I prefer to supervise the whole operations of the government myself, rather than intrust the public business to subordinates; and this makes my duties very great."

Mr. Polk had much of Old Hickory's dislike of financial monopolists. While looking after the Treasury during Secretary Walker's absence, at the time of the Mexican war, he was greatly worried over what seemed to him a criminal abuse of official power, whereby a draft for two million dollars for prospective disbursements in the quartermaster-general's bureau had been lodged with private bankers, to be checked out as might become needful. To one of his own simple integrity in money matters, defalcation appeared imminent; but the Secretary exculpated himself from misconduct, and assured the President that the banking credit behind the draft was strong and adequate. Still probing into the transaction, the President found that confidential favors in the way of a special deposit were part of the consideration upon which our war loans had been negotiated; and others of the Cabinet coming to the rescue of their associate, and declaring such an arrangement legal in their opinion, the matter appears to have finally rested.

In various other respects our eleventh President bore strong resemblance to his immortal fellow-townsman, as the disciple to the master, the less to the greater. With the qualities of civilian and legislator, instead of warrior or forceful leader of the mass, he had nevertheless a corresponding tenacity of purpose within the circumscription of strict party lines. Andrew Jackson was his great patron and exemplar, and from that idolized Democrat of the Democracy came doubtless the chief inspiration of his own foreign policy; though Jackson died too soon after this new administration came into power to influence it greatly in particulars. Polk's affection and veneration for the general appear, however, in various letters copied among these papers; and Jackson wrote frequently from the Hermitage in confidence, being overrun with applications for office, not a few of which he pressed upon the new Executive with characteristic comment. We here see injected into the tale of his own bodily ailments some sensible political counsel as against the "Whiggs" and those "who run with the hare and cry with the hounds;" and Polk took strongly to heart the language of one letter which he sometimes quoted afterwards, — to take principle for his guide and make the public good his end, "stearing clear of the intrigues and machinations of political clikes." Indeed, the new President of the Democracy valued so greatly the good will of his early predecessor, though not always free to follow his advice, that upon Jackson's death, in June, 1845, he sought eagerly a last letter written him, to show to incipient enemies that their cordial relation had continued to the close. This letter appears to have been mislaid, in the midst of household confusion at Nashville, and political treachery was suspected, until, after much anxious inquiry, it reached Washington with a suitable explanation. To Polk's dismay, however, the hero's dying communication proved unsuitable for publication, since the burden of it was, in all friendly confidence, to denounce Polk's chosen Secretary of the Treasury, whom Jackson much disliked, and to guide the chief Executive into a train of inquiry regarding this man and a former government official, also stigmatized by the writer as dishonest, which might elicit certain facts and blow them both "skyhigh." Some interesting accounts of Jackson's last hours and funeral are contained among the Polk papers; and it appears that in the last simple service at the Hermitage the hymn given out (most inappropriate to the exit of such a character) began, —

"What timorous worms we mortals are!"

Within the horizon of his mental vision President Polk was singularly clear-sighted and sensible; but he was hemmed in by partisan and religious prejudices which limited the range of his comprehension.

His private and public writings alike afford full proof of this. In his Diary, the Whigs he persisted in styling "Federalists," until the political strength of that party with the people, and the genial influence of Henry Clay, who paid him a notable visit on returning to the Senate, won his fair respect as the canvass of 1848 approached. He records his disbelief in judges of opposition tendency who might become "Federalists" upon the bench in their construction of the law. Office-holders under Tyler's administration who claimed that they had been conservative Democrats found no favor with him; and when the Mexican war broke out, though he candidly admitted that Whigs must have some of the military appointments, his repugnance for Winfield Scott as the major-general commanding proved inveterate, and he began disparaging Zachary Taylor as soon as the latter's renown attracted those opposed to the party in power. More and more did he convince himself, as Taylor's star rose, that this favorite of the Whigs was without soldierly qualities except as a fighter; and he refused to allow a salute to be fired, on the news of Buena Vista. While trying earnestly, moreover, to assuage the factional quarrels of his party in New York State, he pressed constantly the idea that principle and public good were bound up in the continuous success of the Democracy. In religion he showed, as a Presbyterian, the same rigid and inflexible adherence to his faith; being devout and devoted to public worship, decent not to fail in attendance upon the congressional funerals at Washington, of which there were many; and so much of a rigid Sabbatarian withal that he repeatedly recorded his regrets when forced to transact public business on Sunday, though some of the most crafty work of his whole term was despatched on that day. With something, perhaps, of religious fervor, he seemed imbued with the idea that he led God's chosen people; whatever possessions his fellow-countrymen might appear to covet he was ready to go for, and fetch, with little scruple for the ownership of others. Like the great Jackson, he felt that "might makes right" in national policy, and was ready to despoil our Spanish-American neighbors, who were trying, in their own poor way, to emulate our example of self-government.

Polk's deficient ideality blinded him to some of the inevitable results of such a spoliation in debasing American character and engendering strife; and the gradual alienation of Democratic leaders from his support during the Mexican war he ascribed, possibly too closely, to personal grievances. In the sectional struggle for partitioning our conquered domains between slavery and freedom he could see nothing but "a wicked and senseless agitation," of which selfish statesmen were seeking to make a hobby. His lost political friendships he imputed unhesitatingly and altogether to political disappointments. Calhoun, he recalled, had been dissatisfied "ever since I did not retain him in the Cabinet." Benton, whom he certainly tried most assiduously to please, was uncivil to him, and threatening "from the day I appointed a court-martial on Frémont," his son-in-law; and he says, not untruly, that Benton "is apt to think that nothing is properly done that he is not previously consulted about." Van Buren took early offence, he thought, because the new President would not let him make the selection of the Cabinet. "I have preserved," he writes, "his most extraordinary letter to me on that subject, making no reply to it; and I have since had no direct correspondence except to frank him two annual messages, and to receive his acknowledgment." Van Buren's acceptance of the Free-Soil nomination for President in 1848 against the regular Democratic candidate moved Polk greatly. "He is the most fallen man I have ever known," records the chief magistrate in his Diary; and he promptly removed Van Buren's personal friend from the district attorneyship in New York, appointing another in his place.

Mr. Polk's wife, who was a devout religious worshipper like himself, and whose decided views of social decorum strongly impressed the White House entertainments of her day, seems to have shared in some of her husband's personal dislikes, with that redoubled intensity to which many good wives incline. Her antipathy to the Van Buren family was shown in her bearing towards the ex-President's son, familiarly styled "Prince John." Her husband relates his amusement at finding that she had on two or three occasions countermanded his own order directing this schismatic Democrat to be invited to a White House dinner, and that on one occasion she burned a dinner ticket which the President had requested his private secretary to send him. The reason she assigned was that John Van Buren had not called on her; but we may question whether this was the only one.

In the presidential canvass of 1848, when for the first time our national elections were held on the same day throughout the Union, under an act of Congress, Mr. Polk felt strongly interested on behalf of the regular Democratic ticket. Lewis Cass, the party candidate, was a personal friend, considerate enough to show his letter of acceptance, and modify it upon President Polk's advice; particularly on the point of announcing that if elected he would carry out his policy according to the convention platform; a pledge which Mr. Polk thought inexpedient as a rule. Over the successorship itself Polk had maintained a strict neutrality; inflexibly refusing to run for a second term, or to allow the use of his name before the convention, though many urged him to do so. He passed many sick days during this campaign, and had much apart from the political contest to worry him. But disastrously as the election turned out for his party, he gained in composure and spirit when all was over, and his own public work was substantially done. He felt proud to think that, after all, he had finished the Mexican war successfully before his retirement, and had commenced reducing the public debt besides; that he would leave office with foreign relations everywhere at peace, and no troubles to transmit. Towards the New York "Barnburners," or Free-Soil Democrats, his resentment was implacable; and when his Secretary of State, always bent on conciliating the doubtful elements, selected a Rochester newspaper of that party, soon after election day, to publish the laws of the United States for a year, he sternly countermanded the choice, refusing to allow the patronage of public printing to any press which had not approved his administration. Buchanan, unable to satisfy him by alleging that this newspaper had been moderate in its opposition, put upon the President the whole responsibility of revoking this appointment, and Polk accepted it; the Secretary drew up a letter stating that this revocation was at the President's special request, and the President permitted it to be sent.

Mr. Polk has recorded with evident relish and good nature whatever signs of civility and popular respect he observed during the last few weeks that he occupied the White House. Hundreds of callers greeted him in the East Room at a January reception, and he walked through the parlors, delighted, with the famous Mrs. Madison on his arm. He thought it worth while to write out in his Diary a recipe for presidential handshaking, which he gave to some of his friends orally about this time: "If a man surrendered his arm to be shaken by one horizontally, by another perpendicularly, and by another with a strong grip, he could not fail to suffer severely from it; but if he would shake and not be shaken, grip and not be gripped, taking care always to squeeze the hand of his adversary as hard as the adversary squeezed him, he would suffer no inconvenience from it. I can generally anticipate a strong grip from a strong man; and I then take advantage of him by being quicker than he, and seizing him by the tip of his fingers." "I stated this playfully," he adds, "but it is all true."

When his chosen successor reached Washington, in February, 1849, the administration naturally felt some embarrassment, for the President's treatment of Zachary Taylor during the Mexican war had given the latter great offence. The two had never met in person, and Buchanan, over-anxious as usual, would have strained official etiquette in the endeavor to reconcile them. But Polk stood properly upon his executive dignity, which was far better, and waited for what was due him. Nor did he lose by doing so; for Taylor, bred to military habits, considerate and kind-hearted, paid his ceremonial visit to the White House in company with political friends; and Polk, reciprocating the courtesy, gave his fellow-Southerner an elaborate dinner party, which was attended by all the Cabinet officers with their wives, and many eminent men of both parties. "All went off in the best style," says the Diary, "and not the slightest allusion was made to political subjects."

Finally, on the 3d of March, our Democratic President closed his work by visiting the Capitol to sign bills during the last night session of Congress. He carried with him a carefully written veto message on internal improvements, to use if needful; but no bill of that character passed, — possibly, one might surmise, to his own regret, for he made record that he considered that unused message one of the ablest papers he had ever prepared.

Vice-President Dallas, who served through this whole four years' term, eulogizes Mr. Polk as plain, unaffected, affable, and kind in his personal deportment, with a consistent simplicity of life and purity of manners; as temperate but not unsocial, industrious but accessible. Concerning Polk's secretive disposition and quiet persistency in his plans, more might have been added. But Dallas says very justly, "He left nothing unfinished; what he attempted he did." That Polk desired to be well remembered by posterity appears from his will; for, being childless, he devised his estate in successive interests to the worthiest who should bear the name of Polk. But this singular provision was lately set aside in the Tennessee courts, soon after the widow's death, as void for perpetuity, and the property passed absolutely to his legal heirs, — a new instance, among the many which our present age supplies, of the vanity of testamentary wishes.

In another article I shall consider President Polk's public policy and achievements, as illustrated and made clear by his private papers.

PRESIDENT POLK'S ADMINISTRATION.

THE great achievements of President Polk's administration were four in number: the full establishment of the independent treasury, which divorced government dealings from the banks; the low tariff; the adjustment of a northwest boundary with Great Britain, which secured our title to Oregon; and the management of our annexation of Texas, by diplomacy and bloodshed, so as to despoil Mexico of a still further portion of her domains, and gain a broad southerly area to the Pacific, inclusive of California and New Mexico. All four of these achievements were clearly purposed by our eleventh President when he entered upon his executive duties; in all four he took the initiative, so far as possible, before Congress assembled in its first session under his term; and, with the co-operation of Congress, he accomplished, before that first session ended, every one of the projects except the last, which, proving slow and difficult of fulfilment, and withal developing only gradually before our people as the extent of his secret purpose revealed itself, he despatched as rapidly and surely as the exigencies would permit. Before another presidential election he had wrought out his task to completion.

I shall in this paper[1] consider those four cardinal points of policy only so far as the testimony afforded

Re-printed from Atlantic Monthly, September, 1895.
[1] See also "President Polk's Diary," p. 121.

by Mr. Polk's papers, and especially his Diary, may furnish to our own age plain illustration and proof of historical importance. The first three topics may be passed over rapidly. The sub-treasury or independent treasury plan originated under President Van Buren, as a Democratic measure; but when the Whigs came into power, they at once repealed the sub-treasury act before a fair trial of the experiment, meaning to restore the former national bank system, which, however, Harrison's untimely death and the Vice-President's recreancy debarred them from doing. In this respect, therefore, Polk, as a Democratic President, had simply to restore Democratic policy to the national finances, and the Van Buren measure was re-enacted, to remain enduring. "I have always been for the independent treasury, like Silas Wright," records this new President, referring to the immediate author of the original bill. Next, as concerns the low tariff, that most admirable achievement of this new administration, Polk was a strong pioneer in the reduction of duties, and neither the fears nor the opposition of his own party friends could divert him. He had, to be sure, equivocated somewhat in his opinions in the presidential canvass of 1844; and when, in his first presidential message, he boldly proposed tariff reform in this open-trade direction, ably seconded though he was by his Secretary of the Treasury, the consternation was very great among Pennsylvanians of his party. Secretary Buchanan, as I have mentioned elsewhere, would gladly have left the Cabinet and gone upon the supreme bench of the United States, so as to shirk the issue with his political friends, had not Polk kept back his promised appointment to the place until the legislative struggle was over, thereby committing to his own policy the aid which he needed. Mr. Polk is entitled fairly to the fame of a successful experiment on the basis of non-protection and liberal trade which gave to this country great mercantile prosperity and commercial expansion down to the Civil War, and won the approval of all political parties. "The tariff portion," as he states, of his first annual message, in the Diary, "is mine, and all the message is mine." He evidently, and with good reason, cherished the belief that such a tariff, framed in co-operation with Sir Robert Peel's corn laws and England's new departure for free trade with the world, would aid in uniting the two countries more closely in reciprocal commerce, and in reconciling Great Britain to concessions most desirable for settling the Oregon question. While procuring the needful enactment, Polk's Diary shows him in his former and most familiar character of a driver of business through the national legislature. We see him, by the light of his private revelations, strongly interesting himself in the progress of this tariff-reduction measure through the two Houses during every stage, setting his heart upon accomplishing the work wholly and at once during the first and long session of Congress; and, with this end steadily in view, we perceive him forcing it through with indefatigable zeal against all factional opposition among his party supporters, and in spite of foreign war and other dangerous responsibilities which had accumulated upon his hands in those same early months. A tariff-reduction act was not unpopular with the country at large, and hence the House passed it with comparative harmony. But the real struggle came, as such struggles will, in the Senate and confederate branch; and upon the Democrats of that less responsive chamber he next brought to bear all the personal arguments he could urge in private conference, all the persuasion of Cabinet officers, all the patronage at his official command, for gaining his end.

The executive anxiety was not without good cause, for Polk's party friends were so much divided upon this vexatious issue that, after the best efforts of the White House were exhausted, the fate of the measure was found to depend finally on the uncertain vote of a single Democratic Senator. The casting vote of Vice-President Dallas, however, carried the bill through its most critical stage, after which the act passed the Senate by a majority of one. On the 29th of July, 1846, the President rejoiced that his tariff measure was finally passed, and he felt himself free to veto a river and harbor act which came also to hand for his signature.

Upon the Oregon boundary, Polk's Diary opens with confidential interviews which Buchanan had with him upon the subject, while negotiations remained at a stand after the compromise of boundary suggested on our side had been rejected by the English minister in discourteous language, which Polk quickly resented. And now we see the Secretary of State timorous over the situation, while the President, confident that reflection would bring the adversary to his own proposition, waited for British overtures, betraying no nervousness and willing to bide his time. In spite of Buchanan's dread, our people had no fight for the line of 54° 40′, though there was abundant bluster in Congress over the subject. The fair compromise line was in due time proposed again, this time by Great Britain's negotiator, and a treaty based upon that settlement was promptly ratified by our Senate before the long session ended.

Thus happily was an old controversy laid at rest; and so far honorably, as Jefferson had borne us beyond the Mississippi, did this new Democratic Executive plant American colonization firmly upon the Pacific strand.

But the fourth object to which the President had devoted himself from the outset was not gained so readily; and vainly imagining that he could buy out Mexico through its rulers, and gain the new domain he wanted by threats or cajolery, he was cast upon the undesired alternative of war to gain his end; and the war once begun, he found it far more stubborn and protracted than he had looked for, though a weak nation was our foe. The love of liberty and of territorial integrity burns strong in the breasts of the humblest of republican communities; and, whatever their dissensions with one another, they will turn their arms unitedly against invaders from without, and even their corrupt leaders would rather encourage than betray them. Polk saw clearly what our superior American people, or at least the Southern portion, coveted; and surely, could the new acquisition have been fairly gained, the precious soil was well worth our permanent acceptance. But what we could not obtain by fair means Polk set himself to acquiring by foul; and while "Texas re-annexation" had been the immediate aim of the party that came with him into power, he planned and carried out with remarkable secrecy and constancy a dismemberment of our sister republic far beyond what this rallying cry had called for or expected. The Diary and Correspondence, with their private disclosures, confirm the worst that was ever imputed to this administration in its deadly and depredating course. But Polk was one of those to whom the end justifies the means;

he was fully imbued with the reckless spirit of manifest destiny which was so rampant in that era, and he felt himself God's chosen instrument, in a sense, to advance the stars and stripes, and despoil the weak of their inheritance. Such was the prevalent perversion of the Monroe Doctrine that we seemed actually devoted to the idea of making converts to the republican faith of the rest of this continent, and encouraging all Spanish-American neighbors to emulate our national example to the point of casting off European allegiance, and experimenting in the same direction with ourselves, only for the sake of leading them to misrule and internal disorder, so as to make them the readier prey to our own territorial greed. Mr. Polk meant to vindicate his Mexican policy by the private papers which he preserved so carefully; but this vindication was evidently staked upon the expectation that public gratitude would redound because of the splendid expansion that he gave to our national boundaries. He toiled and he despoiled for the glory of the American Union; but he could see nothing wrong in his despicable treatment of Mexico, in the crime he perpetrated against liberty and the sacred rights of property. He was not the kind of patriot to place himself at another's point of view, and could feel no tender compunctions for an adversary, and least of all for a weak one.

Those familiar with our annals will recall the leading facts regarding the admission of Texas into the Union in 1845. Wrested from the Mexican confederacy and people by American colonists and adventurers who had settled within its neighboring limits by foreign permission, this independent, or rather revolutionary Texan republic sought constitutional alliance with the United States; and after that successful presidential canvass in which the Lone Star issue became so prominent, our Democratic Congress, shortly before Polk's accession, passed a provisional act for admitting into the Union that foreign but adjacent jurisdiction as a new State capable of subdivision. But in order to unite the wavering party elements in Congress, this admission act placed upon our Executive the alternative of accepting Texas immediately under the provisions therein specified, or of beginning negotiations anew with that republic which Mexico still claimed, and postponing annexation indefinitely. The real intent of Congress was, of course, to trust the incoming President as umpire; but Tyler, the retiring Executive, eager for his own glory, at once, and just before retiring from office, chose the first alternative, and despatched his swift messenger to Texas with the tender of immediate annexation and admission to State membership. Polk might consequently have disclaimed the responsibility of a decision; but, as his papers show, he assembled his Cabinet soon after his term began, to consider whether to adopt the late President's action or not: and upon the advice of these counsellors he pronounced for pursuing the same line of policy, and issued appropriate orders. Francis P. Blair, who, like Benton of the Senate, had desired indefinite postponement under the second alternative, angrily charged Polk, during the hot canvass of 1848, with having pledged himself to the second alternative while the act was pending. This, however, Polk has emphatically denied; and those who best knew the surrounding circumstances and had been intimate in the confidence of the President-elect — among them Secretary Buchanan and the manager of the Texas compromise act, Secretary Walker — corroborate by their written statements, preserved among Polk's papers, what Polk himself asserts, and all those cognizant of his traits of character might naturally look for: that he kept his choice of plans strictly to himself, and made no pledge in advance whatever. But this, at least, Polk declares unhesitatingly: that his constant desire had been to have Texas admitted into the Union as soon as possible, by one means or another, and hence that the first alternative was his silent preference, since it best secured such admission practically. "For had annexation by negotiation been adopted," is his just comment in the retrospect, "Texas would have been lost to the United States."

The alternative of immediate annexation once decided upon, there was no sign of feebleness in Mr. Polk's pursuit of the chosen course. To Andrew J. Donelson, despatched upon this mission, the President wrote June 15, repeating his desires, already expressed, that the Texas convention, then about to meet, should accept annexation to the United States unqualifiedly and at once. "That moment," he writes, "I shall regard Texas as part of the Union; and our army and navy will defend and protect her by driving an invading Mexican army out." Donelson was by that time in Texas; and Polk promised to send an additional force to the Gulf the next day, leaving him to his own discretion in employing our troops or vessels should a Mexican army cross the Rio Grande. All we want, he says, is for Texas to assent to the terms of our statute, and he will not wait for the tedious process of forming a new constitution. "Of course," he adds, "I would maintain the Texan title to the extent which she claims it to be, and not permit an invading enemy to occupy a foot of the soil east of the Rio Grande." In this strain President Polk wrote to Sam Houston, also, assuring him that all rights of territorial boundary would be maintained, if only Texas would accept unconditionally the act of our Congress. Here we have the key to Polk's whole Mexican policy: which was to adopt the pretentious claim set up lately by the Texan revolutionists, that the boundaries of that republic extended to the Rio Grande, and over unsettled soil which the Mexican State of Texas had never included; and then to manipulate a treaty settlement with Mexico which should give to our Union another immense fraction of that unhappy nation's domains. By pressure upon that impoverished country Polk thought himself capable of driving a money bargain with her pride. Texas embraced her opportunity to the fullest extent, and voted in convention to accept the terms tendered by Congress, and enter the American Union as a new State; and by September 16, as the Diary informs us, the President announced clearly to his Cabinet that he should try to adjust, through this Texas question of limits, a permanent boundary between Mexico and the United States, so as to comprehend Upper California and New Mexico, and give us a line from the mouth of the Rio Grande to latitude 32° north, and thence west to the Pacific. For such a boundary he was willing, he said, to pay $40,000,000, but could probably purchase it for $15,000,000 or $20,000,000. In these views the Cabinet unanimously concurred, and instructions were given, accordingly, to John Slidell, who went at once as a special minister to Mexico, that republic having previously broken off its relations with us because of our league with Texas. But this September conference followed preparations which the President himself had already secretly started. Slidell, a member of the House, was at his home in Louisiana when sent off; but there are indications in the Diary that he had been fixed upon for such a contingency as the present, and had received from Polk himself oral and strictly confidential instructions before he left Washington in the spring. Meanwhile, Dr. Parrott, Slidell's prospective secretary of legation, who had been in the city of Mexico as a secret emissary, wrote from there, August 19, that Mexico was not likely to fight the United States over the admission of our new State, that there would be no invasion of Texas, and that our Executive ought to restore Mexican relations if he could.

In much of the underhand work of 1845 — in the instructions sent to our naval officers who were cruising off the Pacific coast, for instance — Polk dared not trust himself to writing out contemporaneously in his own journal; he would instruct various persons by word of mouth, and enjoin upon them the utmost secrecy; but his Diary's later allusions aid historical testimony already gathered from other sources. The Diary of May 30, 1846, contains the President's incidental admission, at that tardy date, that in Slidell's instructions of 1845 "the acquisition of California and New Mexico, with perhaps some northern provinces," had been included. Polk's reticence to others he practised with constant constraint for himself when committing his Mexican plans privately to paper; for in all this he meant to forestall public opinion, not to court it, believing that the public results would justify him before the people.

In Polk's private correspondence may be found General Scott's report with the President's indorsement, dated January 13, 1846, in justification of the famous order which required General Taylor to advance from Corpus Christi to the Rio Grande. Its preamble is worth quoting in this connection, inspired as it probably was in expression by the commander-in-chief or Secretary of War: "Congress having accepted the constitution adopted by the State of Texas, in convention assembled, in which constitution the Rio Grande del Norte is, at least in part, claimed as one of her boundaries, — subject, it may be, to future modification in part, by a treaty of limits between the United States and Mexico," — the President of the United States, through the War Department, had deemed it his duty to give instructions to General Zachary Taylor to advance and occupy such positions at or near Rio del Norte as might be necessary.

President Polk has been greatly blamed for precipitating the United States into an unrighteous war with Mexico, and at the same time placing the onus of hostilities, most craftily and dishonestly, upon that republic. The familiar phrases of his message will be recalled: "Mexico has passed the boundary of the United States, has invaded our territory and shed American blood upon the American soil;" "War exists, and, notwithstanding all our efforts to avoid it, exists by the act of Mexico herself." The real climax as shown by the Diary makes his dissimulation even greater than has been supposed. Saturday, the 9th of May, 1846, was a memorable one. Slidell was now in Washington, having returned from a mission for purchase utterly fruitless; and Polk, feeling convinced that nothing but war would give us the treaty of ample cession that he was bent upon procuring, took up a war policy. It was not the original Texas which had won its independence that he wanted to annex, for Mexico sought no recovery; nor was it Texas as voted to the Rio Grande, for Taylor held that disputed solitude by military possession, and was the real aggressor; but it was a new and broader belt to the Pacific, whose clear title could be won, as now seemed clear, only by force of arms. Congress being in the midst of its long session, the President summoned his Cabinet on this Saturday, and stated that it was his desire to send to the two Houses an immediate war message. But no news of any armed advance or opposition by the Mexicans, or of bloodshed or collision of any sort, had yet reached Washington from the front, where General Taylor with his command was already posted to make the disputed area of Texas our own. The Cabinet as a whole advised the President encouragingly, but Buchanan not without hesitation, while Bancroft, the Secretary of the Navy, gave his candid opinion that we ought to wait for some act of hostility before declaring war. Polk's Diary shows, however, that he preferred to recommend war as matters stood, for after the adjournment he made his preparations to write a message. But a new and sudden turn was given to the situation about sunset of the same day, when despatches from General Taylor reached the White House by the Southern mail, reporting that slight and casual attack by Mexicans and loss of life on the line of the Rio Grande which has since passed into history. Here then was the opportunity for throwing all scruples aside; and that Polk made the most of this *casus belli*, of this shedding the first drop of blood by Mexico, the American world is well aware. The Cabinet were summoned once more, in the evening; and they agreed unanimously that a war message

PRESIDENT POLK'S ADMINISTRATION. 151

should be sent into Congress on Monday, based upon this new state of facts. But would not that war message have been sent the same, had not this opportune intelligence arrived from the front? All now, says the Diary, was unity and energy. Mr. Polk worked all Sunday over the message, except for his attendance on morning church; Secretary Bancroft, who took dinner with him, giving his skilful literary aid in the afternoon. There was great excitement in Washington, and confidential friends of the Democracy were preparing to have Congress co-operate. "It was," records the President piously, but with no apparent sense of the unrighteousness of his secular task, "a day of great anxiety to me, and I regretted the necessity for me to spend the Sabbath in the manner I have." On the morning of Monday, the momentous 11th of May, Mr. Polk shut out company, and carefully revised this war message, which he sent in to Congress about noon; and such was the haste of preparation that he had not time to read over the accompanying executive correspondence, though he had seen the originals. Slidell, in the afternoon, called upon him, to announce that though the bill for declaring war with Mexico passed the House, the Senate had adjourned without action, and evidently not united. But the bill went through that branch on Tuesday, with a slight amendment, in which the House concurred. The act was brought to the President soon after the noon of Wednesday, May 13, and he approved and signed it; and an executive proclamation was forthwith issued which announced the existence of war, following the example of President Madison in 1812.

But there were already symptoms of national dissension to impress the Cabinet circle; Buchanan, at least, among Polk's chosen advisers, showing, besides his characteristic timidity, some forecast of the public dangers which would attend this new greed for expansion. In draughting a circular to our ministers in Europe, which announced the Mexican war, he stated expressly, and as though to allay suspicion, that our object was not to dismember Mexico nor to make conquest; that our boundary line as claimed against that republic was the Rio Grande. This draught was read at the Cabinet meeting on this same 13th of May; and the Diary gives a full account of the conference. "I will not tie up my hands by any such pledge," declared the President at once and decidedly. "In making peace with our adversary, we shall acquire California and New Mexico and other further territory, as an indemnity for this war, if we can." A warm discussion now arose in the Cabinet, Buchanan contending on his part that England and France would in that case help Mexico against us; for as yet the Oregon line was still in controversy with Great Britain. But again did the President refuse to embarrass his course by any such pledge; nor, he added, would he tolerate any intermeddling by European nations. The Secretary of State, says the Diary, stood alone in this matter; Marcy being absent on account of business pressure at the War Department. Secretary Bancroft, the Attorney-General, and the Postmaster-General all sided strongly with the President, while Secretary Walker spoke with much excitement against the draught as Buchanan had prepared it. At last, to end discussion, Mr. Polk stepped to his table and wrote out a new paragraph in place of that which had disclaimed all intention of further dismemberment; and Buchanan's despatches, when sent abroad, substituted the presidential paragraph for his own. "This," records Polk, "was one of the most earnest and interesting discussions which have occurred in my Cabinet," and it ended a day "of intense application, anxiety, and labor."

Some authentic explanation has long been wished of Secretary Bancroft's naval order, dated on May 13, when war was declared, which instructed our blockading squadron in the Gulf to permit Santa Anna, as a returning exile from Havana, to pass through with his suite, unmolested. The historical suspicion has been that this ex-President and military chief of Mexico was in secret concert with our administration; and the Polk papers make that suspicion a certainty by their revelations. It appears from the Diary that about February 13, 1846, and before our Mexican relations had culminated in war, a Spanish-American officer and revolutionist — Colonel Atocha by name — held a secret interview at Washington with President Polk, and gave the latter the impression, while Mexico was in strong public commotion, that Santa Anna had sent to arrange for his own restoration to the head of the Mexican government, on the assurance that our ends would be gained in return. Mr. Polk consulted his Cabinet upon such an arrangement, and with their consent, though Buchanan opposed, despatched his confidential agent to Havana, when war broke out, to confer with the distinguished exile. That agent was Commander Alexander Slidell Mackenzie, of the navy, to whose rumored mission Mr. Benton alludes in his "Thirty Years' View," though more slightingly, perhaps, than the facts justify. Mackenzie's despatches to the President, which were received at Washington on the 3d of August, are contained in full in the Polk Correspondence. It appears that the President made the Bancroft order to our blockading squadron the occasion for an oral message to Santa Anna, which Mackenzie reduced to writing and read to the Mexican general; thereby exceeding his authority, according to Polk's Diary record of January, 1848, since he should have delivered it orally. In course of the two interviews they held together, Santa Anna, as Mackenzie reports, asserted that, if in power once more in his own country, he would make concessions rather than see Mexico ruled by a foreign prince; that he preferred a friendly arrangement with the United States to the ravages of war; that he desired republican principles and a liberal government, excluding all mediation of England and France. Santa Anna advised that Taylor should advance his forces to Santillo. He also expressed a sense of his own kind treatment while a prisoner after the battle of San Jacinto, and said that if he did not return to Mexico he should like to become a citizen of the United States, and live in Texas. Santa Anna wrote a paper, it seems, for submission to our State Department. It is hard to say whether Polk's administration, in thus co-operating with the ablest of all Mexicans of the age, civil or military, in a subtle and sly intrigue for revolutionizing the republic with which we were now at war, was not overreached in its own game; at all events, Santa Anna, with his suite, passed our blockading line to Vera Cruz under the Bancroft order, not many weeks later, re-entered his country, and placed himself at the head of affairs; proving himself, however, after having done so, the most energetic and persistent of all Mexican opponents in the field, instead of our artful ally for dismemberment.

Most of the familiar episodes of the Mexican war

are strongly lighted up by the daily entries of Polk's Diary: his strong dislike of Scott, and his increasing disparagement of Zachary Taylor as the latter began to be talked about for the next President; the earnest intrigue in the administration circle to supersede both of these Whig generals by the Democratic Benton, under a projected measure for creating a lieutenant-general to outrank them both, — a scheme in which Benton personally was most active; the failure of such a bill for want of a party support in Congress, followed by Polk's abortive effort to bring Benton into the field as one of the new major-generals, and Benton's haughty refusal of a commission because the President would not retire all the existing major-generals in his own favor, and give him plenary powers to arrange a treaty besides;[1] the Calhoun "fencing in" plan for conducting the war by seizing and holding simply the territory we wanted, which appears to have been first broached by a military officer, but was dropped upon full Cabinet consultation, because such inactivity would not give us a parchment title, and might make the war too unpopular at home to be borne; Polk's disgust upon finding that the Whigs were having this war to their own party account, while he bore all the odium of it; Scott's quarrels at the front, and his recall after the capture of the city of Mexico; Trist, the clerk of the State Department, and his troubles over a treaty which he could not procure in a satisfactory form until he had ceased to be an accredited agent for negotiating one. Many were the mean expedients brought forward from time to time for heading off

---

[1] "The difficulty," records Polk in his Diary, "is about recalling Butler and Patterson" (the Democratic major-generals). "I would have recalled Scott and Taylor."

public opinion in the unhappy republic whose patriotism thwarted us. Our Executive at first employed Roman Catholic priests with his invading army, — "not," says the Diary, "as chaplains," but because "they spoke the Mexican language" and might "undeceive" the adversary; and in their last straits, Polk and his Cabinet had nearly decided to help the peace party of Mexico into power if they would execute in due form the desired treaty of peace and dismemberment.

At last, however, with all this fair domain our own prize, Mr. Polk viewed with alarm and evident surprise the portentous aspect of the slavery struggle which this war had aroused among his own people. He feared that such an agitation would "destroy the Democratic party, and perhaps the Union;" though slavery had, as he believed, "no legitimate connection with the war into Mexico, being a domestic, not a foreign question." But with this premonition, and to check the "worse than useless discussion," this "wicked agitation," he publicly proposed extending the Missouri Compromise line across to the Pacific, and considered himself a national umpire in doing so. This adjustment failing in Congress, it is due to President Polk to say, further, that during the last weeks of his official term he showed himself in private counsel a true lover of the Union, like Jackson before him, strongly contrasting with Calhoun and many others of his own slaveholding section. The Diary records an interview which he held at the White House with Calhoun January 16, 1849, at the time when the latter was gathering Southern congressmen into caucus, and trying to combine them for an inflammatory appeal to Southern constituents. Mr. Polk thought that movement mischievous, and on this occasion expressed to the great nullifier his own strong attachment to the Union and his wish to preserve it. With reference to our new domain, which was being peopled so rapidly in the Sacramento region since the gold discovery, Polk now took the very ground which Zachary Taylor occupied soon after as his successor. "California might be admitted into the Union as a State, and so might even New Mexico; and thus we should get rid of the Wilmot antislavery proviso," said Polk: "and this is the only practical mode of settling the territorial question, — to leave the new States to themselves and arrest this slavery agitation." To this Calhoun expressed himself opposed. He said California ought not now to be admitted as a State, because slaveholders had found no opportunity to go there, and it was sure to become a free State; now was the time for the South to resist Northern aggressions. The two parted in disagreement; and the President, commenting in his journal upon this interview, declares himself satisfied that Calhoun does not want the question settled, that he desires disunion. "I set my face against all this," he records: "let California decide slavery or no slavery, and no Southern man should object."

Polk's Diary discloses a secret chapter in the expansion policy of this industrious administration which deserves a final notice. No sooner had the Mexican war been brought substantially to a close before our untiring President undertook the annexation of Cuba. On the 30th of May, 1848, just as a new presidential canvass was opening, and even before ratifications had been exchanged and peace secured with Mexico, Polk broached this other matter to his Cabinet; but by this time he had learned a lesson in self-constraint, and restricted his proposal to that of a fair purchase, disclaiming all wish for a forcible annexation. His Cabinet were evidently divided at first on this subject, and the Northern portion of it nervous and distrustful; Robert J. Walker and John Y. Mason being his chief supporters in the council. Buchanan objected that it would be a firebrand in the presidential canvass; but Cass, the party candidate, had declared himself quite ready and willing to risk his chances upon such an issue. On the 6th of June Polk brought the subject up again; insisting that a proposition of purchase should be made through our minister in Spain. A day or two after came confirmation of a speedy peace with Mexico, and Polk made it clear to his doubting advisers that he had no treacherous plans in reserve. Cubans were at this time in insurrection; and General Quitman, so gallant on the Mexican battlefields, would gladly have sailed with a force of our returning volunteers upon a filibustering expedition. But this, said the President, he could not connive at; he proposed taking no part in Cuban revolutions, but to let Spain know that we meant to keep back our American troops; at the same time notifying that power of our willingness to offer a price for the island. In this form, says the Diary, the Cabinet unanimously agreed to the President's proposal; even Buchanan assenting with the rest. A few days after, Mr. Polk made his offer in due form by a despatch transmitted to Minister Saunders at Madrid; sending him a power to treat for Cuba, with a hundred million dollars as the limit of a purchase, — and all this "profoundly confidential." There is a later record of September 16 in Polk's journal, stating that an important despatch from Minister Saunders at Spain was read in the Cabinet. What its purport was the Diary does not indicate, but doubtless Spain repulsed our overtures; and there the matter dropped. With a Whig President chosen by the people a few weeks later, this subject, and in fact all schemes for further territorial aggrandizement, became indefinitely postponed.

FINAL NOTE.—The two foregoing articles seem to embrace by statement or allusion all the valuable historical matter to be found in President Polk's Diary. One special subject of Polk's repeated comment is perhaps worth adding, however, in connection with our diplomatic intercourse at Washington, as he found it. The President was not a little amused, as well as annoyed, over a custom which prevailed, as he tells us, among the European ministers, of making each royal birth the occasion of a formal call and pompous announcement at the White House. "Amusing and ridiculous," he calls this custom; and he records an instance where the Queen of Portugal had a still-born child, and the representative of that country, making his ceremonious visit, dilated upon the Queen's sufferings "as minutely as though he had been the midwife or attendant physician." Polk, it will be remembered by our reader, was a childless married man. His usual response at these parturition interviews, so his Diary informs us, consisted in a grave congratulation that the direct royal line was not likely to fail; and this assurance he found himself giving repeatedly in the case of Great Britain, whose minister informed him that he was in the habit of making such announcements once a year.

REFORM IN PRESIDENTIAL ELECTIONS.

For more than a hundred years our Federal Constitution has been in full operation; and yet ninety years have elapsed since the proposal and adoption of any amendment to that instrument except those three which abolished human slavery and closed the Civil War. Not a single State of the Union shows such stagnation in constitutional reform. On the contrary, our increasing States, each in its own jurisdiction, have modelled and remodelled their fundamental institutions, to check legislative and other abuses and yield more closely to popular control; yet the antiquated machinery of the Federal Government still creaks on in its operations unchanged, exposing us repeatedly to the dangers of national anarchy and confusion.

I speak of constitutional machinery alone; for as concerns the general scheme of our government and the general distribution of State and Federal powers, I offer no criticism. Our fathers framed wisely in those latter respects, and custom and precedent have aided the development of good results. A national policy may well be an elastic policy, leaving much for contingencies to shape. It is not to the fundamental system, then, of our American Union, but to the mode of bringing rulers and representatives into power, that I would ask the reader's attention. The

Reprinted from "The Forum," January, 1895.

recent proposition to choose Senators by the people of a State is well worth considering; so, too, are some of those checks upon legislative action now so common in our modern State constitutions, such as might, for instance, prevent a mere casual majority in the two branches of Congress from annexing foreign territory or admitting new States capriciously without reference to popular approval or sanction. I confine myself here to desirable reforms in the method of Presidential elections, and in the relation of both Presidential and Congressional terms to the popular elections of a biennial November.

In the first place, our anomalous method of choosing the Chief Executive by electoral colleges has become, in the course of a century, not only a senseless but a dilatory and dangerous duplication. We know how utterly the expedient of 1787, for obstructing popular suffrage on a national scale, has failed of its original purpose; and how truly, in consequence, the quadrennial assemblage of our present age, when millions of voters undertake on an autumn day to choose by their own ballots a President and Vice-President of the United States, has become in spirit a complete perversion of what the Constitution itself intended. Yet the letter of that instrument remains; and the people of each State still choose, after all, simply Presidential electors, just as the several legislatures chose them formerly, and as South Carolina's chose them continually down to the Civil War. So far as Federal fundamental law is concerned, a State legislature may still at any time take the direct choice of Presidential electors to itself, depriving the State voters of such suffrage; and more than this, Presidential electors, whether popularly chosen or not, have only a moral obligation to cast their votes afterward, in the college, for the candidates previously designated. The whole sanction, in short, upon which popular expression rests in the selection, every four years, of President and Vice-President of the United States — the whole assurance of legal title to a valid succession — is each individual elector's own pledge of honor to vote in the college as he was chosen to vote in November.

The original provisions of our Constitution, indeed, were soon found so faulty with respect to Presidential elections in other particulars, that after the famous tie vote in 1800, between Jefferson and Burr, when President and Vice-President were not named apart, those provisions had to be amended. But two prime evils of the original plan still confront us, showing how utterly unsuited are those provisions to the present republican age: (1) Colleges of electors still elect the Executive; and consequently the choice of a Chief Magistrate is not legally made in early November, but about a month later; and in addition to the injurious delay, the voter who casts his ballot for electors at the polls is exposed not only to peculiar misconceptions concerning his own functions, but to the far more insidious danger that corrupt and crafty politicians may yet, at some later crisis, when voting runs close, baffle the wishes of the people. (2) Nor does a plurality of votes, even in the electoral colleges, finally elect the President; for the Constitution still adheres to the eighteenth-century rule requiring a complete majority, in default of which the eventual choice devolves upon the Legislature, or rather upon one branch of it. To this latter solecism, common enough in State politics a hundred years ago, but long since repudiated upon bitter State experience, public attention has not been drawn as it should be.

All American experience is to the practical conclusion that, desirable though a majority choice must always be, it is much better to let the candidate who has a popular plurality on the first trial at the polls come in over all competitors, than to vote over again, or to refer the ultimate selection of a Chief Magistrate elsewhere.

Nor is it to an incoming Congress, but to a retiring one, and often in effect to a defeated and dishonored one, — and in fact, to a House of Representatives, voting by States, which was constituted two years earlier, — that our Federal plan confides this momentous choice of a President whenever no candidate has received an electoral majority. What State would trust any assembly for so solemn an arbitrament short of that Legislature which was chosen at the time when the Executive was voted for? Our national perils in this respect have been less only because the national choice was more seldom; but with each new election the results at stake become more tremendous and the temptation to trifle with public opinion more pronounced. Whenever, as happened in 1892 and may happen again, some third party is strong enough to carry a State or two, or political issues have temporarily faded out, and the choice lies chiefly as among individuals, "bargain and corruption" may once more be the cry over an election by the House, as it was in 1825, and with far more substantial reason. Two years ago, during the last Presidential canvass, and while the chances appeared close in October, two distinct conspiracies, for forestalling final results and controlling the succession lest the choice should devolve upon a House already Democratic, were divulged by the press to augment the popular uneasiness. One was for the friends of the third candidate to keep an eventual election for the colleges to decide in December, by causing their own Presidential electors to invite bids for Populist principles from the two highest candidates, and then turn the scales as between them. The other plan was from another quarter, to resist all choice by the House as then constituted, upon the claim that its representation had not been based upon the new census of 1890, and ought, therefore, to be changed. From such dangers, which might otherwise have become positive ones, a sweeping majority of electoral votes for Mr. Cleveland delivered us.

Still another Constitutional change is highly desirable in the same connection, and, I might add, for all our biennial elections to Congress, in order to give symmetry to our national system of government and to adapt it to this modern age. We should abridge the present long interval which elapses between the popular vote and the entrance of a new Administration and a new Congress upon their several responsibilities. Considering that a new Presidency lasts but four years and the term of a new Congress but half that time, our present waste of national energy is very great, and needlessly so. We have profited much in the advance of popular suffrage by leaving tests and qualifications in all national voting to State discretion. We have gained in national concentration by compelling a uniform day to be observed throughout the Union for choosing the Presidential electors. But another change still more desirable (could only a Constitutional amendment be had) would be to bring a newly elected Administration more speedily into power, and a newly chosen House of Representatives and Congress besides.

Ever since 1804, "the fourth of March," originally

an accidental date, has been graven into the very tablet of our Federal Constitution. That day of the month and year, with its variable weather, is hardly suitable in the Potomac latitude for out-of-door pageants and parades, as we well know. In fact, inauguration weather at Washington on the two latest occasions was as unfit as possible for the military procession and the ceremonials at the east front of the capitol. But what then? Some have seriously proposed, in propitiation of the weather, that the Constitution be so amended as to inaugurate each new Executive toward the close of spring. But this would be reform in the wrong direction. Mere ceremonials, anywhere or at any time, are liable to capricious weather, and may readily conform to circumstances. The paramount interest, however, of the people of this Union is to have their declared will carried expeditiously into effect; and from that preferable point of view, whatever Constitutional amendment substitutes some other date for the fourth of March will require America's inauguration day to be moved backward and not forward.

Constitutional reforms are, indeed, difficult to carry; but this is, more than anything else, because the people are not aroused to considering them. Where the change proposed is not likely to excite party opposition, nor to inflame State or sectional jealousy, it is worthy, at least, of consideration and effort. State constitutions have borne much salutary improvement; and we ought not to persuade ourselves that constructive inspiration in whatever pertains to the welfare and stability of the whole Union perished with the Revolutionary fathers. Let us set ourselves, then, to repairing the weak joints of this constitutional armor, where almost all else is strong.

The present basis for an electoral proportion by States has its merits and need not be exchanged for a numerical poll of the whole Union; but, in either case, we should sweep out, once and for all, this dangerous and superfluous electoral college, and set each State to devoting the month which follows the November vote to its own official registry of State results. We should abolish the present intervention of a House of Representatives, or reduce it to the remote contingency of a tie between the candidates, trusting, as in State elections, to the rule that a popular plurality shall elect, once and for all. The House of Representatives, and the Congress, to revise results and formally announce the choice, should be the incoming and newly chosen, and not the outgoing, one; and all concerting opportunity for mischief between a Congress and an Administration already delegated to retirement — all such opportunity as embarrassed and paralyzed the country so greatly in 1860 if not in 1876 — should be reduced to a minimum. With a month gained by the abolition of electoral colleges, it would not be difficult for a newly chosen Congress to enter upon its functions at New Year's; and for the new Executive in alternate Congresses to be installed then or soon after, following the common example of the States. An adjournment of Congress, long enough to give a new President time to make up his Administration and formulate a policy, might perhaps be provided; but the United States is scarcely a representative government at all, if public agents elected to meet existing conditions must invariably begin their work under later ones, at the same time that they are liable to stand long in the way after they have been superseded.

BIOGRAPHY.

BIOGRAPHY.

I.

THEY who counselled the present collection of fugitive essays, thrown off in the intervals of a more laborious occupation, have wished it accompanied by a biographical sketch of the author more complete and confiding than the Cyclopedia is supposed to contain. They have claimed that the memoir of one who, in spite of peculiar drawbacks, has gained already so just renown in the triple pursuits of law, history, and University instruction, deserves to be written out. Many among the thousands who have studied with profit one or another of his books or listened to his class lectures, desire to know something more regarding the methods of work and the personal experience of a scholar whose prodigious industry and productiveness they better apprehend than the actual course of his somewhat secluded life. And there are others who ask information concerning the author's father, — a prominent figure in American journalism and politics for so many years, and Adjutant-General of Massachusetts through the Civil War, but whose memory since his death has been fading into oblivion. A disposition to gratify such wishes should not be ascribed to personal vanity; but rather to a genuine desire to be helpful. It is not necessarily the most romantic and adventurous lives that call for description. There is room besides for heroic example in the pathway which lies beaten by common travel. The silent power is often found the strong power. Triumph over obstacles remains the theme that most strongly appeals to the human heart; and such triumphs should be the lasting theme of biography.

JAMES SCHOULER, the subject of our present sketch, was born in West Cambridge (now Arlington), Massachusetts, on the 20th of March, 1839, the second of a family of five children, and the oldest son of William and Frances Eliza (Warren) Schouler. So singular a surname has misled many as to its spelling and pronunciation; and the more so in these later years, when we find the German stock entering so largely into American life, and the German language and literature so familiar. Not unfrequently the first three letters of this surname receive the soft German sound, as though the word were some variation of the German "Schuler." The hard sound is the proper one, and the word if fully Americanized would be "School-er." For the real surname is not German but Scotch; its true Scotch spelling is "Scouler," and while our author comes of good Massachusetts and Revolutionary stock in the maternal line, he belongs on his father's side to the first generation of the family born on American soil.[1] "My paternal grandfather," he writes, "from whom I am named, and who first brought our 'Scoulers' to America, appears to have judiciously adopted for a while the American spelling of 'Schooler;' but

---

[1] Other Scotch "Scoullers," it appears, have established themselves in America at one time or another. There is a Pennsylvania family, for instance, which traces its emigration to 1752 from Lanarkshire.

about the time his sons grew to manhood and he himself became a person of some property and consequence — partly perhaps as the result of a visit which he then made to the old country and his Scotch relatives — our surname on this side of the water acquired its present hybrid form, complimentary to both Scotland and America, but characteristic of neither. I should have gone back to one or another of the former modes of spelling, when striking into manhood for myself, had not the American 'Schoulers' by that time become so fairly rooted in popular renown that filial respect forbade new experiments in nomenclature."

The "Scoulers" are still to be found in Scotland, and in the region, more especially, of Glasgow, Paisley, and Ayr, though scattered elsewhere about the lowlands where probably they are indigenous. Slight variations of this spelling may be traced, such as "Scoular" or "Scouller." One of the more distinguished of this family, who was entertained in Glasgow at a public dinner about half a century ago, stated in a speech that he could trace the Scoulers back in Scotland for two hundred years; but the race appears to have been modest and self-respecting on the whole, rather than illustrious, and not much given to boasting of pedigree. Probably the Scotch "Scouler" or "Scoler," like the German "Schuler," has the same root as the English "Scholar;" and it is certainly a family tradition that the Scoulers, whatever may have been their educational disadvantage, in any sense, are much given to books and reading, — a trait which is strikingly exemplified in various instances on this side of the water. Reading and writing, as Dogberry would say, seem to come to them by instinct. Indeed, the Scouler coat-of-arms, which some Glasgow merchants of the family displayed fifty years ago, exhibits a hand holding an open book, with the accompanying motto "Pro virtute;" a crest which would indicate a strong predilection for the arts of peace. But as the high-born Scottish chiefs of old were always given to war, or at least to brawling, we may assume, perhaps, without diving into Scotch genealogy, that the Scoulers are of no great lineage on their native soil, but a plebeian race of bread-winners, supplying to the world the usual plebeian complement of plain farmers, artisans, and merchants, with now and then a trained professional man of marked ability who holds his head above the rest. Marriage alliances of the Scoulers with more illustrious families, such as the Macarthurs and Macallisters have produced some Scotchmen of distinction: such, for instance, as the Hon. Arthur Macallister of recent memory, who went out to Australia and was twice made Premier of Queensland. He was a near connection of our author's father, and born about the same year. But a still nearer connection and a closer contemporary, though born ten years earlier, was his first cousin, Professor John Scouler, who, so far as we can discover, gave to the Scotch patronymic more decided lustre than any one else in the old country who has yet borne it. He had a precocious bent to botany and natural history. He received the best of liberal training in Glasgow and Paris for his special pursuit, and was for some years Professor of Natural History in the Andersonian University of Glasgow, and afterwards Professor of Mineralogy of the Royal Dublin Society. He was President at one time of the Glasgow Geological Society. The degrees of Doctor of Medicine and Doctor of Laws were conferred upon him. He made important scientific discoveries in the region of the Columbia River while on an expedition with the Hudson's Bay Company; and the large illustrated History of Glasgow refers to him repeatedly on local points as an eminent authority in archæology. His bust, which is still preserved in the library of the Andersonian University, shows a strong profile resemblance to our author's father, with whom in later life he carried on an interesting correspondence over the family history, which has been unfortunately destroyed.[1]

Professor John Scouler was buried in a corner of the quiet churchyard of Kilbarchan, where the remains of his wife (who died soon after marriage) and of his parents are also interred, the spot being marked to this day by a plain monument. From this same Kilbarchan went forth the "Schoulers" (as now entitled) to the United States. It is a small, peaceful village of about twenty-six hundred souls, accessible to the populous manufacturing town of Paisley in the same county, and about ten miles distant from Glasgow. An omnibus which toils along an up-hill road conveys passengers thither nowadays from the nearest railroad station. Kilbarchan has at present the not uncommon aspect in the Scotch lowlands of a sturdy village which has seen better days — though never very good ones — when humble hand-weaving

[1] The letters received on this subject by General William Schouler were doubtless contained in an office desk, which was consumed in the great Boston fire of 1872, a few weeks after his death. His son read most of them when they arrived and remembers their substance. Professor Scouler died in 1871, a year earlier than his American kinsman and correspondent. A full sketch of his life is contained in Glasgow Geolog Soc. Transactions (1873), and his papers on the Columbia River expedition are to be found in the Edinburgh Journal of Science for 1826.

flourished and the printing of cloths by the block method, pursuits both favorable to village industry before the large towns sucked in the rural population. Its long rows of little stone cottages defy the ravages of time; while its two kirks, the "Established Presbyterian" and "United Presbyterian," symbolize that freedom of discussion which divided the Scotch communities long years ago in religious creeds. Kilbarchan has its inn, the "Black Bull," kept after a country home fashion, with a bar served by women folk. It boasts, too, a new town-house which stands in presumptuous contrast with the old and forsaken one, and rears a high white tower.

In this little village during the last and culminating years of England's tremendous struggle with Napoleon — and while, too, as a minor enemy the mother country was fighting in a second unwelcome war the United States — dwelt two Scouler brothers, engaged in carrying on together a calico-printing factory of the sort then common, within an easy teaming distance from the market town of Paisley. William, the older brother, was father of the young naturalist of whom we have spoken; while James, the younger, was the destined emigrant and founder of an American race. William owned the factory, being a man of large means, enhanced by his prosperous marriage to a daughter of the Glasgow Macarthurs, a noted family. James held a responsible place in managing the business; and he, too, had happily married in Glasgow, his wife being Margaret Clark, a woman of superior endowments and family,[1] whose strong character bore well the

---

[1] Margaret Clark used to visit an aunt at Stirling, who lived upon an ancestral estate granted by King Robert Bruce for distinguished services.

test of vicissitudes in store for her. James's dwelling-house in Kilbarchan was a spacious and comfortable two-story stone house which he probably rented. It was near the village, on a rising slope, with hills seen undulating in the distance, which are now studded by residences of the Scotch gentry, and afford fine views for miles about. Here were born in succession three sons and a daughter, the third son being William, our author's father, who first saw the light of day on the 31st of December, 1814. "Fore-house," as this family mansion is styled in modern years, still stands almost unaltered in outward aspect since James Scouler lived there, except for more modern plate-glass windows. A high stone wall separates it from the road; and entering the gates either by the pretty carriage-drive or on the long gravel walk, one sees among fine trees, and beyond a rich green lawn, naturally sloping, on which sheep browse lazily, a solid house of a slate-colored stone, with substantial steps and a stone portico, honestly and squarely facing the road, with a green hedge just in front of it, and a kitchen garden flanked by a high wall in its rear.

The circumstances under which our American progenitor left his thriving business in Scotland and this pleasant and attractive abode, to expatriate himself and settle among strangers across the ocean, were peculiar and highly creditable to him. It was in 1816 that the change in question occurred, and just at a period of wedded life when one's domestic roots begin to strike deepest; for James Scouler, born in 1786, was by this time at manhood's full stage, and father of a growing family. Political reasons were the occasion, as a Scotch obituary notice hinted at his death; but during his life, so reticent had he been on the subject of his removal to America, that this hint was a surprise to his own children. "He told me the whole story," relates our present author, "about the time I graduated from college; and had I then thought how closely he had kept his secret, I would have written down the details at once. As his namesake and oldest grandson, and a liberally educated youth besides, he perhaps meant to show me an especial confidence. It appears that the Scotch brothers, William and James, differed strongly in politics, William being a Tory conservative, while James was a liberal and attended liberal clubs. In 1815 or thereabouts some plot against the government was in progress (and as my impression is, a liberal one) which had its ramifications in my grandfather's vicinity. He found himself one night in a store with others. The shutters were closed, and treasonable plans promulgated. Grandfather listened to all he could bear, and then put on his hat and left the meeting. 'I cannot,' said he plainly to the others, 'raise my hand against my King and country!' Whatever the plot it failed ignominiously, and the officers of the law were soon in pursuit of the parties implicated, desiring to capture grandfather as a government witness. Hearing of this he fled, unwilling, as he strongly expressed himself to me, to help put a halter on the neck of any personal friends; and facilitated by those who dreaded his testimony, he kept in hiding for a week and was then smuggled out of Scotland in a small sailing-vessel bound for the United States. His wife, who knew neither why nor whither he had gone, bore her first daughter not long after his departure. More precise details of my grandfather's story may have escaped my memory; but the main facts evincing his own attitude to the political plot in question, whatever that plot might have been, are just as he related them in his own vivid and impressive manner, and with the aspect of perfect honesty. 'When I first came to the United States,' he added, 'I only expected to stay a few months until the trouble blew over. I had no idea that I should make this country my permanent home.'"

II.

The emigrant and grandfather, James Schouler, — to whose surname we may henceforth give his final American spelling, — landed in New York City when about thirty years old, an utter stranger, without letters and with little money. This was at the time when our people, jubilant over an honorable peace with Great Britain, had just begun to repair the ravages of war. Business shook off its long stagnation and sought new enterprises. Like most emigrants who keep their self-respect, our present one looked first of all for honest work; but the solitary search did not bring quick results. Being, however, a good musician, he would go down to North River in the evening and play for solace upon his flute; and while thus occupied, he attracted the notice of a benevolent citizen, who opened conversation with him, and on learning his wishes procured for him a first situation.

The employment, we may imagine, was humble enough; but James entered upon his work with such a will that before the lapse of many months he had concluded himself capable of making a living in this new world, and sent for his wife and children to join him. Of their voyage in 1816 (or possibly 1817) more is known in the family than of his own. They left Scotland in a ship which occupied seven weeks in crossing the Atlantic; and a young physician on board, their fellow-passenger, showed great kindness to the mother by entertaining her two older boys, John and Robert, while she was nursing little William (or "Wallie," as she always called him) and her infant daughter Jane. Reunited in this land of adoption, the family followed loyally the husband and father, in such wanderings for the next fifteen years as his trade might require, and from one new home to another. In Brooklyn little Jane died. But the three sons who had crossed the Atlantic survived to ripe manhood. Two more daughters and another son were born to the same parents in the United States; and each son and daughter marrying in due course and rearing a family of American grandchildren, our Scotch progenitor made good his transfer of faith and allegiance to the United States.

James Schouler, the grandfather, was a man of industry and perseverance and of perfect sobriety, and he kept a steady regard for his opportunities in life, cheered constantly, as he was through the whole straitened period, by his admirable helpmate, who bore all hardships with courage and good humor. Learning presently that calico print-works were to be set up at Staten Island, he offered himself for employment; and the proprietor, quickly perceiving him to be no common workman, but one who understood the business and had conducted it abroad, gave him at once a good position and salary. Here Schouler would have been contented to remain; but he found the climate of the neighborhood unhealthy, and chills and fever were the consequence. Warned already by death in the family, he resolved to leave; and the proprietor, unwilling to lose him, then offered a partnership. "I would not take your whole factory," was his reply, "at the cost of my wife and children;" and he removed from New York State to Massachusetts. Here employed for a few years longer on a salary, in mills at Taunton and Lynn, he prepared to set up cloth print-works of his own and become himself an employer. He bought for $2,100 in March, 1832, a mill site which pleased him, in the town of West Cambridge, with a water privilege from an upper pond, and a factory and dwelling-house already built; mortgaging the premises to secure about half the purchase-money. Here settling with his family at an opportune time, he soon began to make money and established a handsome business. The county land records, which preserve his first purchase as made by "James Schooler of Lynn, calico printer," show in the course of the next twenty years many more real-estate transactions which indicate that this new freeholder of the town grew rapidly in wealth and extended his thriving business. The site of these picturesque red factories, multiplied by his energy, down in the hollow through which ran the mill stream, can be still identified in Arlington, while his mansion on the upland, with porches and a pillared piazza, which stood at the right-hand side of the highroad to Lexington, guarding the factory and its lane like a sentry of the Revolution, is yet visible; but the factories themselves were destroyed by accidental fire some years ago and the rubbish cleared away. While directing the new business which he had brought to West Cambridge, he equipped his mills throughout with cloth-printing machinery, and a water-wheel supplied the motive power.

But the immigrant Schouler brought with him one

Scotch trait with which our American over-ambition stands in sharp contrast; and this was to achieve a safe competence and then retire contentedly and enjoy through old age the well-earned fruits of personal industry. This period he fixed soon after reaching fifty; and to his sons, by that time grown up, he turned over his flourishing business and sought recreation and a change of scene. About the year 1838 he revisited Scotland and his foreign relatives, bringing back with him among other curiosities wax impressions of the Scotch family crest to which we have referred, and profiting possibly by that renewal of family acquaintance, as well as his pecuniary independence, to conform the spelling of his American surname more closely to the Scotch standard. Unwilling upon his return to remain entirely idle, he bought another mill site and mansion at tranquil Burlington, a few miles beyond Lexington, making this his place of residence while he dallied with his former pursuit just enough to make idleness less irksome, and then he moved back to West Cambridge. Here his wife, the long partner of his joys and tribulations, died July 24, 1851, at the age of sixty-three; and life among the familiar surroundings then grew to him so intolerable that he soon returned to New York State, and for the remnant of his long life resided in the little town of Westchester, not far from the great metropolis and the scenes which had witnessed his first struggle for a livelihood in this new world. He retained still the legal title to the factory premises at West Cambridge, selling out his Burlington property; and he would come occasionally to Massachusetts to visit his sons and daughters, whose homes, like their interests in life, had begun to diverge.

Our present author records a first and only visit which he paid to his grandfather in this Westchester home. "It was in April, 1860," he writes, "and nearly a year after I had graduated from college, that I left New York by the trim paddle-steamboat with a sentimental name, the 'Sylvan Shore,' and at the Harlem landing-place in early afternoon entered a lumbering stage which took me on to West Farms. Thence I proceeded on foot to Westchester, not very far distant, and by inquiring the way soon found the house. Its situation was pretty, and the mansion a snug one for a quiet old couple. Domestic companionship, I may here remark, had proved so essential to grandfather's comfort in life that he had by this time married again and brought into his household a good woman, of congenial Scotch connections and about his own age, whose anxious solicitude for her worshipful spouse was constantly visible. Both received me very kindly, and I made over night a charming visit. The grave simplicity and force of grandfather's conversation was never so felt by me as on this evening, when we sat together and he appeared in his best mood. A man of habitual reticence, who never wasted words on any one, he felt perhaps a special disposition at this time to express himself. I was a favorite grandson, and he cherished some appreciation perhaps of the peculiar dignity attaching to my college diploma. Our discourse turned much upon life, — I looking forward to it and he looking back; and, having an excellent memory, he recited in a manner that much impressed me, with his Scotch accent and melodious voice, a part of that essay by Goldsmith which begins, 'Old age that lessens the enjoyment of life increases the desire of living.' Another passage which, in connection with American politics, he quoted at length from Scott's 'Quentin Durward,' so sank into my thoughts that I looked it up afterwards and found it in the sixteenth chapter. It is where the hero of the novel carries on an argumentative dialogue with the vagrant who has no home, no country, no religion; but who claims, as sufficiently remaining for his recompense, 'I have liberty.' In the course of the evening I played at his request upon the piano; and presently when I struck into an *andante* from one of Mozart's sonatas which he liked, he brought his flute and played the air as he stood by me."

So far as the world took notice of him, Schouler was a plain business man; and the three business traits which marked him and contributed most to his success were good judgment, perseverance, and thorough honesty. There was a genuineness about him, an unassuming self-respect, which inspired confidence; so that where he needed money for his projects he raised it readily and repaid with punctuality. He was high-principled, true as steel, faithful to whatever interests might have been committed to him. But he was not like our American men of business, who make great haste and try to achieve the colossal. He had no wide range of ambition; but a "wee house," a "wee fortune," contented him. He minded his own affairs, and was willing that others should do likewise. We have already noted his disposition to leave money-making when he had made enough to retire upon; the devotion of his last long years to a rustic domestic ease, to tranquil independence and tranquil self-improvement. His just sense of right put bounds to toil, and gave to individual success its due reward. He deemed it enough for his sons that he handed over to them the business that he had so well established, at a time when they all might make together a living from it. He did not choose, for his own part, to slave all his life for posterity, nor to leave an ambitious fortune for idlers to dissipate. He remained Scotch, too, in eschewing all tricks for increasing his own estate by overreaching others. For that American "booming," as we call it in later years, he had no turn; nor for over-praising the qualities of a thing and concealing its faults, so as to drive a sharp bargain. At one time after he had given up the mills, he was induced to go into a Boston partnership in wholesale dry goods, as his eldest son did later. But he soon took his capital out of the concern, disgusted with the prevalent trade methods. "I couldn't lie and I couldn't steal," he would say afterwards, "and so I left the business."

Whether in household or social relations, grandfather Schouler was the same sober individual, sensible, self-respecting, and tenacious of his own opinions. He kept up through life his fondness for the simple customs and the simple people of his native land, and he employed in his factories many who had come over from the lowlands like himself, maintaining his authority all the while by a certain reserve of manner, at the same time that his quiet, unobtrusive interest was kindness itself. The great minds of Scotland were his constant admiration. Burns and Walter Scott he read through and through; and his ideal of worldly happiness seemed comprehended, as so many Scotch songs have expressed it, within the "ingleside" and its domestic accompaniments. And yet, though by no means unsocial with callers or his own family, he was rather taciturn and seldom if ever jocular of speech and familiar. Except when stirred to elevated expression, he was simple and judicious, listening readily to others, giving his opinion in a few fitting words, if asked for it, but not given to trifling discourse, slang, or gossip. But it was easy to see that he appreciated more than he expressed; and to his grandchildren, at least, who stood somewhat in awe of him, he would show by some little attention that he was not unthoughtful of their happiness. They never saw him in a passion nor thrown off his balance of equanimity on one side or the other; but when highly pleased his grave features relaxed into a smile, and when something went wrong he would vent his displeasure by a severe and caustic remark, whose effect was heightened by a tight compression of his thin lips and a peculiar clucking of the tongue within. His whole aspect was that of the master and disciplinarian, though a just one certainly, and after his own silent fashion a kind one.

All this was much in contrast with his wife, the mother of his children. She was a woman of decided strength of character and an admirable complement of such a husband, to temper his justice with mercy and loving-kindness and make him respected by the world to the utmost. Though not educated beyond Scotch women of her day, nor possessed of any marked accomplishment, she was an admirable housekeeper and manager of a family. She had strong native talent, was merry and bright under all vicissitudes of life, entertained admirably with her conversation, which turned much upon her varied personal acquaintance and experience, and had a great faculty for drawing out and making friends of whomsoever she might encounter. She was full of good-humor, and could make others listen to her and laugh by the hour. Her sons have been heard to express the love and gratitude which they felt for her beyond all others. While she lived she held up the children to their best and kept the family united, and after she died the strong bond of union was forever gone and missing. Such of her grandchildren as lived early enough to know her, welcomed her family visits, which were apt to be sudden ones; for with her jovial greeting she always brought them some present or another. And her generosity and good deeds among her neighbors, which fortunately her husband's means after a time enabled her to bestow liberally, so endeared her to the people of West Cambridge that it seemed as if the whole town, rich and poor, poured out to attend her funeral.

The early home life of the Schoulers in this town of West Cambridge is described by the surviving daughters. They and their friends would gather round the mother in a room upstairs and frolic to their hearts' content, while the father passed his evening by himself, reading or playing on the flute; but whenever they wanted him to play for a dance he was ready to gratify them. His love of music and his skilful playing were remarkable for an amateur not much instructed; and his soul was full of Scotch ditties grave and gay, of marches, reels, and mournful minor dirges, in great variety, which he had constantly at command to pour out through the hollow of his silver-keyed instrument with the aid of his nimble fingers. His oldest granddaughter grew to be a great favorite with him, because she not only had a responsive heart, but loved the music that he loved and could play it for him upon the piano.

Grandfather and grandmother Schouler were a pleasing pair, and in aspect and accent of speech bespoke their Scottish origin. She had a dark and sympathetic eye, strongly marked features, more furrowed through hard experience than her husband's, and a face which beamed kindly out from one of those old-fashioned ruffled caps which seemed inseparable from her. He was a man of medium height, perhaps five feet eight, compactly built, and looking like one who would hold his own with any man and ask no more. His hair was plentiful, inclining to gray ringlets. His features had the Schouler cast, observable since in others of the family, with the outline of a handsome forehead, nose, and chin. His mouth was firm-set and secretive; his eye a penetrating blue; and his whole expression, of which a razored face left no concealment, was that of a self-contained man, who had been schooled into sternness and almost severity by the stress of circumstances. Yet though Scotch of aspect, and of sound moral principle, there was no tinge of rigid Scotch intolerance about either of the pair. They seemed, indeed, to fit into their later surroundings better than their earlier ones. The husband was Republican in sentiment, a believer in equal rights, and as soon as our Civil War broke out he called in some money he had out on mortgage and invested it in United States bonds. Yet he would sometimes speak with contempt of the men who managed the politics in his New York vicinity, as scorning to have them for his masters. He was of irreproachable habits; always temperate in drink, though not a teetotaler; a snuff-taker, but not otherwise much addicted to tobacco; moderate in all things and under strong self-control. In religious belief he affiliated chiefly with the Universalists; and of the whole family that he brought up not one strayed back to the old Presbyterian faith of Kilbarchan.

Our exemplary emigrant died at Westchester, February 24, 1864, at the age of seventy-seven. His remains were brought on to (West Cambridge) Arlington to be laid in tenderness by those of the wife who had been the friend of his active years. The life we have described was not historically conspicuous nor ever dreamed to become so. It is paralleled in America by doubtless many others; but of such hidden fountains come the springs that nourish this land of opportunities into greatness. This Scotch founder of a new family in the new world had accomplished something. Landing in our chief seaport friendless and penniless, he had begun a new prime, leaving the earlier one of equal promise behind him. He had in a quarter of a century achieved here a competence, to enjoy it for another quarter of a century. A troop of bright and promising grandchildren gathered at his funeral. His two daughters, both American born, had married merchants of local wealth and eminence. His eldest son, at whose house the last ceremonies took place, had grown up with the town, and as one of its foremost citizens in all enterprises had received its highest honors as selectman and in both branches of the Legislature. His third son, also present at the funeral, was now a Massachusetts military officer, second only to the Governor himself in sending Massachusetts regiments to the front and guarding well their interests. In the quiet Arlington cemetery on the Medford road, from whose hill one might look towards the crowning scenes of his life's labor, James Schouler was committed to his last mortal resting-place. Two marble slabs side by side commemorate husband and wife; and on the headstone of the former is an inscription suggested probably by himself as an emblem of his simple creed, "God our Father, Christ our Saviour."

III.

1839–1846.

WE have seen that William (afterwards Adjutant-General of Massachusetts), the father of our present author, and the third son of James and Margaret Clark Schouler (or Scouler), was born in Kilbarchan, Scotland, on the last day of 1814, and in early infancy was brought over to America by his mother, with three other children.[1] Except for these immediate parental influences, his youthful memories and associations were American from the cradle, as was also his education; but through life he cherished a romantic fondness for his native land, its statesmen, its warriors, and its literature, and hailed as doubly brethren all who bore their credentials of origin from the same rugged soil. Once and only once, in early manhood, he found opportunity to revisit old Scotia, and it was the unfulfilled dream of his later life to revisit it again.

Of William Schouler's experience in childhood very little is preserved, nor was the subject ever much alluded to in his own family. But we know that with his older brothers he followed his father's wanderings to Staten Island, Taunton, and Lynn for manual employment, pursuing, when at work, the

[1] See pages 175, 178.

same trade. He acquired as he might, at one place or another, the elements of a good common-school education; and of his mother's helpful sympathy and encouragement all these years he has spoken to his own children with the utmost tenderness, as though no praise could be too great for her. In one racy and familiar speech which he made in the Massachusetts Convention of 1853, as its reported Debates show, — a speech whose special purpose was to put the assembled body in good humor at a time when irritations were becoming very great, — he alluded with more freedom to his early life than was usual to him. And thus we find that he had worked while young in the mills "and pretty long hours, too;" that both he and his father had inclined politically to Whig rather than Jackson traditions; and that taking earnestly to political controversies when very young, he had been brought up and almost rocked in them, as he expressed it. We see, too, that his bent had been pronounced from childhood for books and self-improvement. "I have read," he says, "a little. I have read some authors in English politics. I have read some Grecian and Roman authors. It was the study of my youth, after mill hours were over, to read these books."[1] And thus had William Schouler, though to a considerable extent a self-made man, laid very broadly the foundations of public statesmanship by the time he was capable of voting, and gained a considerable mastery of the English language for fluent writing and speaking.

William Schouler was in his eighteenth year when his father bought the West Cambridge factory and became a mill-owner for himself; and from that time forward the son's work in the mills was of course

[1] See Debates, Mass. Convention, 1853, 639, 640.

confined to a family establishment, of which he was presently to become a joint proprietor. He married October 6, 1835, in anticipation of pecuniary independence, about three months before attaining his majority; and his father, generous for him as for the other sons, gave a lot of land and built him a house as a wedding gift. It was the only home during his whole life which this son really owned. While still a resident of West Cambridge he bought an eligible building lot in another part of the town, and then removing from the town he sold out at once and forever all his real estate in the world. Frances Eliza Warren, born in West Cambridge, January 10, 1816, was thirteen months younger than her husband. Their match was a love match and their marriage a true companionship of hearts, scarcely in death to be divided. Frances was of a superior Middlesex County stock, identified with the English colonization of Massachusetts in 1630, and with the prowess of famous Lexington and Concord minute-men in the early Revolution, and connected not remotely with the noblest blood spilt at Bunker's Hill. Rev. Dr. Henry Cumings, for many years the parish pastor and leading citizen of Billerica, was her great-grandfather, dying in 1823.[1] But simple and country bred, all this seemed of little consequence to her or her future station in life. She had been brought up as the ward of a leading citizen of West Cambridge, Colonel Thomas Russell, and while yet a girl she became engaged to the man of her choice in one of an emigrant race, new to the town, and newly prosperous. Fortune was no gift on either side, but high

---

[1] See the "Genealogy of William Wilkins Warren," prepared and published for family information by her only brother; and see also the well-known printed volume relating to the "Warren family."

aims, sound health, sound morals, and sound character. Frances was bright, lovely in person and disposition, accomplished for the times and locality, an admirable housekeeper. Her lover appeared by contrast tall, ungainly, homely, rather unconventional; but they grew into a handsome couple, he developing quickly the masculine graces, and no two natures ever proved more congenial. She became the conscientious and devoted mother of his children, and no mother ever gained or deserved more devotion from children in return. Patterning herself after the Christian example, meek, domestic, and quiet in her tastes, self-sacrificing and caring little to shine, she moulded others for conspicuousness by the force of her gentle yet pervading will in the home circle.

The wooden house which William Schouler had built for him and occupied is still to be seen on the Main Street of Arlington, midway between the railroad station and the former site of the factories, though on the opposite side. It is a plain two-story mansion painted white, and still well-preserved; the hills are still seen rising in its rear, but the handsome trees which once shaded it in front have disappeared. Situated close to the sidewalk at a sharp turn of the road to Lexington, it seems to an approaching traveller journeying in that direction to stand across the highway on the left, as though to obstruct his passage; but the optical effect diminishes as he draws nearer. To this house, then newly built, the young manufacturer brought his younger bride; and within its walls were born to them in succession their three oldest children, Harriet, James, and William. James, the future historian, was born March 20, 1839, as already stated; the other two in the years 1837 and 1841 respectively.

As a resident of West Cambridge, William Schouler still followed with his brothers the paternal calling until about twenty-seven years of age. But he had a soul above cloth-printing, and as a public-spirited, energetic, and popular man he inclined to solid literature and politics. He was in much local demand for occasional addresses. Loathing always the Jefferson and Jackson school of national statesmen, and enthusiastic for Clay, Webster, and Harrison, he joined heartily in promoting the good Whig cause through Middlesex County. He would write leaders for a little Whig newspaper in Concord which William S. Robinson, a young journalist of rising fame, then conducted; and in the great campaign of 1840, which carried "Old Tippecanoe" into the Presidency, he took an active part in the local speech-making and enthusiasm, recognized at once as a ready and effective speaker among rural audiences.

With this happy initiation into Bay State politics under the auspices of a new party, unlucky enough in its national triumphs, but immensely strong in the affection of Massachusetts while it lasted, William Schouler forsook West Cambridge and the red factory industry for the more congenial calling of journalism. He now bought the "Lowell Courier," and moved to the thriving city of spindles in 1842 to edit and publish it. With the help of young Robinson, who had printed his earlier effusions and now needed friendship, he made of it quite a famous Middlesex Whig paper. "Indeed," comments a veteran editor, "for those years from 1842 to 1846 we think it was the best piece of journalism in Massachusetts." Middlesex County had been much demoralized by earlier political coalitions, and this Lowell paper now did much to bring honest voters round to the Whig cause. Though supporting in his paper Whig protective principles, such as mightily pleased the great mill capitalists of this enterprising young city, Schouler regarded well the interests of the operative class among whom he had been brought up; and abominating all demagogues and stirrers of envy among the wage-earners, he gained great popularity by his honesty, tact, and generous dealing towards employers and the employed. While a resident of Lowell he was elected four times to the Massachusetts House of Representatives, extending his fame and personal acquaintance to the great civic centre of New England influence. Taking an active interest, moreover, in the militia in these early years, he was chosen Colonel of a Middlesex County regiment, and became known by one military title or another for the rest of his life. Two other sons of Massachusetts, who rose to greater national renown, may be mentioned as his junior field officers, — Henry Wilson and Nathaniel P. Banks. Independent now in fortune and in the control of his own newspaper, Colonel Schouler gave it, as editors usually did in those days, the flavor of his own personal qualities, which were genial humor, courtesy, and good sense. He carried on political controversies in his columns, and wrote pungent paragraphs against opponents without creating personal enmity. He argued convincingly, but with candor and fairness; and as a fellow-journalist has said of him, though full of amusing stories, and rich in conversation and good-hearted mimicry, he was incapable of ill-natured mirthfulness. Such was William Schouler through his whole editorial and political career, as developed in this earliest stage.

The strong religious element in his character should not be overlooked. His children well understood it and saw its purer image in his wife's unworldliness. Whatever may have been his frailties or temptations at any stage of life, William Schouler had the strong root of Christian endeavor and philanthropy. The touching scenes of his last hours revealed its depth, and so did these earlier years of aspiring energy. In politics or journalism he was honorable and unselfish. At some young period of life he had become attached to the Episcopal Church and joined its communion, and his wife and children all embraced and were brought up in the same faith. This was a little singular; for the other Schoulers, not less strenuous in religious tenets, chose rather to be Unitarians or liberals, like modern proselytes of New England; and a certain conservatism of political and social temperament, perhaps a slight family estrangement, seems traceable in consequence. While a mere boy at Staten Island, William so endeared himself to an Episcopal clergyman there that the two renewed a strong personal intimacy almost fifty years later on the strength of that brief acquaintance. While living at West Cambridge, William and his wife (whose relatives likewise were Unitarian) used to ride down on Sunday to old Christ Church near the colleges, whose rector, Rev. Nicholas Hoppin, baptized their three eldest children. When at Lowell the family joined the parish flock of Rev. Theodore Edson, and William was a zealous worker in St. Anne's Church, serving as Sunday-school teacher and superintendent. Both these two clergymen, when in venerable life, conducted the services by request at William Schouler's funeral; and Dr. Edson, a man of wonderful memory, recited at a lapse of nearly thirty years the incidents of his young parishioner's life and rare example at Lowell. "I suppose," said he, "there is no position so trying to a Christian character as that which he filled so satisfactorily to his friends,— the editor of a political paper. I had supposed it impossible for such a man to keep himself unspotted and to preserve a spirit so sweet as his. His mind was always unruffled by the perplexities and provocations of the position, and I came to the conclusion that he drew the spirit from a higher source than this world."

Of his own first recollections as a child our present author writes: "The first consecutive incidents of boyhood I associate with Lowell; and by the time we moved to our second house there, in Tyler Street, the course of my life begins to unfold as clearly as a panorama. I often visited Arlington (or West Cambridge) while a child after we had moved from the place, for my grandparents were still there, and uncles, aunts, and cousins had not begun to scatter; but being only about two years old when my father moved from the town, there is but one childish incident connected with our residence there which I can recall. On one summer's afternoon I had lingered lonely about the house, missing my parents and sister, and most likely crying in my grief. Father presently appeared, and taking me on his shoulder, carried me some little distance across the street to a neighboring house, where a large party had collected in the garden; and crowing at sight of my mother and sister, I entered the company, looking down from my lofty perch in glee and triumph.

"The earliest distinct associations of one's childhood seem to be with particular objects, such as wall-paper patterns, a blue mug, a coral rattle, or with particular faces growing out of primeval chaos, none of which one can connect with special incidents.

Then come one or two scenes which the memory holds, cast permanently upon the retina of the inner mind like an instantaneous photograph. And thus, without any distinct remembrance of a house on Appleton Street where we first lived in Lowell, I remember a vesper service closing at the Roman Catholic Church on that street, to which my nurse had taken me; and I still see the long-robed priest holding up something at the shrine of the high altar, while censers swung and a little bell was tinkling. So, too, visiting the Irish abode of this nurse on another occasion, I see her family paying me attentions; and I recall the peculiar musty smell of another house, but nothing else. This nurse figures in my earliest recollections; and so does another and a Scotch one, most likely of some later date, who frightened me into a nightmare by showing me the picture of a celebrated New York murderess, Polly Bodine.

"When we moved from West Cambridge I was about the same age that father had reached when leaving Kilbarchan and Scotland. From the time I became four years old, life and the identity of existence stand out clear and continuous. The white wooden house on Tyler Street, one of a pair, with its pretty garden on the right-hand side of the entrance, which sloped behind in a grassy terrace, at whose edge grew hollyhocks and sunflowers, while morning-glories adorned the front entrance; the interior of the house, with its regular bedrooms and front staircase in the main building, and its narrow entry of sleeping rooms and backstairs in the ell, while midway was the connecting chamber, where brother Willie and I occupied a trundle-bed; the aspect of the quiet street and of neighboring houses, with the cross-street visible at each end which marked our terminus, and the single outlet opposite our house towards Middlesex Mills, — of these and much more in our Lowell home surroundings the picture is as bright with its colors as though painted yesterday. Brother Willie and I played much together on the pavement, and attracted attention where we went, because dressed much alike in blue or Scotch plaid suits, and yet unlike in features; I with straight dark hair and a high complexion, and he with a delicate face and golden locks, which were kept at this stage of life in long curls. With our sister Harriet we had much indoor delight in the attic, which here, as afterwards in Boston, and until we grew much older, served as our common play-room. We would mimic grown people, dress up in the cast-off clothes of our parents, play school-keeping, housekeeping, and store-keeping, much the same as other children do, and act out scenes of the many fairy books we had absorbed and of 'Pilgrim's Progress,' particularly in the fight of Christian and Apollyon. When approaching seven, I began to play with other boys; and several of the leading residents of Lowell seem to have drawn me in, at one time or another, to visit specially their own children and stop to tea; on one of which latter occasions the hostess read aloud 'Lord Ullin's Daughter,' a poem over which I almost sobbed.

"We children took especial delight in those bright Sunday evenings of the summer season, when father would take us out on a walk, often bringing up at some fine mansion in Belvidere, a suburb of the city, where he would stop for a conversation on the piazza while we made the bashful acquaintance of other children. On very rare occasions, under mother's direction, we entertained other children ourselves; as where on one of our birthdays we made up a little picnic to a neighboring hill, and Harrison silk badges, commemorative of the Whig President's death, of which there were a number about the house, were adapted for a decoration quite unfunereal. I seem to have been launched early into political knowledge; for when about six I received for my Christmas present a gayly painted sled upon which was a well-mounted engraving of all the Presidents of the United States from Washington to Polk, so that I got tolerably familiar with their names and faces as I coasted in their company on many a cold winter's day. Of exhibitions that I remember while in Lowell, 'Bunker Hill,' with its miniature soldiers and conflagration, deserves a special mention; and I remember a moderate-sized audience room, where was seen General Tom Thumb, with whom I was measured as we put backs together standing on a table. Theatricals and the footlights, which I so much enjoyed later in Boston, I was not yet fit to appreciate; but some of the bigger boys on Tyler Street admitted me as a spectator to their own performances one week when the stage fever was epidemic among our youth. A mask through which a pretended tooth might be pulled was the source of untiring entertainment at one of these exhibitions; while at another, which I attended by night in a cellar dimly lighted by candles, duels with wooden swords dealt infinite death, and one of the boys — 'Stuttering Sam,' as we called him — ran from the right wing with drawn weapon in hand, shouting: 'W-h-hat made you kill my brother for? St-t-and back there, st-t-and back.' Demure spectator that I was, these older fellows little knew my young talent for mimicry, or the sense of humor which has predestined them for print.

"The first school which I regularly attended was

kept by Miss Whittemore, an elderly family acquaintance who came from West Cambridge and lived with us during the brief time that she remained in Lowell. She understood well the art of teaching, and had a good number of boys and girls, some of whom had even reached their teens. The school, situated in a lane which made a good ten minutes' walk from home, was a detached building, provided with long desks and benches after the old fashion, which were painted green and ornamented with putty to hide the marks of earlier defacement by the jack-knife. I should judge that this was some deserted district school hired for private occasion. The teacher sat by a stove, behind which we would gather in turn on cold winter days to get a supply of animal heat sufficient to carry back to our seats. A large open lot in the rear of our schoolhouse made an ample playground for recess, especially when a pile of lumber upon it gave us something to climb upon and explore, or when in some large cart belonging to the mill just beyond we could sit close and eat a watermelon which the oldest boy divided among us. In my school life and lessons I progressed tolerably well for so juvenile a specimen; and in reading, spelling, grammar, and writing I must have proved quite proficient; for I read whatever I could lay hold of in school or out, as I long continued to do, and knew the contents of the 'school readers' almost by heart. A pathetic poem or bit of prose roused my emotions deeply, and I seem to have had some unusual gift of entering into the feelings of others and interpreting them. An imaginative passage in our little reading-book, which I still recall, stirred me so as I read it aloud one afternoon in my turn while we sat in class, that I made a visible impression upon the school; but the boy who followed me started off with such emulous exaggeration upon the next and tamer paragraph, that the whole class burst into a laugh, for the anti-climax was too much for them.

"After Miss Whittemore gave up teaching, and for about a year before we moved from Lowell, I attended the public grammar school, of which a Mr. Balch was head master. Children older for the most part than myself occupied the main hall, the girls ranging on one side of the centre aisle, the boys on the other; and there were side-rooms for special recitations of the several classes of each sex. Here I became painfully aware of the flogging abuse which in those days made so prominent a part of public-school discipline; and though never chastised personally at school in my life, I was tortured in soul, here and under one particular usher afterwards in a Boston school, by the pain and indignities which I saw inflicted continually upon other male companions, often, as it seemed to me wantonly, and for such trivial offences as an imperfect lesson. Certain boys were called forward day after day to writhe and distort their faces upon the platform before their assembled fellows of both sexes, as a regular interlude of instruction, until I would feel towards them as though they were education's martyrs. Young children must have taken in the satire of all this, for whenever they played school together, they did little more than whip each other round. But Mr. Balch, who had an agreeable way with most of us, and I dare say a kindly heart, gave a comical air to his castigation; for he would point to his young victim, stigmatizing him as 'thou lazy, loafing, idle boy,' and calling him up, make him take hold of his toes before the dread cane was laid on from behind. I must have impressed this master by my proficiency for a boy of six, for upon my entrance he placed me among big boys in one of the higher classes, where I readily held my own. On Saturday afternoons in winter the Lowell 'Paddies' and 'Yankees' used to have snow-ball battles, one faction chasing another through the street; and in one of these encounters I handed over some well-iced missiles of my own preparation as a party of school-boys charged past my front gate. 'Who is that?' asked one of another as they ran by me to the fray. 'Oh! that's the little cuss in the third class!' replied the other. Going into the house I asked what 'cuss' meant, and was told that it stood for 'customer.'

"Our religious education in the family was well heeded by my good mother. At her knee we prayed and learned and listened to the Bible; and a little book 'Line upon Line,' one of a well-known series which tells the Scripture story for children, imparted such delight from her reading, that to this day the patriarchs of Genesis, Joseph and his brethren, and the conduct of the Israelites from Egypt to the promised land, have an unwonted hold upon my religious feelings. Mother watched the growth of our young natures, and in her solicitude to make us good tried various experiments from time to time, such as recording our Christian progress through the week, which record she would read aloud on Saturday night, or making a little weekly allowance on that day conditional upon good behavior. To her unerring sense of justice and proper discipline — for father tended a little to indulgence — and withal to her gentle prudence, her children owe more than they can ever express. On Sundays we went to church, or to Sunday-school at least, and enjoyed doing so. Dr. Edson, our pastor, among other gifts, had that of remembering names and faces, like the great Henry Clay, to whom he bore some personal resemblance; and living so many years in Lowell, as he did, it used to be said of him that he knew every man, woman, and child in the city, and kept the trace of each individual's career in life. In the rear of our stone St. Anne's Church were two Sunday-school buildings of plain wood. To the smaller one we were consigned until well grounded in the church catechism, after which we were promoted to the larger one. This promotion I gained in good time, with others of our little class, one of whom, now rector of one of the most influential churches in New York City, and famed throughout the land, became, as chance directed long after, a college classmate and dear personal friend. Our teacher herself accompanied us into the large Sunday-school, rather than be separated from such pupils. Here father was superintendent, and in the smaller Sunday-school, at one time while the over-crowded church was being enlarged, he assembled many of the younger folk of the parish for morning prayer, conducted by himself each Sunday, and read to us some suitable tale in place of a sermon.

"I showed early a fondness for music, and through life until my deafness became too positive an impediment, I would gather tunes and strains quickly by the ear, which mingled with my visible impressions of events and served easily to recall them. My brothers and sisters were also full of music, — a natural gift inherited perhaps from grandfather, though father played the flute and mother sang simple airs in the earlier years of our childhood. Sometimes when at a neighbor's house, in these years, they would put me forward to sing one of the Whig campaign songs with which I was familiar. Of church tunes, too, of psalmody and church organs, I took early cognizance, not to add of churches themselves of various denominations, of their sextons and their bells. So fond was I, while a boy under ten, of seeing a bell swing in the belfry of mill or meeting-house, throwing out its clear tones and then pausing inverted on the wheel, that I would climb up into an attic window to watch some of these monitors performing their functions together at the appointed hour; and I remember that on the Fourth of July which followed our removal to Boston, I pulled by a string an old dinner bell which I had hung in an upper window of our house, at the hours of sunrise, noon, and sunset, agreeably to the published civic programme of the day; in blended unison, so far as might be, with the metallic friend whose motions beckoned from a church steeple visible not far distant. With these musical fancies to cherish, I wandered one afternoon while very young into the basement of a Baptist church in Lowell, where a singing-school was in progress; and being well received, I readily learned the catch 'Scotland's burning,' as the trifle appropriate to the calendar. My good parents, appreciating this love of music, allowed me presently to attend for a term the best singing-school in the city; and there I picked up some excellent tunes adapted from such masters as Bellini, Weber, and De Beriot, which have stayed by me all my life. One of them I afterwards heard played by a brass band which came one night to our house for a serenade after the November elections.

"While we lived in Lowell father took his first

and only trip abroad, remaining several months in and about Great Britain, and describing his sights and impressions in a series of editorial letters for his newspaper. During his absence mother once journeyed with us children to Boston, where our daguerreotypes were taken in a group for the benefit of Scotch relatives who still preserve them. This day's visit gave me my earliest recollections of the more solid and sombre brick city which was to become our domicile a year or two later. Another trip thither was made on my express account, and merged into a three months' stay at West Cambridge with my grandparents. I had passed too much time, it appears, in stooping over my books, and malformation of the chest was threatened; but the Boston physician who was consulted prescribed a simple regimen which resulted in an entire cure. Grandmother gave me a shower-bath every morning, and administered regular doses of a bitter sarsaparilla, beyond which I had simply to idle about in the open air, enjoying myself as I might, and let all reading and study alone. The three months passed thus happily in the society of the two old people, whose thoughtful kindness was unfailing. Framed engravings hung on their walls of 'Waverley,' 'Fergus MacIvor,' and 'Sir Walter Scott, Bart.,' all of which they patiently explained to me. I would gather burrs (not flowers) on a neighboring bank, in company with another boy, and then pretend to peddle them about; and I paid constant visits in person to the factories, where I became acquainted with every workman, young or old, and learned the whole process of printing satinets and calicoes, and the minutiæ of the machinery, from the cool water-wheel where motive power began to the heated calender and the brushing machine which gave to the figured cloth its final finish. A brown-paper hat was made for me, such as the operatives wore. I would rig up contrivances of my own on the premises so as to imagine myself hard at accompanying work; and once or twice the good Scotchman in charge of the printing-cylinder admitted me to the supreme dignity of moving the lever that started or stopped its copper plunge through the dye-trough. Grandfather took me with him on various rides which I greatly enjoyed. Together he and I went one evening to old Cambridge to see a circus, the first I ever witnessed; and perhaps the long drive tired me out, for the illuminated tent, the rising benches filled with spectators who drank lemonade, the spangled riders, the chalky-faced clown, the horses that pranced about the ring to the music of a brass band and of cracking whips, left in my little brain but a confused impression.

"I said and did some droll things about the house on this visit, which my mirthful grandmother never ceased to talk about in the family. One evening some elderly neighbors called, one of whom turned to me, as callers will do when they want to compliment their host by taking notice of his young folk, and asked me what I meant to do when I grew up. Taking the question in all seriousness, and having in memory a passage from one of my books, I at once replied that I didn't know whether I should be 'a machine-printer or a minister of the gospel.' This amused the whole room, and the story got repeated. Another day, after returning from a pleasant forenoon's ride to Woburn with grandfather, in the course of which I had found many objects to notice and ask about, one of them being a saw-mill, I proceeded to the covered side porch which I had decorated with my sign as a 'slate-drawing room,' and made a picture of a horse and chaise on my slate while dinner was preparing. Grandfather and I were sketched as occupants of the carriage, while the saw-mill rose from the background. After flourishing with the pencil as children will do, and giving to horse and chaise some peculiarly elegant trappings, it occurred to me to add, as a title for so artistic a production, 'Rich people going to Woburn;' and with the picture thus inscribed, I showed it at dinner to my grandparents. The laugh with which they greeted it I had not looked for; but this tale, too, they sent upon the family rounds; and upon the whole, fond as they evidently were of me, I think they gained and gave the impression that their first grandson was rather an old head.

"During this three months' visit, which, by the way, made quite a distinct epoch of my early childhood, a little sister was born in Lowell, who died within a few weeks. Of both her birth and her death I was apprised at West Cambridge by my grandparents, and she was the only member of my father's immediate family whom I never saw nor knew; for a kind Providence spared all the rest of us, whether born already or later, for many years of united sympathy and happiness."

IV.

1847–1855.

COLONEL SCHOULER'S marked success with the "Lowell Courier," and his increasing renown as a legislator and political speaker and manager, attracted by 1847 the attention of Daniel Webster, whose personal acquaintance he had already made, and of other Massachusetts leaders in the great national party whose fortunes he served. William Hayden now retiring from the chief editorship of the "Boston Atlas," the recognized organ at this time of the intellect, culture, wealth, and power of the New England Whigs, Schouler was induced to become the conductor and a co-proprietor of the paper in his place. He sold out the "Lowell Courier" accordingly, and moved to Boston in the spring of 1847 to enter upon his wider vocation as a journalist.

In after years William Schouler spoke often of the "Lowell Courier" as his "first love." It had been his own newspaper as well as his earliest, and he had so widened its influence and circulation as to leave it a handsome property. He carried the same ambition into the "Atlas," and showed talents and energy worthy of a successor in the enterprise which had made Richard Haughton and William Hayden so illustrious. American journalism in that day did not, as it does now, depend greatly upon costly competition in the gathering of news; but editorial leaders from day to day, which discussed the immediate political situation to influence voters, were the main reliance of the daily press for power and fortune; and a continual sparring was withal kept up in the editorial columns with journals of the opposition, so that editors themselves maintained a certain personality before their readers which has long since passed away. Cordial generosity, fairness, and kindliness of heart had been Schouler's strong characteristics in conducting his Lowell paper; upon which he had employed other pens in subordination to his own good temper, restraining the bitter and slashing style of the talented assistant who, unlike himself, was wanting in reverence and fixed opinions. That same good temper and high honor shone from all that he ever afterwards wrote, or spoke, or did, as editor or statesman. "His editorial bearing," says the Democratic journalist of Boston with whom he now sparred most, himself a man of the utmost urbanity and good feeling, "was ever marked by the discreetness that includes consideration of others, by gentleness as well as a masculine courage and strong self-assertion, and by those indescribable courtesies and amenities which are the offspring and evidence of a kind and generous heart. In his professional contests on political questions with this journal, he excited no feelings but those of respect for his ability, of esteem for his integrity of opinion, and of affectionate regard for his rare qualities of amiability and genuine goodness."

For a while all went smoothly and happily with the "Boston Atlas" under the new direction. Schouler's associates were all loyal, true, men of unblemished honor, capable of appreciating and of co-operating with him. An editorial correspondence from Washington was kept up by one or another of the two nominal proprietors while Congress remained in session; and Colonel Schouler, in the course of a considerable sojourn at the national capital now and later, profited by a wide personal acquaintance with our most eminent national statesmen of the period, many of whom he has described in his "Personal and Political Recollections." This day of the "Atlas" was the day in Massachusetts of Webster and Ashmun, of Edward Everett, Abbott Lawrence, and Robert C. Winthrop, and abounded in public men of the most brilliant and powerful qualities. Schouler was admitted to their secret councils, and shared the responsibility of their political plans. One of the most touching obituary notices of Daniel Webster, in 1852, was from his pen, and recalled personal scenes at Marshfield when Webster was in his grandest mood of elevated thought. The influence of the "Boston Atlas" soon culminated, as did that of the Whig party, in the election and succession of Zachary Taylor to the Presidency; and by 1850 this newspaper was recognized and pronounced the leading Whig paper in New England, and that upon whose support Daniel Webster chiefly relied. But when Webster made that year his famous 7th of March speech, in which he abandoned the strong ground against slavery extension which the soundest Massachusetts Whigs, and Schouler among them, had occupied, and supported the compromise palliatives proposed by Henry Clay, the "Atlas" denounced the speech and refused to follow him. Webster had long been political dictator to the leading Whigs of Boston, and this rebellious protest of an imported editor was a daring and dangerous act of independence, though the administration office-holders in that city and the popular conscience of Massachusetts which Schouler well understood, sustained the newspaper. President Taylor's sudden death, soon after, which upset the best Whig calculations, the accession of Vice-President Fillmore with Webster as premier in his cabinet, and the actual passage of the compromise measures against those wiser plans which Taylor and Seward had formulated, brought serious embarrassments upon the "Atlas;" taking away the pecuniary support of many who had been Schouler's warmest political friends, and seriously and, as it proved, fatally, in the inevitable final rupture of the great Whig party, injuring the prosperity of his newspaper. For editors in those days rose or fell by party politics. Schouler had Massachusetts and the mass of northern Whigs on his side, as the Presidential nomination of Scott showed, whom the "Atlas" supported, and the Presidential vote of the State in the fall of 1852; but Webster's disappointed ambition and death during the canvass were reflected in the Democratic vote of Boston, and the "stop my paper," and "stop my advertisement" of Boston merchants and financiers which now followed, compelled the independent editor to sell out from the concern and retire to some distant State. Upon the advice of Horace Greeley and others he made Ohio and the West his new home; purchasing an interest in the staid and respectable "Cincinnati Gazette," of which he became the responsible editor. He left Boston and New England in the fall of 1853, and in the spring of 1854 removed his whole family — permanently, as he believed — to the Buckeye State, with whose flourishing emporium he had become already identified as a journalist since the previous November.

But Schouler's popularity in Boston had been after all abundant; and many who shared his own clear insight into the future of American politics loved him the more for having so courageously opposed that grand but fleeting compromise of 1850. Before he wrote his leader in the "Atlas," in November, 1852, upon the "Waterloo defeat of the Whig party," he had been repeatedly chosen as a Boston representative to the legislature, as before he had been from Lowell. As an offset to his non-election, this year, the Whig House of Representatives of the Massachusetts Legislature of 1853 chose him

Clerk by way of compliment; and this same year, a few months before he moved to Ohio, he served as a member of the Massachusetts Constitutional Convention of 1853, in whose proceedings he proved himself a progressive but judicious advocate, midway between the strong opposing forces, and one of the best tacticians on the floor.

A growing disrelish for that sycophantic relation which custom in those days assigned to political editors may be traced in the following passage of Schouler's speech in the Convention from which we have already quoted:[1] "A great deal has been said about the licentiousness of the public press. Now, sir, I happen to have had a great deal to do with the public press, and I must say that the most licentious part of my experience connected with it has been the defence of men in high stations." This sally provoked great laughter and merriment, as he had meant it to do; but there was a touch of secret sadness in the confession. His connection with the press was destined to last several years longer, in one precarious sense or another; but he never again felt such enthusiasm for the editor's vocation as he had felt before.

"During the seven years that we lived in Boston before moving to Cincinnati," writes our present author, "we occupied three different houses in succession. First we went to Harrison Avenue, at that time a fashionable street for residences; next to an ample old house on Pearl Street, just at the foot of Fort Hill, with attractive private grounds close by, and mercantile business creeping towards us; and last to a lovely cottage on the beach at Jeffries'

---

[1] 1 Mass. Debates 639; *supra*, p. 189.

Point, East Boston, which commanded a full prospect of the harbor, and where I passed the three happiest years of a very happy childhood. Another brother and sister by this time completed the family circle, — John, who was born in Lowell, November 30, 1846; and Fanny, born in East Boston, January 19, 1852. A closer equality in age had bound the three eldest of us more closely together in childhood's companionship; but we were all affectionate."

James was placed in the Brimmer School when the family first moved to Boston; but when the Quincy School district was set off, a few months later, he became one of the original pupils of this new institution. Under its first head master, John D. Philbrick, the Quincy School furnished Boston's grand model of public instruction; and the conspicuous success of that illustrious educator in organizing and directing so large a body of pupils led to his later promotion to school superintendence. James graduated from the Quincy School in 1851, first on its list of Franklin medal scholars; and then entering the Boston Latin School, he remained there long enough to become well grounded in the Latin language and grammar and insensibly to pave the way to a college education. But James at that time had no idea of entering college; and with a sturdy idea of earning his own livelihood, he prevailed upon his parents, when about thirteen, to let him go into a bookstore. A few weeks, however, of early rising and hard drudgery convinced him that a little more school was preferable, and, sent this time to Chauncy Hall, a private school, he zealously pursued once more his other studies, letting classics alone, until the family removal West in 1854.

As a Boston school-boy the youthful James showed

a certain conspicuousness of his own which strongly attracted the affection of his teachers, at the same time that his modesty and unobtrusive disposition made him less of a leader among school companions, less, perhaps, of a recognized hero, than a boy of his mental attainments is apt to be. Children cannot analyze a subtle character, but trust to surface appearances. Something of domestic seclusion clung to him. If ambitious, it was not along the lines which other boys most sought for distinction; and the impression he chiefly gave to his mates was that of a genial and gentle fellow who got on well and made friends, but left others of more daring self-assertion to lead. His home life wove about him a web almost impenetrable to others; nor had he any great taste for the usual boyish sports, though he bore his moderate part in base-ball, swimming, coasting, skating, and the like athletics of the day. His strong physical endurance as he grew older owed nothing in fact to athletic training; but sound health and morals, a cheerful temper, and simple out-of-doors life explain the whole of it. While living at East Boston he walked about five miles each way to school and back, in all weathers, and made no merit of it.

Theatre-going, concerts, and most of all the Museum fairy spectacles and the Ravel family (to all of which performances editors had free passes) were now his great delight in holiday recreation; and with spools and shifting books for his actors and scenery he would reproduce what he had witnessed by the hour together before his nearest sister and brother, whose tastes were similar; going so far as to purchase play-books and make paper heads and costumes for his mimic stage. Once, with other boys, he got up a very tolerable afternoon performance of "Box and Cox." His love of imaginative books and reading was all the while incessant. From fairy books and Jacob Abbott, he became an eager devourer of poetry and fiction, and in the winter nights he would read aloud the latest number of Dickens' new novel, as the family gathered about the astral lamp. Shakespeare, the Waverley Novels, Macaulay's History, and other treasures of his father's good library he ransacked freely; and upon his father's advice he began in 1853, though with less spontaneous ardor, to dip into the biographies of American statesmen, such as John Jay, Wirt, and Aaron Burr, for the last of whom he conceived somewhat of a romantic fascination until time taught him a better estimate. That "vast vacuity," of which Milton speaks, he was constantly filling up with erudition, worthy or worthless, which enriched his English composition.

At school, from all that we can gather, James ranked high, not by reason of any intellectual brilliancy such as burns out its lamp, but because of a strong healthy all-round development; and his rank was aided by exemplary conduct and a punctual clock-work regularity at his tasks. It was for this manifestation of high marks throughout that his first teacher at the Quincy School, one afternoon, when the marks were read out, bade him take his cap and books and follow him to the highest room, where he was at once installed, skipping the sub-master in the middle of a term, — a public-school promotion quite out of course. The same general thoroughness ranked him first when he graduated; and his principal, John D. Philbrick, long alluded in his educational lectures to this young boy as one who during four years was not absent or tardy but once, when accident excused him. In the mastery of good English at all points James's studies appeared best; his proficiency being most marked in reading, spelling, grammar, and parsing, the choice of words and the construction of sentences. Less for thought, perhaps, than for expression, at so early an age, his English compositions passed for models in his class; fiction, poetry, the discussion of social topics, and historical description furnished the substance of them; and one upon "Napoleon Bonaparte," written at the age of ten, is a good example at hand of his early skill in gathering facts and narrating them. But his literary aptness is still better illustrated by a little newspaper, which he used to write out on double-columned foolscap, and issue (for the home circle exclusively) as "editor and publisher," when only eleven years old, styling it the "Family Visitor and Home Journal." He decorated it with a headline and the motto "Nil desperandum" (which he had picked up long before studying Latin), and a pen-and-ink picture of the Pearl Street residence which constituted his "office." Of this paper, which he carried on in 1850, by way of home recreation, issuing it each week or fortnight, several numbers were preserved by his mother; and the specimen now before us contains, in addition to school items, the seventh chapter of a temperance tale, "It is all for the Best," an instalment of "Alfred the Great" under "Lives of Celebrated Men," and a spirited poem "New England," — productions all original and written out in the neatest chirography possible, without a single inaccuracy in spelling or grammar.

In one other respect, certainly, James's excellence was acknowledged by his schoolmates wherever he went; and this same excellence procured for him a second and then a first Boylston prize when he was at college. This was in declamation, — a talent which first shone out at the Quincy School. At a Boston temperance convention three or four choice boys from the public schools were selected to deliver little speeches arranged for them; and one of these was our present author. "My *début* on a public platform," he writes, "was at the Tremont Temple, when ten years old, and I repeated my harangue from a stand on Boston Common the next day. My chief sensation, I remember, was that of seeing my name in print for the first time upon the programmes distributed in the hall." At all the school exhibitions he attended from that day forward his part was a prominent one; and while at the Latin School, where there was much excellent speaking under Dr. Gardner's direction, he represented his class regularly on the public Saturdays. Though sometimes selecting dramatic poems like "Marmion," his preference was for prose extracts from Webster, Clay, Wirt, Corwin, and some of the Irish statesmen, which he memorized extensively. "A handsome face and figure, with rosy cheeks, typical of health," says one who remembers him, "set off his oratory, which was impressively earnest and was aided by a flexible and melodious voice and appropriate gestures. He threw himself into whatever he had to deliver." The richness of his musical delivery as a school-boy is thus recalled by one who heard him recite Wirt's description of the Blennerhassett island at a Latin school exhibition. Capable himself of strong feeling, and deeply stirred in the soul by eloquent passages, the incessant search which he used to make for them, through prose and poetry, from early youth to manhood, did much to widen his range of thought and confirm his mastery of English expression.

At the age of fourteen, moreover, our author in a marked instance showed himself strongly capable of continuous mental labor during the hours which most school-boys assign to play and sport. While his father was Clerk of the Massachusetts House in 1853 the legislature made an appropriation for copying out some of the old journals of the last century for better preservation. One of these journals — that for 1784 — William Schouler assigned experimentally to his eldest son, who, after a few boyish lapses, buckled himself down to the task and finished it in the course of a few months; aiding his work, as he was wont to do in later years, by closely estimating the daily progress needful to reach the goal by a given time, and then keeping well up to the estimate. A large folio volume of several hundred manuscript pages, substantially bound, and written in a clear school-boy hand with a steel pen, may still be seen at the State Library of Massachusetts as a monument of one's manual toil out of school hours, at the age of fourteen. For this achievement his father praised him as possessing already "a busy purpose, a desire to succeed, and an industrial habit."

James's musical taste and talent progressed in these school years. He would improvise, would play on the piano whatever he heard elsewhere, catching a melody quickly, and applying chords with an almost intuitive perception of thorough bass. At the age of eleven he began taking piano lessons, with an ultimate reference to the organ; and his favorite teacher was a Mr. Leavens, the organist at St. Paul's Church, Boston, and a man of consummate taste in all that pertained to church music. The two grew greatly attached to one another, though in age so unequal, and formed a friendship which lasted for many years. When the hour's instruction was over, the teacher would himself play from the oratorios, or improvise, compare tunes, and discourse with his pupil, until the clock showed that he must hasten out-of-doors for some other engagement; and thus did the boy gain far more in breadth of musical culture than the mere lesson imparted. He exploited all new collections of sacred music, searching every book of church tunes he could find, and buying a number for himself; and before he entered college he had written out with his own hand a choice collection of a hundred tunes, some of which were of his own arrangement. This manuscript book, still extant, he often used while conducting a choir.

That interest in church and Sunday-school which had been inculcated while at Lowell was projected into his whole subsequent life. A struggling Episcopal church at East Boston, which was founded by Rev. Nathaniel G. Allen, who years later married our author's elder sister, appealed strongly to his sympathies. The parish record left by Mr. Allen records "Master James Schouler" among the benefactors, in raising thirty-five dollars for the increase of the Sunday-school library; a task of his own conception, which involved a visit to Lowell, where, under the kindly patronage of his old pastor, Dr. Edson, he made a house-to-house canvass for the money, with two other boys as a local committee. He chose the new books, bought them with the money raised, numbered and catalogued them. Perhaps, however, a more striking instance of his youthful zeal was shown at the same church under Mr. Allen's successor. A young woman who had served as organist married and moved away; and James, who by this time had presided occasionally at the instrument, was urged to take her place. He consented for the rector's temporary convenience, but at once found himself with the entire musical direction devolved upon him, and found no exemption until the family removed from East Boston a year later. "I am sometimes amazed," writes our author, "when I recall the perfect confidence with which, a boy of fourteen, I handled that little organ and drilled weekly a choir of half a dozen adults, selecting all the Sunday music without consultation. At our first rehearsal a man about four times my age undertook to control the choice of tunes, and finding me unyielding, left the room; after which no more loyal or harmonious a set of men and women ever stood up to sing before a congregation, so long as I remained at my post." All who thus aided the music, and our young organist included, did so from good-will and without recompense.

The Schoulers, as we have said, were strongly united as a household, children and parents, and were affectionate towards one another; but between father and eldest son there seems to have been a bond of peculiar tenderness. Each preserved constantly the earliest letters received from the other,— forerunners of a correspondence which was later to reveal much for mutual sympathy and counsel. The first filial letter that James ever wrote bears date December 14, 1851, while his father was in Washington; and the latter's reply, three days later, made mention that Senator Seward, at whose desk he was writing, had read the letter through. "He said that it was written very well, indeed, and that I should feel very proud of you, and he asked your age, which I told him." While at Cincinnati, in September, 1853, preparing to remove his family thither, the father next wrote a long letter to his son James, recalling in a pathetic strain his own early struggles and the blessing a good mother had been to him, and enjoining upon the son a like appreciation on his part, and the cultivation of industrious and self-improving habits; since he, too, must make his own way in life. The son, responding hurriedly from school in recess-time, made laconic answer to all this good advice: "I have your letter to me in my pocket, and I would briefly say that I hope I shall never disgrace the name I bear."

James had much wished that the family journey to Cincinnati should give a chance to see New York City and the picturesque Hudson. This wish the father gratified. Their tarry at the Astor House, in the great metropolis, in March, 1854, with the novel sight of horse-cars running from City Hall opposite, and a World's Fair to visit, was full of delight, but a blinding snow-storm made the steamboat trip to Albany a disappointment. Arrived at their new Ohio home soon after, the child's young mind received new impressions calculated to broaden his conception of American life: he learned to love hill-crowned Cincinnati by the yellow river for the short time he was to remain connected with it; but he pined much for New England, and was homesick for old acquaintances left behind.

In the course of this first summer of 1854 at the west, James's little sister had to be taken to Boston by the mother for medical treatment and a change of scene; he went in charge of the party. Except for this episode, the boy's whole bent was now upon his studies. Sent for the first few months to a private school of half a dozen boys, taught by a Methodist clergyman who had left the pulpit, — a man of much talent and erudition, but as shy and shambling as Dominie Sampson, — he developed at once a precocious intimacy with his teacher; and, drawing out his own programme of studies preparatory to mercantile life, which embraced French and German but no classics, he pursued it in good earnest. But now came up the parental project of sending James to college, — a turn to life wholly unexpected, and yet, when fairly realized, most pleasing to him. It seems to have originated in the idea of others that a youth so exemplary in morals would grow into a clergyman; but when put to the test his ambition in life proved a secular one. Kenyon College at Gambier was first fixed upon; and beginning in the autumn at Mr. Brooks's famous school, where the young scions of Cincinnati's best families came together, James turned back to his classical studies, which for more than two years had been laid aside, and resolved that this first year of genuine college preparation should be his last.

The grammar drill of the Boston Latin School, where rules and Latin words were memorized, gave him an obvious advantage in attacking Cæsar, Cicero, and Virgil; and Greek grammar and Greek authors he also tackled for the first time with assiduity; in English studies ranking already with the foremost in the school. Nominally in the third class when he began, James came quickly alongside of the second and then the first. Mr. Brooks used to say of him afterwards, that he accomplished in one year what took most other boys three years, which was literally true. Meanwhile Trinity College at Hartford had become the parental choice for him; and with the added incentive of returning east, his determination to be fitted in twelve months grew stronger. But in the early summer of 1855, a leading citizen of Cincinnati, who heard James declaim at a school exhibition, said to the father: "Harvard is the institution for your boy. Don't fail to send him there, where I have a son already." The parents heeded this advice, which involved a greater advance in qualifications than the standard previously in view; but, nothing daunted, the son kept on through his school vacation and into the hot summer months, under his teacher's special coaching, to meet the Harvard requirements. His robust health nearly gave way under this new and incessant strain; but he persevered, and at length was ready to take the long journey to Boston and present himself for the second Harvard examination which was to be held at the close of August, just before the commencement of a new academic year. Leaving home and parents for the first prolonged departure of his life, he found at dawn upon the dressing-table of his chamber two parting tokens which he never ceased to cherish, — a long and loving letter from his father, full of sound advice; and a plain gold ring inscribed "from mother," which he wore upon his finger for many years and until a wife's ring displaced it. The early omnibus bore him to the train; three days later he was in Cambridge; and on Friday the 31st of August, he telegraphed his father, "Entered Harvard without any conditions."

V.

1855–1859.

"Until my entrance upon college life at the age of sixteen," writes our historian, "no life could have been happier or sunnier than mine; no home more helpful; no parents kinder or more considerate. For a boy not brought up to luxury, it seemed as though every childish wish had hitherto been gratified. But scarcely had I begun my studies at Harvard when the black clouds began to gather, which, chasing one after another and discharging, have cost me many a sad and sombre day, until I seem to have regained a calm and azure horizon in mature life, chiefly by learning life's deeper philosophy, and gaining patience to endure what Euripides calls, in good classical Greek, ills unbearable that nevertheless must be borne."

Colonel Schouler had sunk more capital in the "Boston Atlas" than he or his friends could at first comprehend. "He has told me with tears in his eyes," relates his son, "that Webster's 7th of March speech marked the turning-point in his pecuniary fortunes." Nor indeed did that faithful party organ long survive the grand Whig procession, for it was moribund when he left Boston. He had as usual trusted too much to the statements of others, when purchasing an interest in the "Cincinnati Gazette;" and though a respectable and well established journal, he found it encumbered with old debts whose payment absorbed all the profits, until in September of this year, 1855, a note fell due which he could not meet.

He had borrowed of his father and brothers, but others upon whom he had relied now failed him. A forced sale of his shares was threatened; and in gloom and distress he wrote to the son just separated from him of new projects in life; of moving east or still farther west; of retiring to a farm in disgust; of coming to Massachusetts once more if only some newspaper could be found for him. This last thought was not to be wondered at, for on a recent visit to Boston Colonel Schouler had received the present of a handsome silver service from "the old folks at home;" and so great a Massachusetts leader of the Whigs as Edward Everett wrote him about this time, expressing the wish that he were back, for things did not go so well in home politics as when he was there. The dishonor of mercantile paper was a new and a sensitive experience for our editor; "this terrible thing of being in debt," writes the father to his son, "weighs upon my mind like a mill-stone." Fortunately, however, he had made a new friend in Cincinnati, of his own generous sort, though of opposing politics, and this friend now came forward. Delinquency was stayed, and things resumed their former course.

But the editors of the "Gazette" did not work smoothly together. Though nominally the chief and held responsible by the public for all that appeared in print, William Schouler could not control his financial editor and co-owner; and when the latter inserted a leading article, purposely, perhaps, which politically attacked Schouler's new benefactor in savage terms, the chief editor, stung to the quick by this semblance of personal ingratitude, tendered his immediate resignation. A truce was arranged; but Colonel Schouler, after a vain winter's journey to Washington in search of a position from the new Congress, whose House was controlled by the composite elements he had helped bring into power, agreed in the spring of 1856 with his two "Gazette" associates to buy them out within sixty days or else sell out to them and retire. He applied to eastern friends, but failed to raise the money; and accordingly he sold his share to his associates and received a small balance in hand over and above the debts he now punctiliously discharged. He left the newspaper by the middle of April, 1856.

All of these successive transactions James at college followed with his epistolary counsel. "You write, my dear son, exceedingly well," wrote the father to him; "your letters display a great deal of matured sense, and I have profited much by the advice they contain." His mother, too, less sanguine and variable in temperament, had detailed with equal confidence the family troubles, and with clear insight from her own point of view sought his advice. "I have often thought," relates our author, "while reflecting since upon this family episode, that I threw away at this time an opportunity in life, not then clear to me, which might have led us on to the flood of fortune and influence. Except for money-making, which Americans rarely lose sight of as a consideration, father certainly achieved a later career outside of journalism, and so possibly have I. But had I chosen to leave college at once and joined father, heart and hand, in this Cincinnati enterprise, I am confident that, youth though I was, we should have raised the money together and made that newspaper permanently our own. We had good mental qualities to combine in such work, — he with his genius for personal acquaintance and popularity,

I with a closer application to details and comparison; and each of us capable of wielding the pen and interpreting events, after his own fashion. Not a suggestion of the kind came to me then, or it might have fructified.* In fact, I was rather disposed, at this early stage of life, to encourage father's increasing disrelish of the press, for journalism in this country had not yet asserted its independence in enterprise, and editors were still too much the bond-slaves of politics and of ambitious statesmen. So I kept on at Harvard, economizing as I might. Father sold out his interest instead of buying out his associates; and the sagacious financial editor of the ' Gazette ' — well known in after years as ' Deacon Richard Smith, the truly good ' — gained that full control of the newspaper for which, I do not doubt, he had been craftily working."

With the trifling balance received from the sale of his interest in the "Gazette," Colonel Schouler now entered the commission business in Cincinnati, engaging a store, and, as he wrote his son, hoping soon to be in the "full tide of successful experiment." His chosen partner, against whom he was seasonably warned as a man of bad reputation in Boston business circles, received nearly all of this money, and went east to purchase goods for the credulous concern; but neither goods nor cash ever appeared, and the partner turned up in a Massachusetts criminal court, a year later, under an indictment for forgery. Colonel Schouler bore his new anxiety with more equanimity than his earlier one; and, having great influence and popularity in Cincinnati, where he had made hosts of personal friends, he was sent to the first Presidential convention of the Republican party at Philadelphia, which nominated Fremont and Dayton, and upon his return presented the resolutions at the large ratification meeting which was held during June in Cincinnati. With renewed enthusiasm for politics he now threw himself into the work of organizing by speech and pen for the new national cause of free soil. His friends had never taken seriously his newspaper valedictory nor his purpose of mercantile life. He had, in fact, been writing leaders constantly for the "Gazette" while waiting for his goods to begin business; and, accepting presently an offer to edit the "Ohio State Journal" upon a salary, he moved with his family to Columbus, and before August was absorbed in editorial pursuits once more. All these home changes transpired during the son's first year at Harvard; and the reverses of another family to whom James had been much attached deepened his intimacy thus early with adversity, and made him prematurely a counsellor of the distressed.

Our author remained at Cambridge, persevering in his University studies and practising a rigid economy. "I cannot divest myself of this sad melancholy when I write you," said his father in a letter, "but I do not wish it to make you sad; you must keep on as you have begun." Remittances from home, however, were of small amount, and necessarily precarious; nor would he have been able to complete his college course at all but for the generous offer of his father's eldest brother, who was a man of means, to make up any deficiency. James inherited a Scotch pride and reticence over all these troubles, and such assistance as the University was wont to render to students visibly in need would have been intolerable to him. In the course of these four years he aided his revenue by teaching school one winter, and at other times by finding Sunday employment as an organist. "The money spent on my music," as he once wrote his father, "was not thrown away; for in this one year I shall make more than all my musical instruction ever cost you." And thus by hook or crook he made his way through college, scrupulous of incurring debt, keeping his frugality out of sight, and sharing fairly in those general calls upon the purse which social companionship made necessary.

Schouler's classmates agree that during the first few months at college he was held somewhat in contempt, and that his rise in the class, though constant, was quite gradual, and due to a better estimate on acquaintance of his genuine talent and goodness of heart. During the first term of his Freshman year he lived at quite a distance from the college buildings in a private family. He was one of the youngest men in his class; among classmates there was no one who knew him intimately already, though several had met him at other schools; and while he did not repel acquaintance, he seemed shy and sought none. Besides being oppressed in fact with domestic troubles, he had been brought up emphatically as a home boy, and was thoroughly home-sick and far away from those he loved. All this made him sensitive and shrinking; and he had furthermore the speedy consciousness that he was misunderstood. The rumor spread that he was "green." Without tact enough to turn the laugh upon fellows whom he saw trying their tricks, he drew rather into his shell; and stories utterly unfounded were told of him, which he had no chance to refute until the Junior "mock-parts" disclosed them. Fortunately for him it soon happened that a table mate began to drop in upon him in the afternoons to study the Greek lesson;

their cordial intercourse grew, and they soon concluded to take a room together in the college buildings at the beginning of the new term.

The friendship of these college chums, admirably fitted for one another, was mutually helpful through their University course, and has since ripened into the intimacy of a lifetime. One of the most sociable of men, fond of class politics and class societies, and possessed thus early of a marked *savoir faire* among callers and companions of all conditions, John H. Ricketson bore well the hospitalities of this conjugal bachelorhood in the college yard, which after all affords the only college life worth living. Classmates now came in upon them for study or fun, and Schouler found himself in his better element, and better understood. To the Sophomore "Institute," he was elected without opposition; he joined one of the boat clubs, and was chosen its secretary; in his junior year he made one of a small and congenial club table, was elected to the Natural History Society, and was enrolled as an original member and first secretary of the Harvard Glee Club. The Harvard class of 1859 adopted a singular course in repudiating all Greek-letter societies, one effect of which was to throw the "Hasty Pudding" somewhat out of balance in its membership; and Schouler took his exclusion in the senior year from that famous society with many classmates of talent and moderate living; but intending to keep out of the new "O. K." as well, which had started in rivalry, he found himself chosen spontaneously and by a unanimous vote. All these and other class distinctions to be presently noticed came to him entirely unsought.

It was impossible that James should prove, as his fond Cincinnati teacher had predicted, the first scholar in his class. That impetuous energy which carried him so rapidly to college and the east exhausted itself with the attainment of its immediate end; and he found himself deficient in training besides, as compared with others of the class whose preparation had been more solid and systematic. His education had, in fact, been hasty, desultory, divided up among various schools and instructors, and only his own constancy had unified the results. From the Boston Latin School he met at Cambridge the most advanced portion of his former class joined to an earlier one; while his average schoolmates of 1852 were among the next year's Freshmen. But his talents and industry assured him of at least a respectable stand. In a college class of about one hundred, he stood just within the line of the first quarter; high enough in rank to secure a part at the Senior May exhibition and on Commencement Day. In Harvard University, as at school, an evenness of development marked his mental progress. In themes and forensics strong power of expression rather than of thought seemed the characteristic, though his marks were high; and at an "Institute" debate of his Sophomore year, and the first in which he ever participated, he held his ground well against two experienced opponents, though contending single-handed in his colleague's absence. He read a lecture before the same society on "Addison and Steele," which showed culture, and was impressively delivered. But he neither won nor sought any of the English composition prizes. To declamation he addressed himself instead, knowing his surer strength, and won, as we have mentioned, a lower and then a higher prize. It was in the Junior year that his chum and he bore off the two first prizes.

An incident is recalled at one of the college rooms about the beginning of Schouler's Sophomore year, when an itinerant phrenologist came in. A number of the class who were present, and reckoned among the ablest, came forward to get their bumps examined; and the comments of the examiner, shrewd and humorous, were more or less complimentary. At length Schouler, who was in the modest background, came forward in his turn; when, to the surprise of his fellows, the phrenologist praised his head above all the others, predicting great things of him. "This was not much relished by the others," says our informant, "for Schouler, though rising in their esteem, was even then reckoned as of no great mental calibre; and they left him to pay the Spurzheim traveller out of his own pocket. But it seemed as if from that day the youth gained in self-assertion among his classmates, — a mental gift in which he seemed always rather deficient. He could arouse and even electrify upon the platform or where he had something special to deliver; but in the general witticisms and conversation of classmates he showed no special exuberance."

This quiet constraint among his fellows, where brilliant talk went on, was greatly due to the gentle home influences which had moulded his character; and moreover to an inbred reluctance to "show off," as he called it, or force his talents upon the notice of male company. But for the infirmity of his later life this peculiarity would have worn off. For at the very time when this modest reticence drew the comment of classmates, James was the life of his home circle, and wherever else he felt intimate enough to make spontaneous mirth. His nicknames, his sport over college incidents which had impressed his sense of humor, his rollicking mimicry and mock theatrical rant, all mingled with his ready musical accompaniment, cheered and delighted such company by the hour together. His mother and sisters would recount the merry pranks of his winter vacation at home, when his spirits were highest, and would hum the lively tunes which he rattled off on the piano; and so was it with dear friends among whom he tarried in the summer. Both in correspondence and personal intercourse, it seemed his mission at this stage of youth to cheer up those whose lives were arched with sorrow, imparting his own buoyancy and hopefulness. In all this young Schouler shone best in mixed company. Women seemed to arouse him to the best play of his intellect; and so quickly attractive was he to the fair sex that he entered the best society without an effort. Before he had finished his Sophomore year he was in the centre of a charming Cambridge set of young men and women, and among the foremost of his class in demand there at dances and evening parties. Though never taught a dancing lesson in his life, he moved with natural grace and rhythm through the quadrilles and country dances that then made the staple of our social functions. With a classmate, too, of congenial tastes and temperament, he was a most entertaining companion, for grave or gay converse, when they were off by themselves.

But if taciturn and disposed to listen rather than talk, where college men were numerous, if unable to make a rattling, off-hand speech, or extemporize a good story, James soon showed a striking felicity with the pen in college diversions. At one of the earlier "Institute" meetings he contributed an effusion to the paper of one of the most popular editors;

which was so well received that the editor got him to write again, and then proposed and carried him in as a personal successor for the new term. The choice was vindicated; and Schouler as an "Institute" editor, particularly in a final paper which was mostly of his own composition, brought a tumult of applause and laughter. A college paper works up mirthful allusions to lessons, teachers, and the college social life, weaving together light analogies, puns, and word-play, all irradiated by the writer's fancy and imagination, whether in prose or poetry. In such literary productions, our author attained marked excellence at college, as did also a classmate and friend, who became class poet; nor was the racy flight of either soiled by a gross or indecent thought. Each in turn, by such a start, gained wider college celebrity, as an editor of the "Harvard Magazine,"—a periodical in whose pages appeared, along with such *persiflage*, some more serious of their literary productions. Schouler's lighter efforts were invoked for another special paper before the class society in his Senior year; and when the class met socially, as mature men, on the silver anniversary of "1859," Schouler was once more singled out for editor. In such literary work, which took many an hour from his college recreation, and doubtless from his studies besides, our author (aside from his gift of oratory) gained doubtless his chief college eminence, and was really a marked man in the class by the time he graduated.

James took no great interest in athletic sports, nor did he ever cherish an athletic ambition. In all recreation, physical or mental, he disliked antagonism, unless, at all events, many shared the burden of it. He would rarely enter a gymnasium; for gymnastic exercise, unless carefully superintended, leads on to feats of daring which to the average boy means injury. But without such special training our author showed sound and robust health, and a capacity for mental and physical endurance, strengthened by temperate habits. He pulled a good oar, and belonged to the picked crew of his boat club while they made use of an old-fashioned barge; but when a light shell and undress succeeded he dropped out. At Fresh Pond he regularly rowed as one of a merry young party of both sexes styled the "Arrow Club." Long walks, at college and in earlier and later life, have furnished his habitual exercise; and these he could enjoy either with company or alone. Convenience, not to add economy, initiated such exertion in his Freshman year; for steam connection with Boston had just been discontinued when he entered college, nor until the following April was the new street railway completed and equipped with horse-cars. Many a Saturday did he tramp over the bridge into the great city, through Boston and back again. Passing one Sunday in the winter with friends in the suburbs, when, after a violent snow-storm the skies cleared at noon, leaving the snow piled high, he walked to Boston to take the Sunday evening omnibus to Cambridge from Brattle Street; and, finding that it would not run, he pursued his solitary march on foot, plunging through immense drifts at Cambridgeport, just beyond the bridge, until at Cambridge he reached his room. Again, on a bitter cold Monday in January, 1859, when the thermometer ranged far below zero, he rose at four in the morning and walked from Boston to Cambridge in the dim dawn, reaching the college yard just as the first bell rang for prayers, which few others attended; and about sunset of the same day, after the usual college routine, he walked back to Boston for an evening engagement. For, punctilious, at this youthful age, in all matters of duty or pleasure, he did not yield readily to external obstacles.

Among his greatest pleasures in Boston were theatres, concerts, and operas, to which his father's newspaper connections afforded him many a free admission. The zest for such entertainments has lasted through his life without leading him to dissipation. The Sunday evening rehearsals of the Handel and Haydn Society he enjoyed quite regularly under a like permit, often walking in and out from Cambridge to attend them. Though in musical demand at Cambridge among the chapel and glee-club choristers as a second tenor, he never made much pretence to vocal skill; but his thirst for good music was intense, and with all the great oratorios, while they were practised, he became quite familiar as a listener. Most of his spare pocket-money in these college days, such as came from prizes or presents, he would devote to classical works of music and standard authors; and he formed a library which seemed to grow, he hardly knew how.

Cultivating always methodical habits, James, upon leaving home and entering college, opened a private cash account of receipts and expenditures, which he has never since discontinued; casting up periodically what he had spent for various objects, and estimating such appropriations as might be needful for the coming year. But not quite so minute as some great men have been, he has found it convenient to embrace various small outlays under some specific head, and then carry out the total. "Sundries" he named such recurring items in his Freshman accounts.

James, also, at his father's request, opened a journal on the first of January, 1856; and this he continued to keep, not only through his college career, but in one form or another, down to the spring of 1868, when the pressure of manhood's cares made it too irksome for continuance. He used plain blank-books for this purpose, writing almost daily, until in 1862 he volunteered as a soldier and went into camp. During his military service, a large pocket-book, which he carried about in the vest, sufficed for diary and cash account together; and finally he made use of an annual printed calendar, which he would post about once a week in very brief phrase. Of his later substitute for diaries we shall speak hereafter. "For a busy man," says our author in reviewing his personal experience, "all such journalizing involves a great waste of time, and I do not strongly recommend it, unless some incentive stronger than the mere chronicle of commonplace life or of commonplace thoughts and emotions presents itself. If you are engaged upon some remarkable exploit or expedition, whose record will prove of historical value, keeping a faithful diary may be of much consequence; but otherwise it seems to me rather out of range with the rush and variety of modern life, and suits better the tranquil ways of the past and that remoteness into which newspapers and the telegraph seldom penetrate. To itemize from day to day in a line or a phrase is of very little use, whether for style or the habit of accuracy, or the delight of fertile reminiscence. Indeed, a well-kept cash account may serve your turn quite as well, besides proving useful in other ways. Self-examination at the close of each day, mental reflection, and the reporting habit, all find scope in such a task, if you find time enough to make the journal in literary excellence what it should be; but in that 'if' consists the difficulty. Literary excellence of expression seems better gained by writing for the press; and furthermore, by laying yourself out in your private correspondence and aiming, with the time thus gained, to describe well your thoughts and feelings, together with what you have seen, in letters to your intimate friends. If you can get these letters back to read in after life, or even retain copies of them when sending them off, you have, with letters received in return, a better means for reproducing your past life than in any diary which one honestly means to remain private." Schouler's college journal, we may mention in passing, struck the medium between dry chronicle and an outpouring of the inner heart. But he has not derived the pleasure in reading over his own production that he had predicted at the outset; and lest some one else might peruse its pages hereafter he has destroyed it.

James's Senior year at Harvard was full of development and activity. As one of the "Harvard Magazine" editors, and the most prominent of them, he took special burdens in its business management, besides composing much and preparing specially the number which belonged to a colleague who was absent, teaching school. By this time he was gaining fame in the class for serious as well as witty productions. His article on the origin of "Class Day," in the October, 1858, number, drew academic notice at a time when the faculty had talked of abolishing the institution; and in tracing out its ancient establishment, he laboriously searched old newspapers and old college pamphlets among the libraries of the Athenæum and Historical Society in Boston; so that we may call this paper his first real essay at historical exploration. Articles grave and gay appeared from his pen in the January, 1859, number, besides what he contributed to the "Editors' Table;" and in "Our Day Dreams," he pleaded earnestly for buoyancy and enthusiasm rather than a cynical spirit when entering upon the battle of life. From June, 1858, he had been an organist and choir conductor each Sunday, — first, at Dedham, and then at the Church of the Advent, Boston, during a transition period of the latter parish, and while its rectorship was vacant. Warmly attached to the Dedham church and its pastor, he was confirmed there, and joined the full Episcopal communion in the first month of 1859. With all these distractions from the curriculum, he kept up well in his studies, and gained in college rank. At the May exhibition preceding graduation, his part attracted unusual applause as a brilliant piece of composition eloquently spoken; "Douglas Jerrold" was his chosen subject, which he had worked up into a character sketch illustrating a warm disposition soured by long, unappreciated labor.

In the mean time, on March 14, 1859, class election day had been reached, — that anxious goal of college politics. Some wished Schouler for class orator, — a distinction which had been his own secret desire; but his star had risen too slowly and too late. Other circumstances were against him; and in a bitter party contest over class favors, from which he had kept aloof, his name was not presented as a candidate. But he received scattering votes for almost every class office, as a spontaneous recognition of merit. "You are honored by the whole class," said one of the class leaders after the meeting, "and you have not an enemy among them; another office would have been given to you if you had signified your wish to receive it."

Ever since May, 1858, his father's family had been back in Boston. William Schouler for nearly two years edited his Columbus paper, and performed effective work in organizing the political elements which firmly seated Republicanism in Ohio. During his five years' residence in that State he gained the personal friendship and confidence of such public leaders as Judge McLean, Thomas Corwin, and the man of massive statesmanship, Governor Salmon P. Chase. Abraham Lincoln once toiled up the "Gazette" staircase, when in Cincinnati, to have a political chat with him; and at Columbus, Howells, the famous fiction-writer of the future, set types for him. But Schouler was heartsick for Massachusetts, and for various friends in the old Bay State, now rising in influence, who urged him to return. A newspaper offer came at length from Boston; whereupon Governor Chase, reluctant to lose him, appointed him Adjutant-General of Ohio; hoping that the legislature would at once increase the trifling salary, and put the Ohio militia upon an organized footing. That bill failed of passage; and Schouler would defer acceptance of his Boston offer no longer. A public dinner was given him at the State capital as a testimonial on his departure; and Ohio long and affectionately cherished his name and political services. Schouler's welcome back to Boston and to the Boston editorial guild was no less hearty; and under his sanguine direction the reorganized "Bee" — or "Atlas and Bee," as he chose to have it styled — started into circulation with some of those strong leaders of other days. But the venture was ill-advised, and with no solid capital behind it served merely for temporary aid in establishing a new political party. Handicapped with indigence and a precarious salary, the editor of this superfluous Boston press did, nevertheless, the expected work in fusing some of the old Whig element of Massachusetts into this new Republican coalition whose national triumph was approaching.

When the son's organ engagement at the Church of the Advent ended in April, 1859, the kind Dr. Shattuck, who was senior warden, offered to the young collegian a place among the instructors of St. Paul's School, at Concord, New Hampshire, — that famous institution for boys which his benevolence was then founding. The tender was wholly unexpected; and as no credentials were asked, he had probably looked up the student's college record for himself. After a visit to the school, whose principal, Rev. Henry A. Coit, received him most cordially, James concluded an arrangement to take effect just after Class Day; and with this suddenly disclosed field of work came a new outlook upon active life. A vacancy in the chair of English literature happened to exist at Trinity College; and with a new hope of influence not unfounded for obtaining it, Schouler determined to devote whatever spare time his next year's work might afford, to post-graduate study in the appropriate branches. Early in his Junior year he had made up his mind to be a lawyer, and his father, when consulted, had approved the idea; but now, exchanging this plan for the other, he presented the set of Blackstone already on his book-shelves to a classmate who was sure to need it. Few Harvard graduates begin their serious career in life on the Senior leave-taking day, so as to make graduation and Commencement Day an episode to toil. But such was our author's experience; and among the distractions of a tutor at Concord he prepared his Commencement part and returned to Cambridge to rejoin his class for the final exercises of July 20. The subject of his Commencement disquisition selected by himself was "Doctor Thomas Arnold," which, inspired by "Tom Brown's School Days," he treated, after much the same fashion as his Senior exhibition part, in characterizing the life-work of that Christian teacher at Rugby. Something in the speaker's manner and matter seems to have made an impression; for a Boston evening paper mentioned that Governor Banks pronounced this the best piece in a programme of thirty or more parts. The class of 1859 numbers many men illustrious in the various walks of life, though others of the highest promise on Commencement Day lost early their lives in the course of the Civil War.

One little incident of this graduation may be here related for the first time. After the degrees had been announced, the class marshals went upon the stage to receive the baccalaureate sheep-skins, adorned with pink ribbon, and distribute them among the graduating candidates. Schouler's degree was not among them, which caused one or two expressions of concern; but he kept silence, mistrusting the cause, and found, on arriving home, that his father, who had undertaken to attend to his term-bill, had been unable to raise the money. "Father's mortification," says our author, "must have been greater than my own; for mother told me afterwards, that he sat under the elms on Boston Common, that evening, and shed silent tears over the want that had caused the son he loved a moment's ignominy." The money was procured next day, the term-bill paid, and the parchment handed over; and James returned to Concord, there to continue work until the vacation of St. Paul's School came in October.

VI.

1860-1866.

JAMES SCHOULER was twenty years of age when he graduated from college; a young man marked among his classmates at Harvard for the happy blending of talent, diligence, and sobriety, — one who personally looked forward and urged others to look forward to active life with high aims and a high sense of honor. He appeared in blooming and vigorous health, with full visage and ruddy complexion, and without a sign of physical defect; his height, which was five feet eight inches, set off a well-proportioned figure. Other young men pronounced him handsome when well dressed, but one who seldom gave great thought to the tailor; to women he seemed always handsome. Praise never seemed to turn his head or make him conceited, but rather encouraged him to do well. His photograph, taken with the rest of the graduating class, was a strikingly good one; showing a well-shaped head, well poised upon square shoulders; a beaming expression of countenance; a smooth oval face (for the mustache was worn later), which exposed a large mouth and full lips, strong index of the thought or feeling that stirred within; a good nose and chin, the heritage of the Schoulers; a high and intellectual forehead; and soft hazel eyes, full of expression, which were perhaps his handsomest feature. "A fine face and head, indeed," said a good physiognomist who was shown one of these photographs. "That young man is sprightly and intelligent; but I should judge from the height of the back of his head that his organ of firmness is pretty fully developed, and that when he takes up an idea he sticks to it."

Of his personal character, as it impressed members of the college faculty, the Plummer Professor [1] thus wrote to a friend a few months later: "He appears to possess excellent qualities for an academic officer. There is a certain soundness in his nature readily felt by all about him; a genuineness which is of the utmost worth in a society of young men. His mind and heart are full of health. There is a fine energy in his will, coupled with a conciliating gentleness and modesty of manner. He at once gives and consistently maintains the impression of a thorough manliness." After dwelling upon his capacity and strength as a scholar, and the concentration of studies which had probably carried him since graduation far beyond the respectable rank he reached in his class, he added: "Should his youth be thought an objection (to a professorship) the dignity of his bearing goes far to outweigh that objection." And a former teacher, the superintendent of the Boston schools, referring to "his scholarly habits, his purity and elevation of character, and his generous ambition," said "without any qualification he is by far the best man for such a post whom I know of his age or very near his age."

"The grand virtue of men is sincerity," Schouler's father had once written to him; and the son did not

---

[1] Since Bishop of the Episcopal Church in Central New York.

forget that precept. In the quiet retreat of New Hampshire, he strengthened his critical knowledge of the Latin tongue, which occupied most of his instruction hours. He also conducted the chapel music, organizing the first choir from among the school-boys; and during all the leisure time he could command from his routine work he studied the great English poets from Chaucer down, and the great prose writers, besides dipping into French and German translation. Modern history and rhetoric found also appropriate hours in a schedule varied by needful recreation, which he prepared, ranging from early dawn until bedtime. The school, since so famous, and now spreading out its vast array of imposing buildings over a large landscape, was as yet confined to a single stuccoed dwelling-house, to which was added a wing for school-room and dormitory. A pretty brick chapel stood close by; and the number of boys had increased to forty, which was thought a handsome limit. Pupils and teachers were so much of the time together under one roof, for meals, studies, sleep, and even recreation, that one longed sometimes to escape from himself and find a solitude. But amid distractions that cost the high-minded Dr. Coit himself many a nervous headache and night of sleepless anxiety the noble work was pursued; and our young Harvard graduate felt and aided the dignity of it. Not familiar with the boys, and yet friendly and considerate towards them, and gaining their warm respect in return, he went through his tasks without serious difficulty, and maintained a steady discipline. In the few instances where boyish mischief tested him to get the upper hand he quietly contrived to disconcert it. His poetical muse did not wholly slumber through all this grind of study and recitation; for on the anniversary day of the school, in January, 1860, an ode was sung of his own composition.

On March 20, 1860, James reached majority, and thus made birthday record in his diary: "If in after years I turn back to this leaf, and read its record of good resolutions, ardent hopes, and earnest prayers for the future, may I be able to add that the life to which I now look forward, was not spent in vain. I commence to-day to keep my accounts in a ledger and day-book (or journal), and shall hereafter keep them thus. I commenced my accounts of cash expenses when I entered college, and have kept them ever since; but to-day I close the book. On taking an inventory of personal effects I find I may consider myself worth $138.12." If all this grand book-keeping seems whimsical for a youth of scanty means to apply to tailor bills and salary payments, the method thus pursued worked out good grist afterwards; for it was largely due to his correct and systematic habits in these petty finances, besides his conscientious distinctions between *meum* and *tuum*, that he secured confidence for the management and settlement of estates which constituted so large a part of his professional business a few years later; procuring him ample bondsmen, while he possessed very little property of his own.

The year 1860 saw a brighter dawn for the Schouler household, and relief, for a good space at least, from the son's family anxieties. His next brother William, whom he had brought with him to Concord, to coach in college studies with reference to the ministry, worked into an admirable arrangement with Dr. Coit, which gave him the full training he had deeply at heart, and his independence at the same time. In Massachusetts, towards the close of March, his father received from Governor Banks the appointment of Adjutant-General of the State, — an appointment promised in old friendship months earlier, but deferred because of some military opposition stirred up by the incumbent of the office. The latter procured a protest from the militia major-generals against a change; and this proving in vain, a complimentary banquet to himself was arranged which three of the Governor's aids attended in rebellious dissatisfaction. Banks promptly revoked the commissions of these aids, fully equal to such an emergency; his staff was reorganized for the better, and William Schouler entered upon the duties of adjutant-general on Monday the 2nd of April.

With this welcome change of pursuits, William Schouler made his residence at Lynn, where, near the Swampscott line, a modest seaside cottage became his family home for the next ten famous years; and where, too, James passed many happy summers, and sometimes the winter months besides. It was part of an estate owned by his wife's brother, who, with his own wife, occupied a neighboring house, making the summer reunion complete. The Schoulers were lovers of nature, and felt always a tenderness for this little cottage, resplendent in the eastern sun, with the changeful ocean in full sight beating out its daily harmonies upon the beach. And at Boston in his pleasant suite of offices on the southwestern corner of the Bulfinch State House, — in 1860 quiet enough as compared with the scenes twelve months later, — our new adjutant-general attended to his easy routine duties, receiving congratulations which poured in upon him from every part of the State. Personal friends presented him with his military uniform and sword, and on the earliest parades honored by the Governor and staff, his popularity was clearly seen. With a single clerk for assistant, as the law then provided, and for himself a salary of eighteen hundred dollars, which in its certainty seemed munificent, he retained the capable subordinate of his predecessor, and began at once to pay from his own quarterly savings the private debts which had greatly harassed him.

A first year's public experience, and the last while our old militia peace establishment lasted, is worth a moment's notice. General Schouler first of all stopped an abuse of perquisites by which his predecessor had eked out an income. A Boston firm which furnished supplies to the State arsenal sent its bill to the adjutant-general, which was paid. Next it enclosed a personal check by way of percentage to the adjutant-general; and he deposited the check promptly in the treasury to the credit of the Commonwealth, and ceased dealing with that firm. In the autumn the Prince of Wales visited Boston with his suite, and special escorts took place; and it pleased Governor Banks greatly to find that his new adjutant-general ended the year with an unexpended balance, having carried his department upon a saving of four thousand dollars over the year preceding, notwithstanding these ovations.

Nathaniel P. Banks retired from office at the close of this year; and the fearless John A. Andrew succeeded him in early January, 1861. Adjutant-General Schouler added paragraphs to his report of 1860, as it now went through the press, forecasting the approach of civil war, and advising among other specific measures the issue of a general order for reorganizing the active militia of Massachusetts, and preparing to place it on a war footing. "You are far too modest, General," said our war Governor to him, a few years later, when a boastful brigadier of the present Massachusetts militia, who rose to national renown, claimed to have inspired Andrew with the famous "General Order No. 4," of January 16: "that order originated in your own recommendation, already in print, and the militia preparations of that winter which equipped Massachusetts for ready action were the fruits of our own concert and consultation." The son remembers well that while many influential citizens of the State were blaming the new Executive in that waiting winter for what they thought rash and incendiary preparations, he had his own grave doubts and stated them to his father; but the response was such as assured him that all was right, and that the father was heart and soul with Governor Andrew in the whole business. Each had his own national acquaintance in Washington, and advices that confirmed his military foresight.

James Schouler had placed a year as the proper limit of his work at St. Paul's School, unless the way proved clear to the appointment he wished at Trinity College. His kind principal, and several influential trustees of that college, were his friends, and aided the promotion so zealously that, a vacancy occurring at this time in Trinity's presidency, the prominent candidate for successor promised, if chosen, to bring him into the faculty. But temporary opposition to this candidate developed when the trustees met. The presidency was offered to another and declined; and meanwhile the vacant professorship of English literature went to a person of means who offered to serve without a salary. James, in consequence, announced his purpose of leaving St. Paul's School when the summer term of 1860 ended, and taking up the study of law. But Dr. Coit, who had more than once urged him to take orders, was reluctant to lose this assistant, and offered many inducements for him to remain and make his life-work at the school with leisure for liberal studies. He predicted the future enlargement of that institution just as came later to pass. Though touched by such deep sympathy and appreciation,— for Dr. Coit was a most lovable man,— Schouler adhered to his own views. "I am not a recluse by temperament," was his reply, "and I must live among men, and not boys." They parted friends for life; and with a brother left behind for a while among the instructors, James often revisited this haven of good influences.

Once more in Massachusetts our author took up his law studies with zest, living at the parental home by the seashore. By early October, 1860, he was deep in Blackstone, which he would study each day at the State library, looking in upon the courts for an afternoon's inspiration, or reciting to himself what he had read as he strolled upon the common. On the 20th of November he entered the office of George D. Guild, Esq., in the famous "4 Court Street" building. He was his preceptor's first and only law student; for that promising member of the Boston bar, honorable and judicious, died untimely in 1862. Here James used the desk assigned to him so long as he continued a law student; finding in an older man who had only taken him in for instruction to oblige a friend, a genial personal acquaintance. Schouler did not confine himself to the law alone; but taking advantage of hours which he was free

to arrange to suit himself, he wrote a sketch of
New England life, which, rejected by the "Atlantic
Monthly," found its way into print, but not fame,
through the medium of an obscure magazine which
paid nothing for contributions, — "a better fate,"
says our author, "than the essay deserved." He also
explored at home by the evening lamp such books
as "Judge Story's Life and Letters" and the
"Federalist." "I am deeply interested in the
political history of our country," he records in
January, 1861; and a campaign book, which fell
somewhat earlier into his hands, "Hall's Republican
Party," with its historical sketch of political parties
in the United States, stirred him earliest to make
that subject his own for literary treatment some
day.

This was a winter of exciting suspense in public
affairs, and the diary of our author shows how deeply
his own interest was engaged. Though entering
upon his majority as a Seward Republican, he had
studied up the candidate, and believed him true and
trustworthy. He rejoiced in Abraham Lincoln's
triumphal election in November, and earnestly hoped
that there would be "no more compromises to secure
the increase of slavery." A passage in one of Judge
Story's letters which he came across seemed so pertinent to the winter's discussion in Congress that he
copied it out and got it inserted in one of the newspapers. He and his law preceptor, whose politics
differed from his own, had many a characteristic
office discussion on this subject, the one in fiery
earnest, the other moderate and calm. At length in
April, 1861, Fort Sumter fell, and all Boston blazed
with enthusiasm as the militia regiments of Massachu-

setts went forth, already organized and equipped, to the defence of the nation.

The adjutant-general had not been home for three days, and the son went up to the State House. "James," said his father, pointing to a heap of unopened letters, "you must help me out in this correspondence; I need your services." So the young law student became installed in the adjutant-general's inner office; there performing the duty of a private secretary, and working off details disconnected with rosters and commissions. He kept informed and imparted information on all topics of interest to soldiers and town authorities, incidentally making the acquaintance of the distinguished callers who thronged the State House at this time, of those earlier officers who recruited and led the Massachusetts Volunteers to the front, and of the Governor and Executive officials besides. The Governor's Council fixed a fair standard of recompense for the new force of clerks in the military department; and out of his salary our author in less than six months repaid the uncle in full who had assisted him at college, and thus stood free from all money obligations. He was not tempted, however, to turn into a new channel and make civil or military service his life pursuit; but pursued his law studies still, as he might, availing himself of the precious hours of evening or early morning, and poring, as he travelled in the train, over the solid volume in law-calf which he carried back and forth. By January 18, 1862, he had passed his written examination before the Supreme Court in Suffolk County — "a very creditable one," as Chief-Justice Bigelow afterwards told him — and was formally admitted to the Massachusetts bar on the 23rd of the same month. When he ended finally his labors at the State House, he found lying upon the desk a commission of justice of the peace issued to him without an application; an unexpected token of thoughtfulness and goodwill from the Governor, such as endeared that famous man so greatly to all who ever served under him.

With an office in Niles's Block, whose expenses were shared by another young lawyer and college friend, and with a shining sign under his window, Schouler sought clients, and was not long kept waiting. A personal friend had handed him a note for collection, as the first piece of business following his admission to the bar. An inevitable swarm of soldier claimants sought him from the State House which his scrupulous father avoided all agency in directing. Our author's decided preference was for jury trials; and his first case of the kind came at once from the adjutant-general's office to launch his reputation. The colored messenger of that bureau, officiously but innocently, and most probably as the dupe of some hangers-on at the State House, had passed a forged soldier's check, and was prosecuted for doing so in the United States District Court. The adjutant-general believed his innocence and stood by him; but in those times an accused person could not testify at his trial, nor was evidence for the messenger procurable at all but that of good character. His young counsel, who served without recompense, conducted the case so skilfully upon his unsupported theory of innocence, and made so earnest a plea that the jury disagreed upon two trials, and the prosecution dropped. This messenger showed his gratitude by constant fidelity to the adjutant-general, serving for many years at the State House, and gaining a life-long renown among his own race for military talent and probity.

With his second brother John appointed to the Naval Academy in 1861, James was the only son left with his sisters in the parental household; and for a winter residence near Boston, where he might vote and claim his domicile, he had chosen Dedham, the county town of Norfolk. Friends welcomed him here, and the good rector of his former church made him the Sunday-school superintendent. His Boston practice brought him a self-supporting income for the very first year. But he followed the progress of the Union strife with a constant uneasiness lest he should fall short of the duty he owed as a citizen. The first Bull Run battle of 1861, disheartening as it was, had impressed him with the true logic of our national situation. "We must now forego," says his diary when the news arrived, "the expectation of crushing the rebellion at once, but must patiently pursue a long war; and a bloody revolution is to be ushered in. I do not despair of the republic; but I think the downfall of slavery is to be a result of this revolution."

The summer of 1862, which followed with its gloomy disasters, deepened his desire to be at the front with braver youth who were sacrificing for their country. He was now twenty-two years of age.

> "Shall I be carried to the sky
> On flowery beds of ease?"

he asks himself in his diary, quoting a well-known hymn. He took part in July at a Dedham town-meeting called to raise volunteers, making there the first political speech of his life. When in early August Massachusetts was called upon for nineteen thousand nine months' men, he could hold back no longer, but enlisted in a Boston company which his office-mate had begun raising. Released from this roll under an authority with a popular Dedham youth to raise a Dedham company, their conjoint appeal, with the co-operation of selectmen and committee, brought the maximum number to their standard in a single day. Young men, the flower of the town, enlisted. Schouler's friend was chosen first lieutenant and he the second. An older man from outside was summoned as captain; and the company soon went into camp at Readville, attached to the Forty-third Regiment of Massachusetts Volunteers. Professional business was now turned over for non-combatants to manage. Drill, tactics, military study, superseded civil pursuits, and, like Gibbon, our author may say that an experience of this kind was not without its later help towards preparing historical narrative. But, as young Schouler wrote his father from the field, he had gone into the service, not for fame nor from any relish for military life; but solely to perform what a young and able-bodied citizen owed to his country.

On the 12th of November, 1862, the Forty-third Massachusetts reached by transport the North Carolina coast; and except for the Goldsboro' expedition passed most of its time quietly about Newbern, like most of the other nine months' troops from that State. But Lieutenant Schouler, detailed at once for Signal Service, on reaching the front, learned the Myer code with some other nine months' officers, and gained a far wider occupation than would have been possible in the regimental line. He served thus in various staff positions with illustrious officers of the army and navy. He was with a river fleet of gunboats which were sent to co-operate with the Goldsboro' movement, being once under fire, but otherwise encountering incidents more humorous than heroic. He took his turn with flag and torch in charge of a lonely signal-station on the line of the railroad between Newbern and Morehead City. He served on General Naglee's staff in a winter's expedition to South Carolina, and after being detached for duty in that department, he accompanied General Stevenson's forces to North Edisto inlet at the close of March, 1863, in which harbor he served on board various naval gunboats, communicating with the shore, until, towards the close of May, at his own request, he was sent back to North Carolina in season to rejoin his regiment on its return home. While at Edisto inlet he went on board some of the new and curious ironclads brought thither. He saw the splendid fleet of Admiral Dupont sail forth on a bright Sunday morning to capture Charleston, and then return crestfallen after a mere reconnoissance. Reconnoitring previously before Charleston harbor in the vessel to which he belonged, he discerned Fort Sumter and Sullivan's Island through his signal telescope. Homeward bound from Newbern in June with his regiment once more, he passed a night off Yorktown, went into temporary camp at Old Point Comfort, and touched port at Baltimore about the first of July. The glorious news of Gettysburg was here received; and part of his regiment, though claiming that their time was up, went towards Harper's Ferry to aid in the effort to intercept Lee's retreat. While on Maryland heights doing provost duty as officer of the day, among these grand and picturesque surroundings, our young lieutenant saw the tattered Army of the Potomac pass by in vain pursuit of the enemy. Back once more by slow trains to Baltimore, and entitled for this special service to the badge of the Sixth Army Corps, the fragment of this Forty-third Massachusetts Regiment proceeded to Boston, and on the morning of July 21 the troops breakfasted and greeted their rejoicing friends on Boston Common; next proceeding to Boylston Hall, where they broke ranks and dispersed.

James's pocket diary and letters to the family describe very fully this army experience; and whatever his secret dread or privations, they kept up the constant strain of loyalty and cheerfulness. In personal habits he had always been abstinent, though by no means an anchorite; and during his army life, with so many young men of good parentage under him to whom example was everything, he resolved not to smoke nor drink a drop; and that resolve he faithfully kept. As for smoking, he has often said, that though his father was an inveterate consumer of the weed, he went through college and through army life without ever indulging the habit; after which he took it up in moderation for social companionship alone. From the day of his enlistment he appeared constantly confident that he should return home in health and safety; and he was so carelessly secure of life, that, having his revolver stolen soon after reaching the seat of war, he finished his long campaign with no weapon about his person except his sword. Camp life had at once made him rugged and hearty, the picture of health when he started on his perilous mission; and so it continued until the journey home. But while encamped on Federal Hill near Baltimore, a night's exposure to a heavy rain brought on a fever and ague so acute that he dragged his way on the Harper's Ferry march with the utmost difficulty, and reached home again pale, feeble, and utterly exhausted. A few weeks of tender care at the seaside cottage brought him out, as it seemed, all right again; after which, at the close of August, 1863, he was sent to Washington, under special State House orders, to procure copies of the deficient muster rolls of Massachusetts troops at the war department. This first visit to the national capital, though in the hot season of recess, was an unfailing delight, and fixed him in the wish to connect himself more intimately with the historic district upon the Potomac. While at Washington he gained a vivid impression of our capital city in its war aspect: he strolled through its deserted temple of legislation and the busy Executive buildings; he met President Lincoln four times face to face; he conversed with Secretary Chase, who received him cordially; he dined at the family table with Secretary Seward, — a special attention with incidents which he never forgot; and he took in the faces and forms of Stanton, Welles, Halleck, and others of the magnates who then presided over the gigantic strife. Returning to Massachusetts, he adjusted mistakes, whereby he had been drafted in two places while soldiering the past winter; and by the first of October, at the age of twenty-four, he was once more in Niles's Block, Boston, with his former law companion, sharing a more commodious office than before, and starting the professional life anew. As a tribute to his military efficiency he received from Washington headquarters the tempting offer of a captaincy in the new Signal Corps, which had been lately organized under an Act of Congress, and, as its officers hoped, was virtually and permanently a part of the regular army; but he heeded his mother's wishes and declined all further military life.

Clients now poured in upon young Schouler again; and most of all the war claimants, whom he tried vainly to bar out, so as to give to court practice the full precedence. In November, 1863, Governor Andrew appointed him a public administrator of Suffolk County; an office still retained, which familiarized him with probate business and the settlement of estates. This appointment made it needful for him to leave Dedham finally and make Suffolk County his place of residence; but he still passed his summers with parents and sisters at the seashore, they, too, sojourning usually in Boston during winter months, where he resided. His professional practice was at once lucrative, as recommenced, and yielded him a handsome support; so that with a trifling balance which he had saved from his army pay, he was now able to start his little capital by investing in a government bond. His office-mate soon leaving the legal profession for journalism in another city, Schouler rented the whole office, and then added the adjoining one for his own business needs; presently making room in the suite for his college classmate and constant friend, Ellis L. Motte. He showed himself public-spirited in politics; he read the Declaration of Independence at Boston's Fourth of July celebration in 1864, and next found himself selected to present and read the resolutions at a Presidential ratification meeting held by the Republicans about ten weeks later at Faneuil Hall. After speaking at various local rallies he cast in November the first national vote of his life for President Lincoln's re-election.

But now appeared marked symptoms of a physical disorder which was soon to suppress the social activities of our author and turn the current of impetuous achievement into a new and more quiet channel. He had during his college career perceived a partial deafness in the left ear, of which he only made jest, as a positive convenience whenever hilarity went on too noisily about him. Few noticed this difficulty at all, and none had thought it the slightest hindrance to his chosen pursuits before he returned from the seat of war. Watchful of himself, however, he consulted a physician for the first time in November, 1859, as his diary shows us; and Dr. Edward Reynolds of Boston told him that on the left ear was the scar of an ulcer which hindered the drum from vibrating, — a trouble that could not be remedied. Soon after young Schouler came home from his army service, and in close connection with the fever and ague which he had contracted in Baltimore, deafness spread to the other ear, and those at home quickly detected his difficulty. On July 24, 1863, he began a regular course of treatment with a Boston physician, reputed a specialist in such cases, — "the first," observes our author, "among many courses of one kind and another, which I have patiently tried from year to year without obtaining the slightest relief." Insidious in approach, as it always continued, producing neither dizziness, ringing in the ears, nor other mental inconvenience in the least degree, — the dread foe speedily advanced; and by another year and after a slight recurrence of his army fever in July, 1864, people began to perceive that he heard imperfectly, and they raised their voices slightly when accosting him.

During October, 1864, Schouler consulted in New

York City an eminent specialist, who told him the nature of his difficulty, and strongly advised him to place himself under the care of Dr. Edward H. Clarke of his own city as the very best man for relief. "See," he added, "whether he does not explain your case as I do." Our patient did so, and found that the two physicians agreed in their diagnosis upon a personal examination. There was a calcareous deposit within the drum of each ear, whose tendency, from some inner predisposing cause, was to thicken, and thus prevent the drum from vibrating properly. But whence this predisposing cause no medical adviser ever explained. "All calcareous deposit," once said a European doctor to our author, "originates in rheumatism;" and the rheumatic sickness which he brought home from the war was his first real departure from sound health since an early childhood remarkably free from the average child's ailments. He sometimes caught cold and had coughs; but so, too, have others in normal health. No perceptible relief has come from treatment on the catarrhal theory nor by electricity or massage. Allopathy, homœopathy, perforation of the drum, have alike failed to improve his hearing or even to check its deterioration. To various doctors he has suggested that perhaps a scalp-wound or a laceration of the right hand, both injuries of boyhood which left permanent scars, had something to do with this deposit; but they reject each hypothesis. No hereditary deafness is traceable in the parental stock. But as for Dr. Clarke, of whose advice he now availed himself in Boston while he could, that eminent physician inspired him with great confidence by the skill he showed, by breadth of information, and by what among medical advisers is so often lacking, — fertility in resources. His own professional effort was to produce absorption of calcareous matter in the blood; but at the same time leaving no other experiment untried, he sent out his patient to try electricity, and afterwards recommended him to a young aurist who was fresh from European schools and the latest discoveries. When friends of the author had spoken of a wonder-working German instrument for operations upon the deaf, he produced such an instrument from his closet and showed very clearly why it could not benefit one like him.

In short, from all the many medical men here and abroad, whom our author has since consulted in the vain hope of at least arresting the progress of his physical disability, he has extracted no advice more alleviating than that which this most admirable physician bestowed as the epitome of his own experience in the case, — to "avoid over-work and take care of the general health."

VII.

1866–1872.

General William Schouler, by virtue of the exalted military station which he filled in Massachusetts, during the whole period of our Civil War, and while the noble John A. Andrew was Governor, remains among the devoted citizens of that State who best deserve an imperishable remembrance. With such a chief to serve under in his full prime, and such a chance for public usefulness, he felt the stimulus to high exertion, and did his best faithfully, patiently, and patriotically under the immense pressure of new labors which were imposed upon his office. In the fearful trial through which Massachusetts was now summoned to pass, he showed in all their strength the shining qualities of his character; so that whatever fellow-citizen might possibly have excelled him in a certain polish that comes from scholastic training, no man could, all in all, have been so well qualified for the adjutant-generalship at this time as he who went through these tremendous years of war with his executive commander-in-chief to the costly goal of victory.

Our adjutant-general was not content with the orderly functions of a bureau which, of all others, is apt to get all too readily into the grooves of martinet and punctilious authority. He organized and recruited Massachusetts regiments, consolidating fragmentary bodies in the State camps, and applying immeasurable tact and kindness to reduce the friction so constantly engendered among raw military aspirants and raw enlisted men, and to draw all together into harmony for the common weal. Besides other high officials and legislators in his own State, he had national military organizers and officials to encounter, and to move smoothly with, in a common task which could not possibly escape asperities on the one hand nor permit of haughty compulsion on the other. "It was in this place," records one good observer, "that he had the best opportunity to show that warmth of sympathy and true democratic instinct which no man ever possessed in a higher degree." Nor did his labors cease with the routine performance of such duties. "He worked for the soldier," says another, "with all the devotion of a personal friend. While marshalling and directing large numbers of armed men, he did not forget that they were torn from the homes of a lifelong peace to do the unaccustomed work of cruel war. Not a man went to the front from Massachusetts during the whole of that dreary period, without feeling that the friendship and sympathy of the adjutant-general accompanied him. He knew the stuff of which our regiments were made."

Easily assumed by spectators to have failings for such a task, though admitted by all who knew him as one of the most genial of men, having qualifications of zeal, industry, and honesty which none could deny, he proved his higher directing qualities from year to year, until executive and legislature accorded in their full confidence. In fact, his long and intimate knowledge of Massachusetts, not to add of men and politics in Washington and at the northwest, was beyond that of all others who worked at the State House; while his long journalistic experience made him fluent and expressive with the pen, — an advantage by no means slight in those times of multitudinous composition. As for the more technical work of his bureau, Senator Wilson conveyed the commendation of the war department at Washington that Massachusetts rolls and records there were the most perfect of all the States. Nor content with this, he wove into his annual reports, which were marvels of spontaneous industry, such full and accurate accounts of the experience of Massachusetts volunteers in the field, as circulated those public documents far and wide for fireside reading, and furnished to other States an example of adjutant-general and war annalist at the time wholly unique. And thus it worked out that the new Governor, who himself had not fully understood the capacity of the man whom he found already in place, began the military labors which our President's first call devolved upon him, by detaching the quartermaster and ordnance bureaus from the control of his adjutant-general, and transmitting orders to his chief of staff through a coterie of military aids; but as time went on he drew more and more closely into a personal military relation with his adjutant-general, attracted by the latter's sagacious counsel on all difficult points, his faithful disinterestedness and wide experience, his unassuming talents, and, not least of all, by those traits of good fellowship which they had in common, and which gradually endeared them to one another like brothers in arms. "The relations that existed between these two men," it has been well said by a contemporary, "were of the closest and most affectionate character;" and "their friendship grew out of the innate generosity and manliness of both; for neither could brook meanness or littleness in any of its manifestations."

The adjutant-general's intercourse with his own bureau subordinates was marked by the tenderest solicitude; and while he kept them up to their work, he erred, if at all, on the side of kindliness and good-nature. For instance, the clerk who succeeded James as private secretary, the son of an old friend, came too well recommended; for though a neat copyist, it proved that he could not compose readily nor accurately; yet, rather than wound a father he loved or a son whose faithfulness was unimpeachable, the adjutant-general went on through the war, bearing the disadvantage as he might, though compelled in consequence to elaborate the drafts of most official letters, while harassed with other drudgery.

While organizing well, General Schouler pursued a primary system of his own; which was to bind his bureau by red tape as little as possible, consistently with general order and accuracy, and to make it headquarters whither all might resort, the highest or the humblest, man or woman, and gain information and comforting words for those far away to whom the nation and Commonwealth owed a debt of gratitude. Accordingly, while he left military commissions and orders to the supervision of his faithful clerk, now promoted to a staff officer, and confided other routine duties to capable heads, he reserved to himself and to his inner office the immense miscellaneous correspondence and public intercourse of the department. Those familiar with our general were amazed at his facility in working off all inquiries by mail or in person, so as to inform without offending; doing, if possible, the thing wanted and in the quickest way. His grasp of the day's duties was remarkable; and his secretary, asking at noon how certain letters by the morning's mail that he had glanced at were to be answered, would find that he had orally responded and settled the point while down town. A flavor of hearty interest quite characteristic pervaded in consequence his busy emanations; few men could so well combine social and political talk with business. The Governor liked to refer papers to him for a formal report, because the general not only stated difficulties well, but was sure to suggest some sensible plan for escaping them. As for those huge annual reports, they, like his volumes of military history afterwards, were planned, arranged, and written out entirely by himself; and he would work over them in the long evening hours of winter as a labor of love while he boarded with his family in Boston. Often, as men passed by on Beacon Street while pursuing their evening pleasures, did they see across the State House terraces the light shining through the brown window-shade at the southwest corner where the adjutant-general sat composing at his solitary desk.

The close of the war found General Schouler happy in his appreciated public labors. The Massachusetts legislature, unsolicited, had passed an Act which raised his rank from brigadier to major-general; it had also increased his salary to a self-supporting standard, though, as he sometimes remarked, he would have preferred his original eighteen hundred a year payable in gold, had that been possible. John A. Andrew, on retiring from office after the war had ended, paid him the worthiest of tributes in an Executive Order which he purposely penned and issued as the last official act of his own illustrious career as Governor.[1] Under his son's legal direction, William Schouler had recently discharged the long-sustained burden of personal debt by assigning over his share in his deceased father's estate; so that if not owning a dollar at this time, he could not be said to owe one. Watchful of convivial temptations, whose danger he well understood, he had lately pledged himself to total abstinence, that nothing might be wanting for leaving to his children the legacy of an unblemished name.

One would have thought that an adjutant-general of such a character and services was sure of retaining

---

[1] As the full scope of the historical compliment thereby intended is sometimes misapprehended, this executive military order, composed by Governor Andrew himself, is subjoined: —

January 6, 1866.

Executive Military Order No. 1.

The Governor and Commander-in-Chief, at the moment of retiring from office, as his last official act, tenders this expression of grateful and cordial respect to Major-General William Schouler, Adjutant-General of the Commonwealth, who has served the country, the Commonwealth, and his chief with constancy, devotion, ability, and success, throughout his administration. JOHN A. ANDREW.

long his place. "You will hold it all your life," said a member of the retiring Governor's staff, a fellow-citizen of the incoming Executive. Yet adjutant-generals hold office in Massachusetts at the sole will of the Governor and Commander-in-Chief; nor did this single year, 1866, end before he had been hurled headlong from his military office with cruel opprobrium and privation. "Enjoy your military honors and let politics alone," had been the prudent advice of his son; but to one of the father's habits and temperament this was scarcely possible. During the war he had applauded the President's sagacious policy like any civilian voter; and after Lincoln's death, he, like Governor Andrew, deprecated vindictiveness in dealing with the South, and believed, with all generosity for the negro, that the lately rebellious States must ultimately depend upon their natural leaders. So when General Benjamin F. Butler, of Lowell, a man of methods and influence long obnoxious, swooped upon the Essex district as a candidate for Congress, pledged in advance to impeach President Johnson and make things hard for the rebels, General Schouler, as a resident voter of that district, opposed the nomination, and, failing to defeat it, announced in a published letter his intention to vote against him. Butler was chosen, however, and demanded of the new Governor in revenge the displacement of the adjutant-general. Precipitately, perhaps weakly, Governor Bullock complied with the demand; Schouler was summarily removed, and in the correspondence which led up to this result, the Executive stated, as the sole reason for such action, that each public officer was under an obligation to vote for the regular candidate of the party.

Though deeply grieved by this indignity, General

Schouler was not ruined or wrecked in consequence. He confided the whole correspondence to his son in the afternoon of December 14, 1866, when the catastrophe was complete, asking him to break the news to the household before his own return home at night. "The only one," says this letter, "with whom I have conferred, and who knows all about it, is Governor Andrew." James did as requested; and by the time the husband and father reached Lynn his family received him with the cheering consolation that a man needs in such moments. James proposed at once a plan for their office connection, more especially in the war-claims branch of his practice; and the offer was accepted. The sympathy of the adjutant-general's warm friends also expressed itself, as soon as the situation was made public, in a circular letter signed by many of the most eminent citizens of the State, which Governor Andrew procured and headed, and which invited him to write a history of Massachusetts in the war. This invitation he also accepted, entering at once upon the collection of materials, but refusing all recompense in advance of publication, such as his friends in their kindness were prepared to bestow.

This work, comprised in two large volumes, the labor of his next five years of prolific activity, was the perfection of his noble memorial of the State's patriotic action and record; minute, faithful, and interesting, as critics have pronounced it, ranking among the best of local war histories, and necessarily engraving the author's name upon each living page. The first volume was given to the political and military development of Massachusetts affairs during those momentous years, — and was indeed a noble tribute to Governor Andrew, whose untimely death he mourned while preparing it; the second grouped, in a more statistical form, the detailed work of the different cities and towns. A third volume, which General Schouler projected, but did not live to compose, would have narrated the tale of Massachusetts regiments in the field, and its basis would necessarily have been his own annual reports. Under the office partnership he had formed he was practically his own publisher; and the Massachusetts legislature, to its lasting credit, rendered the publication a pecuniary success by ordering a thousand copies of each volume for State distribution.

The office partnership of father and son — though the latter alone was a member of the bar — worked out its expected advantage, in the union of high mental qualities and practical experience in which each might supplement the other; at the same time that the war-claims business, which each disliked, was felt to be a dwindling one, and other resources were exploited. Besides the petty bounty and pension cases came in various large miscellaneous claims, to which the late adjutant-general's skill and experience were applied successfully. Their most important work together lay in applying a judicial correction to the discretion of the treasury officials, hitherto arbitrary. James had made a careful study of the history and jurisdiction of the new Court of Claims, which an exhaustive article from his pen on "Government Claims" set forth about this time in the "American Law Review;" and to that tribunal at Washington the Schoulers brought a number of petitions on behalf of war claimants who had been denied relief at the departments by what appeared to them a legal misconstruction. Of these the Hosmer case, the sole and entire triumph of this partnership, is the most remarkable; by whose adjudication thousands of our early volunteers, all through the loyal States, reaped the just benefit of their bounty contract with the President, a fair share of the Massachusetts men interested becoming clients of the firm that tested their rights.[1] The father, who had noted this public breach of contract while adjutant-general, presented the points to his son; whereupon the latter prepared with all legal formality this test case, conducting and arguing it at Washington in person on the plaintiff's behalf before the Court of Claims, and on appeal before the Supreme Court of the United States; for to both of those tribunals he was admitted in 1867 as an attorney. The Court of Claims decided unanimously in his favor; and so on appeal did the Supreme Court, rendering final judgment for the claimant. The accounting officers of the treasury were at once disposed to submit; but the appropriation required for this class of claimants throughout the Union was so great that they waited for the further sanction of Congress, which by 1872 was procured; pending which delay the Schoulers brought similar petitions for other claimants to be advanced if needful. Meanwhile, upon the Attorney-General's advice, the government settled without a contest various miscellaneous suits which this Boston firm had entered in the Court of Claims on behalf of clients. The Hosmer case was in fact the only soldiers' test case arising out of the war in which the Executive department was positively overruled.

---

[1] For the legal issue involved in this celebrated case, which arose upon a discrepancy between the terms of the President's original call for loyal volunteers and the Act of July 22, 1861, by which Congress legalized that call, see Hosmer v. United States, 9 Wall. 432.

There was one more, however, whose justice our Boston firm was equally prepared to maintain, — that of a battalion of Massachusetts artillery pronounced "home-guards;" but a statute of limitations barred the test suit, and this technical defence the Attorney-General gladly interposed.

Local revolt against party discipline and the Executive injustice carried General Schouler into the State senate the next year after his displacement from office; and in the Massachusetts legislature of 1868 he advanced his high public reputation by constant and capable work. Men worked more dexterously in these modern days of politics than in old Whig times for their own selfish advancement; or perhaps he would have mounted higher. A second revolt against Butler in the Essex congressional district followed in autumn of the same year, strongly organized when it started; and William Schouler had modestly hoped that it meant his own nomination by the independents; but the cards were arranged for another candidate, a professional man of eminent talent and principle, but personally most unpopular and with claims to a residence in the district scarcely less pretentious than those of Butler himself. In the disastrous canvass which followed, the son stumped the rural towns in his father's place, more for a brush with the adversary than anything else; but the audacious hero of New Orleans, who put almost every other speaker of the opposition upon his self-defence, bore this young assailant in silence. James declined all recompense for his campaign efforts, and received from the defeated candidate a handsome letter of thanks; but never again in his life did he take part in a political canvass. Not very long after, William Schouler moved from Lynn, from the Essex district, and his seaside cottage, and for the brief remnant of his life resided with his wife and daughters in (Jamaica Plain) West Roxbury; a pleasant suburb of Boston, which has since been absorbed into that populous city.

When General Grant became President of the United States, March 4, 1869, James Schouler went to Washington, and there opened a branch office in temporary partnership with his father and his friend Motte, who managed the Boston concerns in an office on Kilby Street, while he attended to the court practice and such other business as might develop at the national capital. He was a spectator at Grant's inauguration, and has witnessed almost every similar ceremony since. One lives at our national seat of government without residing there; and as our young lawyer had journeyed thither much of former years, with a batch of unfinished matters requiring a personal visit, the traditions of this famous place, its great men and memories, delighted him even more than its easy gayeties and free social intercourse. His father, too, had been drawn to Washington in earlier years, forming there many warm acquaintances who received the son with kindness and hospitality.

But there were other serious reasons for this change of abode connected with the literary plans young Schouler was now forming. He had struck already into the career of a professional writer while exploring government business to its full horizon in articles contributed about this time to the "American Law Review" on "Customs and Internal Revenue," "Public Lands," "Government Loans," and "Government Contracts." Calling, about 1865, upon his office neighbor in Boston, the venerable Judge Redfield, a man immersed in law-book publications, to solicit some copying for a friend: "it is not a copyist I want," was the response, "but a head." Out of that conversation grew an arrangement under which young Schouler did some annotation at his leisure on the judge's law treatises; and out of that annotation came an offer from the judge's law publishers, Little, Brown & Co., of Boston, to publish any treatise which Schouler might write on a good subject, upon the same favorable terms that they gave to the judge himself. After casting about for a topic, Schouler chose the "Domestic Relations," — a choice at once approved and applauded. This Washington abode our author thought desirable for the tranquil task of preparation; and most of that celebrated text-book was composed in the great law library of the Capitol amid fit historical surroundings which inspired him.

Accident turned our author, while this literary labor occupied him, to the new commission of three for codifying the United States statutes, which Congress determined to establish in place of an old commission which had done nothing; and he applied in form for appointment to the third and only place not bespoken upon this commission. "It is the only national office," writes our author, "for which I ever applied in my life; and I applied in the confidence that it was intended to be a place not for politicians, but for expert lawyers who would despatch a needful work." The Attorney-General at a first interview derided to his face the presumption of one so young, "an objection," suggested one of the Massachusetts delegation, "which will diminish every day;" but when young Schouler's credentials came in, from

Massachusetts judges and lawyers most competent, some of whom had just examined the advance-sheets of his new book which was going through the press, this Cabinet adviser became convinced, and recommended the name strongly to the President, — though not without a caution to the applicant that local influences were likely to rule New England men out. And so it proved; for the President sent in to the Senate the list of commissioners with a North Carolina man for the third place.

The year 1870 proved a notable one in our author's chronology. In spring he argued and won the Hosmer case in the Supreme Court; and in June, simultaneously with his defeat at Washington for the codifying commission, his first law-book was issued from the press in Boston, which showed that his professional skill with the pen needed to be taken on trust no longer. Both from the felicitous mode of treatment and the choice of a subject — for, through all the changes of our family law, no comprehensive text-book of the kind had been in the market for forty years, — Schouler's "Domestic Relations" at once took possession of the legal field, and through five large editions has securely occupied it ever since. Reviewers both English and American at once welcomed it, and praised its clear, accurate, and logical expression, its superior literary style, and a certain freshness of treatment, after the deductive fashion, which set the law forth as lawyers had not clearly understood it before. So far as a portly volume of the kind may be thought capable, it has brought to the author solid fame and profit. And on its appearance one Boston reviewer mentioned it as something of an event that a book showing such maturity of continuous power had been written by a lawyer hardly thirty years old.

Nor had Schouler's intimate friends failed to observe that this law of the household was the work not only of a young man, but of a young bachelor. For such a subject, notwithstanding, he had qualified himself to write by a profound thought and experience quite unusual. His intuitions were delicate, and his moral sense tested the family relation in all of its vicissitudes. He had in fact been familiar as an own son in other households which bore trials besides his own. With women and children our author's gentle nature always found ready expression; he has interpreted them and gained their peculiar love without apparent effort; and so, too, upon men and women much his seniors, he seems, by our narrative, to have impressed himself more readily than upon his equals in age. Many a woman, of one social grade or another, has confided in him her secret, and been set on the right road rejoicing; for in confidences he is honorable. He in return, as he has frequently confessed, owes more and more in life to woman's sympathy; for men are apt to be coarse or unfeeling towards a fellow-man's infirmity.

It is not strange, then, that a man like this was thought to have had some unusual experience with the fair sex, — some early romantic attachment or disappointment. Upon all such points our author preserves the closest reticence, except to say that he was never engaged in his life save to the woman he married. But when Du Maurier's two novels were discussed not long ago in his presence, he expressed his strong preference for "Peter Ibbetson," and pronounced it a striking psychological study. "Love," he remarked, "has immense influence in shaping the character and course of one's life; and so, too, have the illusions of love." On the 14th of December, 1870, our young author married Emily Fuller, the only child by a first marriage of Asa F. Cochran, a respected merchant of Boston and New Orleans. She had been long a family friend; and the match, which mutual acquaintances at once pronounced most sensible, proved also a most happy one. With quiet refinement, good housekeeping traits, and good judgment, the wife has aided her husband in working out his most cherished plans of life; and so constant and intimate since marriage has been their personal companionship, that they have rarely had occasion to correspond by letter. One obvious advantage of this alliance has been in the opportunity it gave our author to pursue unremunerative work without tempting him to ease or idleness.

James Schouler brought his wife to Washington City to enjoy the social pleasures of a winter season; and their first summer was passed at the White Mountains. For serious work, he began the new year, 1871, with the first issue of a law periodical at the national capital, styled the "United States Jurist;" an enterprise upon which he concentrated his energy as editor during the next three years, in connection with a new law-book on "Personal Property," which he presently contracted to write for his Boston publishers. Issued in the name of a law-publishing firm, in Washington, at this time prosperous and eminent, the "Jurist" was in reality the project of its editor and controlling owner; whose experiment was to supply a magazine for the American bar of a national cast, an exponent of the best thought and intelligence for diffusion among the legal profession of the whole country. Had this experiment proved a full financial success, Schouler would probably have lived in Washington and confined himself to legal literature and professional pursuits for the rest of his life. He had already become fully aware that the pen must be the chief resource of his future fame and usefulness; for his deafness still increased, and the ticking of the watch by which he had for several years tested his daily hearing ceased to be heard at all at either ear the first summer he lived in Washington.

General Schouler plied his own pen busily at the Boston office during the interval of clients. In 1871, besides finishing the second volume of his war history, he wrote a series of "Political and Personal Recollections" for the "Boston Journal," — articles of great merit, which, if culled in extracts, would make an entertaining book. But their irregular publication depressed him; and often did he yearn for the control of some weekly paper, rustic and homespun, which in some quiet town he might edit and improve. "I would rather," he writes his son, "have charge of a well-established weekly paper than be a field-marshal. That is all I am fit for; and then I could spin out my 'Recollections' as easily and pleasantly as a spider does a web." In other moods, he longed for a restful change, and to see old Scotland once more; in fact, he needed recreation greatly, and the consulate of Glasgow had been the unrealized dream of ten years. One, however, who dwells upon his reminiscences has ceased to belong to the present; and for any political appointment he was too much out of touch with the national politics that ruled the hour. But his pecuniary affairs gained steadily; and when in October his last promissory note was taken up at the bank, "I shall henceforth," he said, "keep my hands from signing and borrowing as I always have done from picking and stealing."

When the new year 1872 began, General Schouler retired from his office partnership upon an annuity whose terms included his wife and daughters; at the same time retaining certain interests in a firm which once more aimed to be purely professional. His son John was a party to this arrangement; and both the brothers, while wishing their father to enjoy the rest he needed, urged him to devote his remaining activity to the third volume of his History, for which the public was waiting; or, if he did more than this, to prepare a second series of his "Recollections," which had not as yet extended beyond the Whig era. But his first leisure at home he gave to sorting out and arranging the large correspondence of his life; and then came the summons of the Presidential campaign of this year, which stirred him like a trumpet's call. Joining once more the independents who called for magnanimity to the South and uncorrupt administration, he was placed as a Presidential elector on the liberal Republican ticket of his district. When at Cambridge, during early autumn, and speaking in the open air, at one of these political meetings, he took a severe cold, and was soon confined to his chamber in consequence. His disease, an affection of the heart and liver, assumed presently a dangerous type. The doctors who were called for consultation told him, as requested, his exact condition; and when they informed him that he had but a few days to live, he met the announcement with fortitude and resignation. Conscious to the last, he now took leave of family and personal friends with a cheering and affectionate word to each. His wife and sisters attended the sick chamber devotedly, and all of his children were present except John, the naval officer, who arrived from his station at Key West too late, and to whom the father dictated a farewell letter. Strong in the Christian faith, our hero gave himself humbly as a child to eternity, and his soul ebbed gently out from its mortal frame like a receding tide. General Schouler died on the 24th of October, 1872. His funeral was simple as he wished it, and the pomp of a military funeral tendered by the State was declined. Family, relatives, neighbors, and personal friends thronged the little Episcopal church at Jamaica Plain without ceremony; and the two venerable pastors of his early manhood, whom we have mentioned, conducted the services, after which his remains were borne to Forest Hills Cemetery, their last resting-place.

"No one who ever really knew him could harbor a feeling of enmity;" "Few men, with such decided opinions, had fewer personal enemies," — such were the spontaneous public expressions which recalled General Schouler's genuine goodness and the many high and noble qualities of his character. In Boston a movement, organized soon after his death, resulted in the erection of a handsome monument at Forest Hills, to which friends, high and low, and men of all politics subscribed; the first donation of all coming from Boston's leading lady of society, Mrs. Harrison Gray Otis, who feelingly expressed her sense of the manifold virtues which had impressed her while in constant communication with him on behalf of the women workers of Boston during the whole Civil War. Upon this monument, chaste in its whole detail, is chiselled a fair medallion profile of the adjutant-general's face, with its regular Scotch features.[1] He was a very handsome and striking man, especially when in full military uniform; being six feet or more in height, well proportioned, and wearing a becoming dignity on serious occasions, though ready at most other times to beam out with friendliness and good-nature. He was a genial and engaging man; a good story-teller, with a great and varied fund of personal experience among interesting men and events to draw upon; a well-read and companionable man for any social gathering, since all human nature interested him. If he ever came short of full social expression, it was chiefly from modest pride and the consciousness of a penury which chilled his generous impulses and made him feel most nearly allied to the poor and humble. And yet, under his son's skilful management, — what with his literary property and his share in fees of the Hosmer claims, which were now being paid, — he left at his death an estate more nearly approaching affluence than he had possessed during most of his life. Entering quite early upon manhood's responsibilities, he acquired a maturity of expression which perhaps was heightened by wearing English side-whiskers; yet he was but fifty-seven years old when he died.

Though foreign-born, William Schouler loved Massachusetts to the core, and knew well its people, civic or rural. In last years his heart recalled many of his earlier friendships; he revisited Marshfield

---

[1] It is to be regretted that there is neither statue nor oil painting of General William Schouler, as he was familiarly seen and remembered; but some excellent photographs, which were taken during the Civil War and later, are still preserved by his children. An oil painting by the celebrated artist Alexander, now owned in the family, was made when Schouler was quite a young man; and tradition says that the likeness is excellent; but there is little about the picture that his children or the later public can recognize.

and the Webster family, and the grave of their immortal ancestor; nor did the casual coincidence escape comment at his funeral that he died on the twentieth anniversary of the death of his first great civil leader. But, with impulses that always warmly responded to the highest ideals of public duty, he to the last revered in memory John A. Andrew above all others. It was his dying wish that the Executive Order, which recognized his associated service to the Commonwealth,[1] should be graven upon his monument; and among his private papers, after death, that order, as transmitted to him, was found carefully preserved, together with its original draft in Governor Andrew's own handwriting.

VIII.

1873–1896.

THE death of husband and father was the first great bereavement of the household we have described; and, oppressed with grief, James Schouler prepared, on his return to Washington soon after the funeral, to detach the strand of two closely interwoven lives which death had separated, and, at the age of thirty-three, to adjust his own career to new conditions. With the inducement of an important trust from his maternal uncle, he presently decided to give up his Washington connections and make Boston once more the centre of such professional activity as remained to him. Fate herself seemed to close the portal upon the past, for very soon after General Schouler's

---

[1] See *supra*, p. 266.

funeral came the great fire in Boston; and its flames, in their devastating progress, licked up and levelled the solid granite building in Kilby Street where their office was situated, consuming the father's desk with its contents and his own, and all the old papers and vouchers in fact of his prior professional life.

The winter of 1873-74 saw a last family reunion at West Roxbury, while James settled finally his father's estate; and in the spring of 1874 his wife and younger sister went to Germany, where he joined them for a summer tour through northern Italy, Switzerland, and France. This was a first and delightful experience abroad for all of them; and, returning in the fall of that year, they prepared for housekeeping in Boston apartments, where the mother, General Schouler's widow, was soon to join them. But while she visited in the meantime her son William in Syracuse, her delicate frame succumbed to pneumonia, and she died there, after a brief illness, on the 1st of November, 1874. James had just time, when summoned, to hasten to her bedside and receive her smile of recognition before she expired. Her remains were laid by the side of the illustrious husband who had owed immeasurably to her devotion; and upon her gravestone it is fitly inscribed that "her children arise up and call her blessed."

Not long after this full orphanage of the children, sons and daughters settled each in separate homes, affectionate still through life, and mindful of the loving and tender influences which had brought them up united. William, married previously in 1871 to Sophia B. Heaton of Brooklyn, has served for many years as faithful rector of the Episcopal Church at Elkton, Maryland; John, who in 1881 married Hope

Day of Catskill, has risen honorably through successive grades in his naval profession, and with a high rank in the active list of commanders, serves at present as executive officer on the flag-ship of our North Atlantic squadron; Harriet, now a widow, married in 1875 the Rev. Nathaniel G. Allen of Boston, an Episcopal clergyman; and Fanny, who was united in 1880 to James H. Williams, a prosperous banker in Bellows Falls, Vermont, died in 1891. Among the marriages of General Schouler's five sons and daughters, those of James and John have borne no offspring.

As incidental to his withdrawal from the national capital, — a city just emerging from a grub or chrysalis condition into its modern splendor, and fascinating him greatly with its warm friendships and cordial social life, — our young author regretfully abandoned the experiment of his "United States Jurist," whose last quarterly number was issued for October, 1873. The circulation and influence of this periodical had steadily increased, but not rapidly enough to warrant him in expending upon it longer both capital and brain-work. During the three years of its existence under his editorial direction, a large share of its material was from his own pen and those of his two Boston partners; but among voluntary contributors who encouraged the enterprise were lawyers of renown, like Justice Miller of the Supreme Bench, Professor Emory Washburn of Cambridge, William Beach Lawrence, and, chief among all editorial friends, the versatile John William Wallace, reporter of the Supreme Court decisions and President of the Pennsylvania Historical Society, — a warm-hearted man whose thoughtful attentions, once begun, ceased only with his life. With reference to James Schouler's retirement in 1873 appeared an article in a Philadelphia paper from the pen doubtless of this last-named gentleman, from which the following is an extract: "We regret this retirement because we have thought that we could see in the 'United States Jurist,' of which Mr. Schouler was the founder and sole conductor, the more than seminal principle of a thoroughly independent and valuable law journal. It began with no flourish of trumpets and no external exhibitions, perhaps rather unimpressively. But we early observed in it the marks of an original, fearless, and thoughtful editorship; and of a pen guided at once by high legal attainments and a very careful consideration and analysis of every subject which it passed upon."

Two incidents, one pleasant and one unpleasant, are still remembered in the annals of this youthful lucubration. The pleasant one relates to the famous New York advocate, Charles O'Conor, by this time an elderly man, who was an early subscriber to the "Jurist," and liked it so well that, when renewing his subscription, in 1872, he paid for five years in advance. When the magazine was discontinued, a check to refund the proper balance was sent to him; but he never transmitted it through the bank for payment; meaning apparently to signify that the amount might stand as his donation towards the concern. The unpleasant incident relates to a change in methods of legal instruction which began at the Harvard Law School while the "Jurist" was published. Mr. Schouler had made "book reviews" a special feature of his magazine, giving full lists of new law-books and preparing notices, whether editorial copies were sent him or not. In reviewing two volumes of "Selected Cases," issued upon the new method, he took issue with the "American Law Review" concerning their merits as compared with legal text-books; writing boldly, and even sharply, under a loyal warmth to some of Harvard's former professors — though he had never attended personally any law school whatever for his own instruction — and for vindicating a class of legal writers among whom he belonged, and who seemed marked for disparagement; but otherwise without personal bias against any one. But he soon found to his surprise that he had given offence in other high quarters of his University, on an issue which he had supposed interested men of the legal profession alone; and chiefly for that reason he resigned in 1873 the class secretaryship which he had held with the favor and confidence of his classmates for eight years.

Boston now becomes once more the regular seat of Mr. Schouler's professional labors in a quiet routine, for the next twenty years or more, which was chiefly varied by brief winter excursions to Washington and a summer life among the mountains. Abandoning, as hard destiny compelled him, all further ambition of forensic triumphs, and of course cutting loose from war claims, he adjusted his professional work to the standard of chamber practice, chiefly concerning himself for the future with the settlement and care of estates in probate. When in 1875 new and commodious buildings went up in the burnt Boston district, he moved into one of them near the new post-office, and 60 Congress Street still remains his most convenient mail address, wherever he may personally be. And by that time dissolving all partnership relations, he retained Mr. Motte still as a constant office neighbor and companion. Thus located in his own business, Mr. Schouler steadily pursued his literary plans, under succeeding contracts with his publishers.

Of his well-known law treatises which followed "Domestic Relations," the first volume of "Personal Property" was issued while he tarried in Washington in 1872; and the latter subject of investigation opened so broad a field of legal study that a second volume (chiefly upon "Gifts and Sales") followed in 1876; a third on "Bailments including Carriers" in 1880; "Executors and Administrators" in 1883; and "Wills" in 1887. "Husband and Wife," an expansion of "Domestic Relations," went through the press in 1882. Six of these seven volumes have sold rapidly, passing into new editions which have cost much editorial labor in bringing the court development of decisions down to date; but with each new edition carefully revised and improved by the author's personal labor. This author's law-books have long had a wide national reputation; they are recognized in the courts as standard authorities on the various subjects treated; and written, as they are, in a clear, lucid style, applying sound judgment with a wealth of learning, these books serve well the use of law-students or of the practising lawyer who wishes to freshen himself upon elementary principles. Besides these creative labors, Mr. Schouler edited "Story on Bailments" soon after his return to Boston; and while doing so perceived that simpler principle of classification which he applied afterwards to his own work on the subject, and which, as taught since in good law schools, is rapidly superseding the nomenclature of Lord Holt and the writers who followed his primitive exposition of the subject. Our author bore also an important part in the preparation of "Myers' Federal Decisions," and has contributed various articles to English and American law magazines, most of which relate to professional studies in connection with his own text-books. Under the pressure of other important work to be presently mentioned, he has firmly declined of late years to take up new professional subjects, though receiving tempting offers from law publishers in all our leading cities; and, in fact, feeling the need of curtailing such labors, he cancelled six years ago a contract for a new legal text-book which he had already entered into.

But Mr. Schouler is far more widely and popularly known by his historical work than by these purely professional productions. His successful occupation of this second field furnishes quite a remarkable instance of versatile literary industry; for while most historians have found historical subjects grave enough to absorb their most serious study, he, to quote his own words, made history "the diversion from literary toil more dull and mechanical, — in other words, a literary lawyer's recreation." From our famous Presidential campaign of 1860, which, as we have seen, intensely interested him just as he had reached majority, our author's early diaries exhibit him as exploring with enthusiasm American politics and the writings of our early statesmen in the midst of his vigorous preparations for the bar. Soon after returning from the seat of war he made a minute sketch of Massachusetts colonial history in a picturesque paper entitled "Sir Henry Vane, Governor," which was sent to the "Atlantic Monthly," but returned to him rejected. That essay has long since disappeared from the author's manuscripts; but in his diary, of November, 1864, he wrote soon after his rebuff: "I shall now betake myself in earnest to my historical studies, with a view of writing in time some book on our constitutional history, — an idea which I have secretly cherished a twelvemonth or more." In 1866 he prepared from an original study of the State department volumes an article upon "Our Diplomacy during the Rebellion," which was published in the "North American Review;" it drew from Secretary Seward himself an autograph letter which to our young author was a great encouragement. Pursuing these diplomatic studies later to the final tragedy of "Maximilian in Mexico," after the French had been forced to withdraw, he wrote another magazine article on that subject; but this failed once more of acceptance. Notwithstanding these literary discouragements, Schouler pursued the consecutive national studies which he had already taken up in earnest; and even while composing his "Domestic Relations" at Washington he was examining with interest the memorable sites about him and making comprehensive notes of the writings of Washington, Madison, Hamilton, and Jefferson during the era which next succeeded our American revolution. His wish, now cherished, was to begin his narrative where the venerable George Bancroft had seemingly laid down his pen, and be the recognized historian to supply the connecting link between our American Revolution and the Civil War. He knew of no other scholar, native or foreign, who had projected such a work. Indeed, during the very same year (1870) that his first law-book, the "Domestic Relations," was published, we find that he completed the first draft of an introductory chapter to such a history, and then laid the manuscript aside for the "United States Jurist," thinking to concentrate his talents upon law literature [1] for the rest of his life. All was encouraging and hopeful here; but as to literary fame and usefulness outside of the law nearly all was discouragement.

After the "Jurist" experiment had been abandoned in 1873 Schouler took up once more in earnest the suspended project of writing a United States history. His Boston law publishers, whose range of general literature was extensive, were well disposed to sustain the venture; but as publishers already of George Bancroft, whose future literary plans were uncertain, they felt themselves unable to decide at once in his favor, and counselled delay. Their suspense continued thus for years; in early 1879 the author made proposals to another leading Boston firm which declined to assume his undertaking; and dreading the ordeal of publishers elsewhere, strangers to him, with a bulk of manuscript which must be finished before being considered at all, he went at once to his former "Jurist" publishers at Washington, the Morrisons, and found them glad enough to stand sponsors for the history under a most liberal publishing contract. With this spur to exertion, he now completed his composition of the first two volumes, and they went forth to the world.

This publishing connection did not prove altogether advantageous for bringing such a work into notice; and, to add to the author's chagrin, his Boston law publishers, Little, Brown & Co., announced themselves at final liberty to take up the history just when it was too late. One of the Morrison brothers died soon after the first volume was pub-

---

[1] See author's original preface to History of the United States, vol. i.

lished; and the survivor, though fairly fulfilling to the best of his ability, was hampered in pushing the work as it deserved. At the same time he held tenaciously to his contract rights until other embarrassments forced him by 1890 to sell out, shortly after the fourth volume was issued. From among various large firms in the great cities who were now ready to assume publication, the author chose Dodd, Mead & Co., of New York, whose services had been tendered him for years, upon their own discovery of the merits of his undertaking; and this choice he has never regretted.

Parallel with his legal text-books, the "History of the United States, under the Constitution," in five volumes, was prepared and issued by our author, as follows: volume i. ("Rule of Federalism," 1789–1801) in 1880; volume ii. ("Jefferson Republicans," 1801–17) in 1882; volume iii. ("Era of Good Feeling," 1817–31) in 1885; volume iv. ("Whigs and Democrats," 1831–47) in 1889; volume v. ("Free-Soil Controversy," 1847–61) in 1891. After this completion of the extensive narrative under his original plan, Dr. Schouler next gave his personal attention to a revised edition of the whole work which comprised nearly three thousand pages; he made entirely new plates for the first two volumes, which he largely re-wrote; and here his facile pen has rested. A life of "Thomas Jefferson" by our author in the "Makers of America Series" deserves a favorable mention.

In recalling those ten earlier years of anxious authorship and depression, while the merits of his monumental work gained with the public but gradual recognition, and there was little business energy or advertising to bring the work forward while it stole into scholarly notice, our modest author loves to recall some of those influential men whose spontaneous commendations cheered him onward in his task. There was George Bancroft, first of all, who had at length concluded to leave the field open; the late Alexander Johnston, an American historical professor and scholar of great promise, who wrote the first strongly laudatory notice of the earliest volume and inserted it in the New York "Nation;" the cultured George William Curtis; John Austin Stevens of the "Magazine of American History;" Samuel Eliot of Boston, Professors MacVane of Harvard, Sumner of Yale, and Herbert B. Adams and Jameson of the Johns Hopkins, together with the President of this latter institution. Most of these gentlemen signified their appreciation by personal correspondence and in other ways; and some writers for the press, whose names are unknown, deserve also a mention. In the course of fifteen years many gratifying letters have come to the author from characteristic though less distinguished readers: one, for instance, from an old Baptist minister in the Rocky Mountain region, who says that the only change of words he could wish in the whole work would be to call the Mormons "rascals;" and another, which came a few weeks since from the managing editor of a large Philadelphia newspaper, who expresses his grateful pleasure after a "fourth perusal" of the five volumes. "There are many persons," observes our historian, "who will flatter you to your bent after a cursory glance at what you have solidly written; but when you find one who has read from cover to cover and then praises, you may feel that he is your friend."

We shall not here undertake to cull from testimonials to the merits of Schouler's masterly work which are contained in the publisher's portly circulars; but we borrow from two tributes only which have reached the author within the past twelve months, and of which the publishers have taken no cognizance. The first is from a personal letter written by the kindly and accomplished President Gilman of the Johns Hopkins University: "You have won unique distinction, not likely, I think, to be taken from you by subsequent investigators. The sense of proportion which has governed your work is valuable; but the candor and fairness and justice which you manifest, in the discussion of critical periods and of influential characters, give it even higher importance." The second we quote from an article which appeared in a New England weekly from the pen of a good literary scholar and clergyman in an article devoted to a comparative estimate of American historians now living: "Mr. Schouler's work is, without question, the most complete picture of the nation from its founding to the Civil War. It is a rapid, straightforward narrative, seldom stopping to quote authorities, but accurate in facts, and possessed of the highest historical genius. The narrative flows on, when well under way, with a marvellous richness and eloquence, midway between the general and the particular, the narrative and the philosophic methods. As an authority, it is going to stand prominent. But what it is to be most valued for is the fact that the author is possessed of a vast synthetic power: a real economic and political philosophy makes the facts he relates bear their true relative position and force. There are instances of special pleading as he reaches periods near his own, and these are to be regretted; but, on the whole, Mr. Schouler has given us a brilliant, vigorous, strong, pithy, stimulating history. He is never tempted to turn aside to lengthy, disproportionate disquisition, but holds his subject and himself marvellously well in hand. He is a condensed, pruned Macaulay."

While thus occupied with a twofold sedentary task which must naturally have increased in tendency his social exclusion while broadening his literary fame, Mr. Schouler received quite unexpectedly an invitation which opened to him a new field of usefulness most welcome and opportune. Judge Edmund H. Bennett, a man of kindred tastes and experience in legal composition, offered him in the summer of 1883 the post of lecturer on "Bailments," which had just become vacant, at the new Law School of Boston University, of which he was Dean. The place was provisionally accepted by our author; and, standing before a class of young men to expound a subject already familiar to him, he found himself at once among fresh and highly congenial surroundings. "The boys like you," said the judicious dean after the first lecture had concluded; and he added "Domestic Relations" to the new lecturer's subjects, and made his engagement permanent upon the Boston University staff.

With this advantageous start as a professional instructor and lecturer, Mr. Schouler found by 1886 a similar position for a few weeks' employment each year at the National University Law School at Washington, with which the famous Justice Miller and a strong personal friend of the author at the district bar were already connected. Annual excursions to Washington, such as he had already been taking for historical study, found henceforth a new motive; and a few weeks of leisure still remaining to him in midwinter and the early spring, application was next made in 1889 by friends on his behalf at the famous Law School of Columbia College, New York, where new courses of instruction were to be established. The veteran Professor Dwight, founder and head of that school, gave, after full inquiry, his written pledge to send Mr. Schouler's name to the trustees, which was thought to be a virtual appointment; he failed, however, to do so, and possibly a schism in the school over modes of instruction which followed simultaneously with Professor Dwight's retirement, in the summer of 1890, may explain a mysterious change of mind. Scarcely, however, had our author rallied from his disappointment in that quarter, when an unexpected offer came from his friend, Professor Herbert B. Adams, and the historical department of Johns Hopkins University, before the year ended, which has led to the happiest possible consummation of his annual work in University instruction. All these staff positions as lecturer our author has since steadily retained, increasing in each instance the extent of the courses for which he was originally engaged, and serving to supplement his labors with the pen.

As a lecturer, Professor Schouler shows most of the qualities which marked him for high forensic promise in his younger days, — an attractive person, an impressive manner, good delivery, and a musical voice, earnest in its deeper utterances. Sedate and moderate, as befits a class instructor, and rather inclining to simple and natural exposition, and yet always full of his subject and at times rapid and vehement when kindled in demonstration, he arrests the attention of his audience and holds it securely till his appointed hour ends. His dignified alertness checks all indecorum; but applause follows an occasional sally or stirring expression. No lecturer could ask for more attentive listeners. Sometimes he turns aside for a comment upon the general aspects of life, and the close of each course supplies usually some eloquent exordium which brings the students to his desk for a last grasp of the hand; but for the most part he keeps closely to his immediate subject, developing the law or narrative just as he had investigated, and with his constant sense of proportion, and making each lecture reach a certain stage or climax. Leading principles are thus elucidated, and their limitations clearly defined, with apt and ample illustrations not only from reports, but from daily life besides; a constant object with him being to encourage the student to observe with his own eyes among daily circumstances where and how a legal principle should apply. He cannot, of course, conduct an oral quiz; but students accost him before or after the lecture with points of inquiry; and wherever they may find him, he makes himself as helpful to his pupils as possible. Written examinations have attested the practical value of the instruction he annually imparts. He does not write out his lectures at length; but, saturated with his subject, he prepares a mere skeleton sheet or brief for his convenience, having ready at his left hand a small package of slips for such special reference or quotation during the hour as convenience may suggest. An impressive thought or illustration gets thus woven specially into his routine exposition; and often does an idea worth inculcating from the platform occur to him as he walks to or from the lecture-room. For nothing can go wholly by rote with so systematic a thinker, who brings all knowledge to bear upon immediate action and events. This fresh contact with young men is to the author himself a well of inspiration. There is not too much of it to tire the brain; and he agrees with a writer who once observed: "I have learned much from my teachers, more from my equals, but most from my pupils."

Allusion is made in some of the foregoing essays to our author's habits of literary work and to his general methods of study and composition.[1] Orderly arrangement and the economy of time are traits strongly characteristic of him from early youth. He originated by experience his own routine of life; and his early diaries show how incessant was his mental training from the time he left college until he became a recognized scholar and writer. A "perambulation book" is repeatedly mentioned in his journals, which he carried in his pocket on his daily walk, with catchwords and cues to refresh the memory of studies as he repeated them aloud. Another book which he kept, such as young students are more familiar with, was the "common-place book;" of which three neat volumes are still preserved, covering the first twenty years of his majority, and traversing a wide field of general reading, prose and poetic, grave and gay, solid and imaginative, from Aristotle to Mark Twain. On the whole, however, these volumes show the special bent of his mind to American history and statesmanship; they are concise rather than elaborate; and, not to be too much harassed by either diary or common-place book in his productive manhood, he contrived, when about forty, a fair single substitute for them both. This was the use of long envelopes of pasteboard or stiff paper marked for

---

[1] See pages 40, 58.

each succeeding calendar year. Upon prepared slips, about the size of an ordinary bank check, he would enter quotations from his reading, or the rough thoughts or comments that might be wrought out for some further occasion, or else some casual diary description worthy of his later reference; all such slips, wherever written, went into the envelope of the year; and it was easy to add to the same collection a contemporary newspaper cutting or printed circular worth recalling. All this served the stead of a blank-book. Out of a year's envelope the contents might be poured upon a table at any time and read over or separated as his immediate convenience required. For lecture purposes the author has kept special and appropriate "scrap envelopes" of this character.

"Method," observes our author, "and frugality of time should be handmaids of all intellectual industry which involves considerable pains and study. And especially in that general range of reading which every accomplished scholar needs to liberalize his special researches, the pen-work should be economized. It is lost labor to carry in volumes of manuscript what ought to be imbedded in the brain; for after all the note-book is mainly for review, for exact statement, and to aid the mind later in its own energizing. A famous scholar has well said that what is twice read is easier remembered than what is once transcribed; and it is my own experience that by jotting down in pencil, while one reads, either on a marker or a fly-leaf, the number of each page which contains a striking thought, and then recurring to those pages after the volume has been finished, a second perusal may confirm sufficiently the mental impression. And as for those extensive commonplace books with topical index, which we see exposed for sale, I cannot conceive of any productive writer going far with it; for all such self-imposed tasks when considerable suit only a literary novice, or the man of leisure and superficial culture who seeks to entertain his friends agreeably. Of the mind, and of memory itself, prodigious feats have been recorded, as to some illustrious scholars, which I am wary of believing. The average player of a stock company shows you, to be sure, how greatly the mere memory may be strengthened by exercise; but the memory an intellectual man wishes is that which puts what others have said to the vital nutriment of his own thoughts. I would rather have a good selecting memory than an omnivorous memory (if such there be) which holds everything and can fetch on demand. One intellectual mind draws one thought, and another mind another, from the same great predecessor; and it must often be a trick of playing off the particular thing that haunted one's memory from association, like an oil portrait that happens to hang over the mantelpiece, which imposed on credulous admirers the belief so often expressed that everything was remembered by that individual."

Thus occupied during the last quarter of a century, our author has made Boston his place of residence; living the hotel life, at the Boylston, the Evans, the Brunswick, successively, with his wife, the sole companion of his home, while using his own quiet office as his literary work-shop. Bright and cheerful situations, with sun and air and glimpses of green, and yet close to the main arteries of city life, have always been their choice; and for six years or more they have occupied apartments at the Hotel Bristol, on a charming corner which commands the most famous residential square and the noblest architectural cluster of buildings of Boston, or perhaps of any American city. But Professor Schouler has passed many winter months in Washington, while busy over his history, "not so much for society," he expresses it, "as for study;" and for the last six years his lecture-work has occupied him there and in Baltimore for two winter months regularly. With old friends and new to thus revisit, two brothers resident in Maryland with their families, and a genial and hospitable society abounding in the region, these variations of a winter season's surroundings are always welcome to him, at the same time that his New England attachment remains sincere. "Boston is *arida nutrix*," he sometimes says, "for such a one as myself; but the best reference libraries of the country are there at my command, and the best means of general recreation; and after all a real Bostonian can never feel so much at home in any other city."

But Dr. Schouler's chief happiness is found at his summer home among the White Mountains, where, with his wife, he spends some five months of every year, and where alone they have the freedom of housekeeping. Both enjoy a simple social life, and are great lovers of natural scenery. Boarding at "Intervale," a hamlet of famed North Conway, during the first three summers following their marriage, and returning thither after two more experimental seasons elsewhere, they fixed upon this enchanting region and the White Mountains for a permanent summer residence. Our author purchased on the main road a disused pasture fringed with stately pines, and having a sloping and graceful knoll, near the road, which commands an enchanting view of the Presidential range through the trees and beyond the green valley; and here in 1878, next to the costly and extensive estate of Mr. Erastus B. Bigelow, inventor of the carpet loom, he built an appropriate summer villa; setting the first example in the town of Conway and its mountain neighborhood of a pretty cottage, artistically planned, with fine natural surroundings, yet such as a city man of moderate means might build for his summer use. With a long and curving red roof sloping on each side to the cedar piazza posts, the plan of this colonial cottage originated in the bright seaside home of our author's boyhood in Boston's island ward, as memory reproduced it; and from each piazza looking northward and southward, as well as from every window of the little wooden house so admirably finished, some lovely mountain landscape feasts the eye with great variety. When this Schouler cottage was built, it stood somewhat remote from the cluster of summer boarding-houses comprising Intervale; but now quite a number of pretty villas adorn the landscape besides the noble Bigelow mansion, and the colony of summer cottagers has become a considerable one. No longer dependent upon North Conway for its mails, Intervale now boasts its own post-office, express, and telegraph, besides a junction railroad-station.

Such have been the neighboring changes within less than twenty years, since our author chose the township of Conway as his dwelling-place for five months of the year; and in this neighborhood he is always happy, being well known and esteemed both by residents and the summer people, whose common interests he has done much to unite. He has been a liberal benefactor of the Public Library of North Conway, founded in 1887, and as its most active director from the start, is still greatly depended upon for selecting and purchasing books, supervising the details of management, and engineering summer entertainments for its benefit. He is treasurer of the Episcopal Church in North Conway, and a leading member of its vestry. As a good churchman he serves, besides, during the winter season on the vestry of St. Paul's Church in Boston. Schouler's fondness for the mountains is shown in all his writings, which abound in felicitous images and metaphors from brook, forest, and pastoral studies; and many a striking passage of his history which sums up individual character, has he thought out while rambling among the pine woods or reclining solitary under a favorite tree with Moat Mountain's outline before his vision pencilled upon a blue sky. Moat is North Conway's appropriate sentinel. There is no mountain region of Europe or America which to him seems so closely blended with human nature in its essential moods as these supreme granite hills of New Hampshire, — neither too awful nor too commonplace for man's habitation; and as for this emerald gateway of the region which North Conway furnishes, so varied, he affirms, are its landscape enchantments within a radius of fifteen miles, that he contrives a new walk and a new ride for every season. In younger years he has travelled in every remote quarter and scaled almost every considerable peak of these White Mountains; and he still enjoys a day's tramp through the level of the region better than any other recreation.

Alternating thus in his external surroundings for different portions of the year, our author is enabled to freshen periodically his literary tasks. What many would find distracting in a change of scene is to him a positive help. Turning from law composition to historical, he diversifies his labor still further by composing in one place and collecting important material in another. No weeks are more fruitful of historical composition than the earlier ones passed at his mountain home, before the hot season fairly sets in, with the summer-boarder crowd and his brief allowance of vacation; for now there is no great reference library to consult, but materials must have been already shaped and at hand. City life, on the other hand, offers the true opportunity for gathering all stores of special information, when composition flags; and while at Boston he writes with the key turned in the morning quiet of his office, which is opened for business at noon hours only; or else composes in the quiet Athenæum or Bar Association Library, where such books as he may need for reference are close at hand.

Steadiness and concentration have served him well habitually in all these years; for the whole pen-work which heavily tasks the brain is completed each day by noon. While in Boston, office business and correspondence come next in order, followed in the afternoon, perhaps, by lectures or some plodding literary task. Under no circumstances is the evening robbed by him of its needful rest and recreation to advance the creation of a book or essay; nor, unless some social engagement keeps him up longer, does he retire later than ten o'clock at night. An early riser throughout the winter months, he breakfasts about seven when in Boston or wherever else he may breakfast alone, and between eight and nine o'clock in the forenoon he is well immersed in the day's chief literary task. For a winter evening he enjoys with his wife an occasional theatrical performance, concert or opera, taking with him a small nickel trumpet that all may not go on as a pantomime; quite rarely he may be seen in city club or society; and, if spending the evening at home, he scans the latest magazines and light literature, often reading aloud to his wife, or takes a hand with friends at whist or euchre. In card-playing, as in all other games of recreation, he would rather play for pleasure than antagonism.

Twenty years of such a routine life have been three times broken. In the winter of 1876–77 our author, with his wife, made a pleasure excursion at the South, visiting more especially Florida and Louisiana, and passing and repassing through Washington. That was the famous winter when the Presidential contest between Tilden and Hayes culminated in the electoral commission established by Congress, which declared the Republican candidate chosen; and upon the constitutional aspects of an "electoral count," as first agitated with pretentious claims made on behalf of a President *pro tem.* of the senate, our author prepared and published an historical essay at his own cost under the pseudonyme of "Jurist," and made free distribution of it among our members of Congress. He saw the rival and distracted State legislatures in session while at New Orleans, and, learning the sentiment of leading citizens there quite accurately, published it when passing through Washington on his return. In 1889, he visited Europe with his wife for a second time, and passed seven memorable months in the complete tour of Southern France, Italy, England, and Scotland, besides visiting the World's Exposition of that year at Paris. Usually in good health, he had broken down by over-work before starting on the voyage from New York, and a rheumatic affection which troubled him upon his travels settled finally in the eyes, and compelled him at the age of fifty to resort for the first time to glasses. "My eyesight," says Dr. Schouler, "had been as acute, all these preceding years, as my hearing was dull, and I suffered undoubtedly in the end by my own imprudence in straining it; for, being bent upon a long holiday, I had labored so incessantly for six months to prepare for it, reading finely printed proofs by night in addition to my daily labors, that when vacation came, I stood in full need of it." The warning monition not to abuse nature's gifts came in good season; and, once more in normal health by the time he returned to work, our author took his lesson seriously to heart, as other literary workers should do. A third European journey by Gibraltar, the Mediterranean, and Genoa, in the spring of 1894, occupied him and his wife in traversing Southern Germany, the Rhine, Holland, and Belgium.

Peculiar conditions of mature existence have caused, as one might say, the insensible formation of a rind over the author's common intercourse which those casually accosting him seldom penetrate; a few pleasant words of greeting and common-place sufficing perhaps with such as find communication an effort and have nothing particular to impart. With such he finds it most natural to lead by asking his own questions and receiving replies. The poet's lines seem often to apply to one who, like Dr. Schouler, never forces nor monopolizes a conversation: —

> "The best of thoughts that he hath known
> For lack of listeners is unsaid."

But it is very different in the home circle, or with sympathetic acquaintances, who can take up the other end of his ear-tube and draw him into congenial talk or discussion. One who by this time cannot hear general conversation, and must endure as a patient looker-on long scenes which under his natural and earlier conditions he would have been quickest to appreciate, is certainly at a social disadvantage. But when given his cue, Schouler is found one of the most lively and interesting of conversers; he is amiable, sympathetic, and considerate of those about him; and most of all he has a mirthfulness which, once aroused, makes him the life of his company, and promotes good fellowship at once. Nicknames, mimicry, droll and taking phrases, repartee, and a scintillation of wit and delicate fancy which lights up all literature and all philosophy pour forth in his talk when he is thus in high spirits. Evanescent and hard as fireflies to catch, but suiting admirably the occasion, impromptu generally and instantaneous, this flitting fun is of much the same sort that made his college papers so attractive; he gets humor out of sober subjects, and has a light way of poking fun at his heaviest tasks, which is one reason, no doubt, why he carries the burden of them so easily.

While tarrying at Washington, when a bachelor, in the house of some personal friends, he would produce his watch and key about bedtime and say: "Now I will wind up my watch and then wind up the stairs." "Ah! the power of money," was the exclamation of one in a family group which discussed the threadbare theme of their poverty. "Yes," was his response, setting them all in better humor; "a stronghold in the day of trouble." When two young ladies, Martha and Bertha, both of whom he much liked, visited his wife at the mountains recently, he amused them on a morning ride by addressing various remarks to them collectively as "Rtha." In his office, as well as in the home circle, his spirits have found incessant play in jests which have a touch of pleasant satire and exaggeration. When young at the bar, and performing that function which all of the profession so well appreciate, he used to remark, "'The lawyer shall have his fee,' saith my Lord Coke." "What!" asked a fellow-lawyer, jestingly, while he was deep in devising the prosecution of claims against the United States, "are you in favor of preventing the public debt from being paid off?" "Yes," was his not less jesting reply, "and in favor, too, of judiciously increasing it." One maternal client called in those busy years to receive her settlement, bringing an adult son with her; and the latter seemed quite desirous of carrying the government draft away to get it cashed by the paymaster, contrary to the office rule, which protected the attorney's lien on the fund for recompense; but, seeing a dubious expression on our young lawyer's face, he added, "I can leave mother here till I come back." "That is not quite the collateral which would suit the transaction," was his ready answer. Honest as the day in all professional relations, and sometimes unreasonably moderate in his charges, Schouler has had many a sly lunge at his sober function of public administrator: "One touch of public administration," he is wont to say in a sort of mock rhapsody, "makes the whole world next of kin." And with reference to his dignified law treatises, he sometimes indulges in the light fancy of an illustrated edition, — dilating upon such fitting wood-cuts as the wife pledging her husband's credit for necessaries, or the judge granting *habeas corpus* for the custody of an infant. All these are fair specimens — neither the best nor the worst — of our author's light ebullitions in social company where he is intimate. There is nothing caustic in his wit, nor the slightest soil of coarseness or indecency. Like his father before him, he enjoys with the young and ingenuous the pretence of misunderstanding what was said; but he rarely relates stories or anecdotes at greater length than did Æsop.

Music, too, is an inseparable element of our author's nature, whether in graver or gayer moods; and in his piano he has found the constant companion and solace of enforced solitude. "My ear for music," he sometimes says lightly, "is the ear that I retained longest." With the classical school which Beethoven brought to perfection, and Mendelssohn delicately fenced in, he is amply familiar; but for obvious reasons the modern technique school and the latest modern masters he has not much cultivated. While he heard easily, all the popular street music of the day he readily caught up and memorized, so that each year moved on with its own musical calendar; and such earlier music he can still reproduce on his instrument by the hour together, — that, for instance, of his military service year, of which not a strain is forgotten. He whistles much while at work in his study, or bursts out with some odd snatch of poetry set to original music. For several summers preceding his trip to Europe in 1889, he presided at the little organ of his summer church at North Conway, organizing and training most acceptably with his wife's aid a voluntary choir each year.

In the summer entertainments, too, at his mountain home, whether for charity or religion, he has long been prominent, as stage or business manager, improvising various performances when younger; and on one occasion he played admirably in private theatricals, and sustained a leading part through long dialogues by reading with his eye the motion of the other speaker's lips. There has been no gnarled or eccentric growth in him of habits or character, such as marked infirmity is apt to engender; but he carries along the affairs committed to him (which are many) with good sense and discretion. A temper self-reliant, and perhaps irritable and stern when opposed, is kept under Christian self-discipline; and the whole tenor of his life has been to harmonize and unite, while in affection he is generous and sincere to tenderness.

www.ingramcontent.com/pod-product-compliance
Lightning Source LLC
Chambersburg PA
CBHW030802230426
43667CB00008B/1031